STUDYING AMERICA PAST AND PRESENT

Volume I To 1877

to accompany

Divine • Breen • Fredrickson • Williams

AMERICA PAST AND PRESENT

Fifth Edition

Donald L. Smith
Houston Community College System

Richard Bailey
San Jacinto College

Charles M. Cook
Texas Higher Education Coordinating Board
Community and Technical Colleges

 LONGMAN

An Imprint of Addison Wesley Longman, Inc.

New York • Reading, Massachusetts • Menlo Park, California • Harlow, England
Don Mills, Ontario • Sydney • Mexico City • Madrid • Amsterdam

Study Guide, Volume I to accompany Divine, *America Past and Present*, Fifth Edition.

Copyright © 1999 Longman Publishers USA, a division of Addison Wesley Longman, Inc.

ISBN: 0-321-00562-7

CRS

99 00 01 02 9 8 7 6 5 4 3 2 1

CONTENTS

PREFACE

Our goal in writing this study guide is to make your study of American history, using *America Past and Present*, Fifth Edition, more effective and rewarding. We hope that *Studying American Past and Present* will help you

- develop the study skills you need to learn history inside and outside the classroom.

- master the text material and demonstrate your knowledge on tests and quizzes.

- develop a clear understanding of the main trends and recurring themes within American history.

- develop map-reading skills and expand your understanding of the relationship between geography and history.

To achieve these goals, we have gathered an assortment of study tips, exercises that require factual answers, and broader "thought questions"—all of which should help enhance your knowledge of the text and America history. These study aids can be divided into two general classes: essays and review exercises designed to improve your study skills and chapter-by-chapter review materials.

REVIEWING THE TEST CHAPTER BY CHAPTER

Each chapter in *Studying America Past and Present* corresponds to a chapter in your text. Each chapter of review materials includes a chapter summary, learning objectives, glossary of terms, and self-test questions that include identification, matching, completion, true/false, multiple choice, and thought questions.

- The *Summary*, which is organized around the heads and subheads within the chapter, highlights the most important points and will help you review your reading of the chapter.

- The *Learning Objectives* pinpoint the most important themes or ideas of the chapter, themes and ideas you should take away from your study. Refer back to this list as you review the text chapter and as you complete the self-test exercises to see how well you have mastered the material.

- The *Glossary* contains a number of terms that may be unfamiliar to you. Besides a definition, we have supplied a quote from the chapter that shows you how the word can be used in a sentence. Learning these words and terms will expand your vocabulary, which will help you in this and other courses in the social sciences.

- The *self-test exercises* cover both specific details and broad concepts. (An answer key for these questions is at the end of the text). *Identification* items ask you to identify key phrases and explain their significance. *Matching* exercises are intended to help you distinguish between similar but different people, locations, or events. By asking you to fill in the blanks, *Completion* exercises will help you relate specific items to their context. *True/False* and *Multiple Choice* questions will give you valuable practice for objective tests and help you check your knowledge of key points.

- *Thought Questions* are designed to meet the objective of helping you develop a clear understanding of the main trends and recurring themes within American history. Answering these questions will help you tie together your classroom lecture notes and the text coverage; this will also help you study for essay tests, a feature of most history courses.

- *Critical Thinking Exercises* are designed to help you learn to analyze and compare primary source documents through a series of readings and analytical questions.

For best results, try to use the chapter-by-chapter review materials in a consistent manner. Read the chapter and then begin working through the chapter's review materials, using the "Summary" and "Learning Objectives" to focus your study. After you have completed the self-test exercises, check your answers against the answer key. When you understand why you missed a question and determine areas of weakness, focus your attention on reviewing those sections. If you do this faithfully, both your knowledge and pleasure in American history should increase. We hope you find your efforts worthwhile and your confidence in your ability to learn and enjoy history enhanced. If so, we will have accomplished our goals.

The Authors

CHAPTER 1

NEW WORLD ENCOUNTERS

SUMMARY

During the sixteenth century the Spanish, French, and English discovered the Americas, displaced Native American cultures, and established colonies in the Western Hemisphere.

Native American Cultures

Humans occupied part of the Western Hemisphere thousands of years before the European discovery of America. For example, the Mayas, Toltecs, and Aztecs in Central and South America created societies at least as sophisticated as that of the Europeans. Along the Atlantic Coast Native Americans formed diverse and mobile communities of hunters and gatherers. The clashes between the many Native American cultures and European cultures that took place after 1492 often resulted in individual and tribal extermination. Many Native Americans who were not killed in battle died as a result of deadly diseases brought to the Americas by the European newcomers.

Aztec Society

Native Americans developed a complex and successful empire in central Mexico.

Eastern Woodland Cultures

Along the Atlantic Coast Native Americans formed diverse and mobile communities of hunters and gatherers.

The Indians' New World

Native Americans were profoundly changed by the discovery. They often sought mutually beneficial trading arrangements with the Europeans, who typically misunderstood native ways. While some tribes and individuals adopted European religion, others tenaciously held onto their own culture and world view.

Disease and Dependency

Many Native Americans who were not killed in battle died as a result of deadly diseases brought to the Americas by the European newcomers.

West Africa: Peoples and History

A variety of intricate cultures dominated sub-Saharan West Africa at the time of the European colonization of the New World. The Portuguese explored the coast of West Africa and began trading in slaves, resulting in a massive forced migration of black Africans from Africa to the Americas.

Europe on the Eve of Conquest

Rapidly changing conditions in sixteenth-century Europe led to the discovery, exploration, and conquest of the Americas. At the end of the latter Middle Ages strong monarchs centralized power, forming modern nation-states. The Renaissance and the invention of the printing press aided in the expansion of new ideas and new technologies in Europe.

Europeans' New World

With explorers like Christopher Columbus leading the way, Spain established the largest colonial empire in the New World. Once in the New World, the strong and independent *conquistadores* led the Spanish in securing this colonial empire. Spanish government officials brought some order, class distinctions, and Catholicism to the empire of New Spain, and pushed the frontiers of their empire north into the lands of present-day Texas, New Mexico, Arizona, and California.

Admiral of the Ocean Sea

Through the insight and persistence of an adventurer from Genoa, Christopher Columbus, three ships from Spain made a significant voyage of discovery to the New World.

The Conquistadores

Strong and independent, the *conquistadores* led the Spanish in carving out a colonial empire.

Managing an Empire

Spanish government officials brought some order, class distinctions, and Catholicism to the empire of New Spain.

French Exploration and Settlement

Later, the French, without much support from the Crown, settled parts of North America, primarily exploiting the valuable fur trade.

The English New World

England began to venture out into the North Atlantic in the latter fifteenth century, in search of better fishing areas and, possibly, a short route to Asia, the mythical northwest passage. The Protestant Reformation permanently shattered English and European religious unity. As Protestantism became increasingly associated with English nationalism, the English longed for victories over Catholic Spain.

Religious Turmoil

The Protestant Reformation and the desire of Henry VIII for a male heir prompted a break with the Catholic Church and the establishment of the Church of England.

Protestantism in Europe

The teachings of Martin Luther and other Protestant theologians permanently shattered Europe's religious unity.

The Protestant Queen

Elizabeth I settled the religious debates and established in England a stronghold of Protestantism.

Religion, War, and Nationalism

As Protestantism became increasingly associated with English nationalism, the English longed for victories over Catholic Spain.

Irish Rehearsal for American Colonization

In the latter sixteenth century, the English established a pattern for colonization in Ireland.

English Colonization in Ireland

The English used Ireland as a testing ground for their theories of colonial rule.

English Brutality

Military governors of the Irish colonies often used brutal means to bring the natives under English rule.

England Turns to America

By the mid-1570s, the English became actively interested in North America.

Roanoke Experiment

An English pioneer of colonization, Sir Humphrey Gilbert, tried unsuccessfully to plant an outpost of the English nation in North America. Later, Sir Walter Raleigh similarly tried and failed to establish a settlement on Roanoke Island, Virginia.

Dreams of Possession

After Richard Hakluyt popularized exploration, the English were anxious to place permanent settlements in the Western Hemisphere.

LEARNING OBJECTIVES

After mastering this chapter, you should be able to:

1. Explain how ice age hunters may have crossed the Bering Straits and began settling North America.

2. Discuss the cultures of the Maya, Aztec, Toltec, and Algonquian; show the impact of European diseases on the Native Americans.

3. Explain why the Norse discovery of America was ineffective.

4. List the changing social conditions and new scientific discoveries that resulted in European voyages of discovery.

5. Describe the economic, political, social, and religious factors of the Spanish colonial system.

6. Discuss the motives, elements, and problems of the French colonial empire in North America.

7. Show the similarity between the British treatment of the Irish in the latter part of the sixteenth century and treatment of the slaves and Native Americans during the Colonial Era.

8. Discuss the early English attempts at planting colonies, including the work of Sir Humphrey Gilbert and Sir Walter Raleigh.

GLOSSARY

To build your social science vocabulary, familiarize yourself with the following terms:

1. **nomadic** wandering, roaming, or migrating. " . . . involved small, independent bands of nomadic people."

2. **technology** the methods, tools, and techniques of accomplishing work. " . . . the early Indians developed many of the same technologies that were just then appearing in other parts of the world."

3. **bureaucracy** significant influence in government by minor officials. " . . . formed complex government bureaucracies that dominated large tributary populations . . . "

4. **allocate** to give out, set aside, or distribute according to a predetermined system or plan. "These senior leaders allocated economic and human resources."

5. **provincial** of or related to a local area, sometimes implying unsophisticated. "Medieval kingdoms were loosely organized, and fierce provincial loyalties, . . . "

6. **feudal** an arrangement or system of service and obligations, based on land, pertaining especially to the Middle Ages. "Before the mid-fifteenth century, feudal nobles dominated small districts throughout Europe."

7. **despotic** like an oppressive ruler or dictator. "While these new rulers were often despotic . . . "

8. **mestizo** person of mixed parentage, especially Spanish and Indian. ". . .unions which produced 'mestizos' . . . "

9. **mulatto** a person of mixed parentage, especially white and black. " . . . unions which produced 'mestizos' and 'mulattoes' . . . "

10. **anticlericalism** a doctrine of opposition to the Roman Catholic Church." Popular anticlericalism helped spark religious reformation in England . . ."

IDENTIFICATION

Briefly identify the meaning and significance of the following terms:

1. Bering Straits _____

_____

2. Algonquian _____

_____

3. Ferdinand and Isabella _____

_____

4. Amerigo Vespucci _____

_____

5. Bernal Diaz del Castillo _____

_____

6. Bartolomé de Las Casas _____

_____

7. Samuel de Champlain _____

_____

8. Sir Walter Raleigh _____

_____

MATCHING

A. Match each of the following people with the appropriate description:

_____ 1. Cardinal Wolsey   **a**. young and sickly monarch of England, under whom militant Calvinists influenced policy

_____2. Anne Boleyn

     b. second wife of Henry VIII, and mother of Elizabeth I

_____3. Catherine of Aragon

     c. first child of Henry VIII; tried to return England to Catholicism

_____4. Mary I

     d. wealthy, powerful officer of the Catholic Church in England

_____5. Edward VI

     e. author of an English language version of the Bible

     f. Spanish wife of Henry VII

B. Match each of the following explorers/leaders with the appropriate description:

_____1. Sir Humphrey Gilbert

     a. able administrator and artist who led the second Roanoke Colony

_____2. Sir John Davies

     b. sea-dog who financed the two attempts to settle the Atlantic Coast in 1585 and 1587

_____3. Sir Richard Grenville

     c. cruel military governor of Munster in Ireland

_____4. Sir Walter Raleigh

     d. courageous sea-dog who returned to England with a boatload of "fool's gold"

_____5. John White

     e. leading figure in colonization of Ireland

     f. leader of the first settlement at Roanoke

COMPLETION

Answer the question or complete the statement by filling in the blanks with the correct word or words.

1. Native American farmers grew _____, _____, and _____.

2. Most tribes located on the Atlantic Coast of North America belonged to a linguistic group known as _____.

3. Eric the Red's son, Leif, established a small settlement in North America in the tenth century called _____.

4. More maneuverable ships built in the fifteenth century with a new type of sail were called _____.

5. The _____, invented at some time in the 1430s by Johann Gutenberg, aided the spread of new knowledge.

6. In 1494, Pope Alexander VI divided newly discovered lands between Spain and Portugal by issuing the _____.

7. The kings of Spain rewarded successful *conquistadores* with a grant of the labor of an Indian village. This grant was called an _____.

TRUE/FALSE

Mark the following statements either T (True) or F (False):

_____1. The arrival of Europeans in the Western Hemisphere had little impact on the lives of the natives.

_____2. Europeans were successful in teaching Native Americans to adopt European culture.

_____3. New concepts in navigation and naval architecture helped stimulate the exploration of the New World.

_____4. Columbus greatly underestimated the distance from Spain westward to Asia.

_____5. The Spanish colonies received little or no support from the government.

_____6. Cortés easily defeated the Aztec empire.

_____7. Montezuma was briefly indecisive because he thought the Spanish may have been messengers from the god Quetzalcoatl.

_____8. Coronado's expedition resulted in quick and permanent settlement of the Spanish borderlands.

_____9. The Act of Supremacy of 1534 made the Catholic Church supreme in England.

_____10. Semi-military colonies were planted in Ireland by the English in the 1560s and 1570s.

MULTIPLE CHOICE

Circle the one alternative that *best* completes the statement or answers the question.

1. As a result of the successful domestication of maize (corn), beans, and squash, some Native Americans
    a. gained greater control over their environments.
    b. became primarily vegetarian.
    c. evolved into a single continental cultural unit.
    d. could continue a wandering, hunting lifestyle.

2. The result of the deadly diseases brought to the New World by Europeans was
    a. an extremely high mortality among the natives, destroying the culture of many tribes.
    b. a diminution of these diseases in Europe.
    c. some deaths, but a low number compared with those caused by guns.
    d. a death rate high only where Indians lived in great concentrations.

3. In what is now Mexico, the Aztecs, Toltecs, and Mayas
    a. lived in huts in small tribal villages.
    b. thwarted the Spanish in their effort to build a great colonial empire.
    c. migrated across the narrow straits from America to Asia.
    d. developed phenomenal cultures prior to European contact.

4. Which of the following was *not* a reason for the rise of European exploration and trade?
    a. an increase in the population of Europe
    b. availability of cheaper land
    c. increased demand for luxury items
    d. centralization of political authority into several strong nation-states

5. A fifteenth-century European development which stimulated later exploration was
    a. the increase in trade.
    b. the rise of nation-states.
    c. the development of new naval technology.
    d. all of the above

6. The English and Spanish colonial systems differed in that
    a. the English Crown totally funded the colonies, whereas the Spanish Crown offered little aid.
    b. the English efforts were private and the Spanish colonies were supported by the Crown.
    c. the English settled the interior lands, while the Spanish settled primarily the coastal regions.
    d. religion played a central role in all the English colonies, but had little or no impact in New Spain.

7. The *encomienda* was
   a. an appellate court in colonial New Spain.
   b. a Spanish town council.
   c. a system of social class distinctions.
   d. a royal grant of Indian labor and land in return for protection and guidance.

8. In Canada, the French colonial empire was
   a. based on exploiting Indian labor for growing staple crops.
   b. based primarily on the fur trade.
   c. a successful transference of French feudal institutions.
   d. overpopulated with rural peasants and urban artisans.

9. John Cabot (Giovanni Caboto) primarily wanted to
   a. finance a new expedition from Venice to China.
   b. find the northwest passage for England.
   c. reestablish the fishing enterprise on the Grand Banks.
   d. convince the English to establish colonies along Hudson Bay.

10. The key to the success of Protestantism in England was
   a. widely popular anticlericalism.
   b. the fact that Martin Luther and John Calvin were both English.
   c. the fervent Catholicism of the Tudor Kings.
   d. the English hostility to the French Huguenots.

11. The religious settlement of Elizabeth I
   a. ended religious controversy in England.
   b. resulted in the restoration of Catholicism.
   c. established a congregational organization in the Church of England.
   d. made the Church of England Catholic in organization and ceremony, but Protestant in doctrines.

12. The defeat of the Spanish Armada in 1588
   a. changed the attitude of England toward colonies and empire.
   b. totally destroyed the Spanish fleet.
   c. had no religious significance to the English.
   d. marked the decline of the Spanish empire.

13. Which of the following is true regarding the English colonization of Ireland?
   a. Its purpose was to spread the Protestant faith.
   b. The experience served as a model for the colonization of America.
   c. The process was mostly peaceful, with the violence being caused primarily by the Irish.
   d. The process was a joint and cooperative venture because the Irish invited the English to their country.

14. In his attempt to settle the Roanoke colony, Sir Walter Raleigh found that

a. inadequate financing and difficulty in communication and supplies doomed the project.
b. the location was so good that other English colonizers competed for the available land.
c. the unwarranted hostility of the Indians made the collection of gold and silver too difficult.
d. Sir Francis Drake destroyed the colony out of jealousy.

15. To keep the dream of America alive Richard Hakluyt
    a. explored the New World and brought exotic products back to England.
    b. interviewed explorers and propagandized their stories in a book.
    c. planted a successful colony that made reasonably good profits.
    d. wrote an extensive work on the variety and cultural diversity of Native Americans.

THOUGHT QUESTIONS

To check your understanding of the key issues of this period, solve the following problems:

1. Describe the settlement of the Western Hemisphere from the perspective of a Native American.

2. What were the main causes, elements, and effects of the different approaches to colonies followed by the English and Spanish?

3. What is the relationship between capitalism and Calvinism?

4. What led to European exploration and expansion in the sixteenth century?

5. In what manner was the discovery of the New World a kind of ecological revolution?

CRITICAL THINKING QUESTIONS

After reading Christopher Columbus, "Letter to Luis De Sant' Angel" (1493), Alvar Nuñez Cabeza de Vaca, "Indians of the Rio Grande" (1528-1536), and Bartolomé de Las Casas, "Of the Island of Hispanola" (1542), answer the following questions:

Christopher Columbus, Letter to Luis de Sant' Angel (1493)

Sir,

As I know that you will have pleasure of the great victory which out Lord hath given me in my voyage, I write you this, by which you shall know that in [thirty-three] days I passed over the Indies with the fleet which the most illustrious King and Queen, our Lords, gave me: where I found very many islands peopled with inhabitants beyond number. And, of them all, I have taken possession for their Highnesses, with proclamation and the royal standard displayed; and I was not gainsaid. On the first which I found, I put the name Sant Salvador, in commemoration of His High Majesty, who marvelously hath given all this: the Indians call it [Guanhani]. The second I named the Island of Santa María de Concepción, the third Ferrandina, the fourth Fair Island, the fifth La Isla Juana; and so for each one a new name. When I reached Juana, I followed its coast westwardly, and found it so large that I thought it might be the mainland province of Cathay. And as I did not thus find any towns and villages on the seacoast, save small hamlets with the people whereof I could not get speech, because they all fled away forthwith, I went on further in the same direction, thinking I should not miss of great cities or towns. And at the end of many leagues, seeing that there was no change, . . . [I] turned back as far as a port agreed upon; from which I sent two men into the country to learn if there were a king, or any great cities. They traveled for three days, and found interminable small villages and a numberless population, but nought of ruling authority; wherefore they returned.

I understood sufficiently from other Indians . . . that this land, . . . was an island; and so I followed its coast eastwardly for a hundred and seven leagues as far as where it terminated; from which headland I saw another island to the east [eighteen] leagues distant from this, to which I at once gave the name La Spanola. And I proceeded thither, and followed the northern coast, as with La Juana, eastwardly for a hundred and [eighty-eight] great leagues in a direct easterly course, as with La Juana.

The which, and all the others, are more [fertile] to an excessive degree, and this extremely so. In it, there are many havens on the seacoast, incomparable with any others that I know in Christendom, and plenty of rivers so good and great that it is a marvel. The lands thereof are high, and in it are very many ranges of hills, and most lofty mountains incomparably beyond the Island of [Tenerife]; all most beautiful in a thousand shapes, and all accessible, and full of trees of a thousand kinds so lofty that they seem to reach the sky. And I am assured that they never lose their foliage; as may be imagined, since I saw them as green and as beautiful as they are in Spain during May. . . .

And the nightingale was singing, and other birds of a thousand sorts, in the month of November, round about the way I was going. There are palm trees of six or eight species, wondrous to see for their beautiful variety; but so are the other trees, and fruits, and plants therein. There are wonderful pine groves, and very large plains of verdure, and there is honey, and many kinds of birds, and many various fruits. In the earth there are many mines of metals; and there is a population of incalculable number. Spanola is a marvel; the mountains and hills, and plains, and fields, and land, so beautiful and rich for planting and sowing, for breeding cattle of all sorts, for building of towns and villages.

There could be no believing, without seeing, such harbors as are here, as well as the many and great rivers, and excellent waters, most of which contain gold. In the trees and fruits and plants, there are great differences from those of Juana. In [La Spanola], there are many spiceries, and great mines of gold and other metals.

The people of this island, and of all the others that I have found and seen, or not seen, all go naked, men and women, just as their mothers bring them forth; although some women cover a single place with the leaf of a plant, or a cotton something which they make for that purpose. They have no iron or steel, nor any weapons; nor are they fit thereunto; not be because they be not a well-formed people and of fair stature, but that they are most wondrously timorous. They have no other weapons than the stems of reeds in their seeding state, on the end of which they fix little sharpened stakes. Even these, they dare not use; for many times has it happened that I sent two or three men ashore to some village to parley, and countless numbers of them sallied forth, but as soon as they saw those approach, they fled away in such wise that even a father would not wait for his son. And this was not because any hurt had ever done to any of them:-but such they are, incurably timid. It is true that since they have become more assured, and are losing that terror, they are artless and generous with what they have, to such a degree as no one would believe but him who had seen it. Of anything they have, if it be asked for, they never say no, but do rather invite the person to accept it, and show as much lovingness as though they would give their hearts. And whether it be a thing of value, or one of little worth, they are straightways content with whatsoever trifle of whatsoever kind may be given them in return for it. I forbade that anything so worthless as fragments of broken platters, and pieces of broken glass, and strapbuckles, should be given them; although
when they were able to get such things, they seemed to think they had the best jewel in the world. . . .

And they knew no sect, nor idolatry; save that they all believe that power and goodness are in the sky, and they believed very firmly that I, with these ships and crew, came from the sky; and in such opinion, they received me at every place were I landed, after they had lost their terror. And this comes not because they are ignorant; on the contrary, they are men of very subtle wit, who navigate all those seas, and who give a marvellously good account of everything-but because they never saw men wearing clothes nor the like of our ships. And as soon as I arrived in the Indies, in the first island that I found, I took some of them by force to the intent that they should learn [our speech] and give me information of what there was in those parts. And so it was, that very soon they understood [us] and we them, what by speech or what by signs; and those [Indians] have been of much service . . . with loud cries of "Come! come to see the people from heaven!" Then, as soon as their minds were reassured about us, every one came, men as well as women, so that there remained none behind, big or little; and they all brought something to eat and drink, which they gave with wondrous lovingness. . . .

It seems to me that in all those islands, the men are all content with a single wife; and to their chief or king they give as many as twenty. The women, it appears to me, do more work than the men. Nor have I been able to learn whether they held personal property, for it seemed to me that whatever one had, they all took share of, especially of eatable things. Down to the present, I have not found in those islands any monstrous men, as many expected, but on the contrary all the people are very comely; nor are they black like those in Guinea, but have

11

flowing hair; and they are not begotten where there is an excessive violence of the rays of the sun. . . . In those islands, where there are lofty mountains, the cold was very keen there, this winter; but they endured it by being accustomed thereto, and by the help of the meats which they eat with many and inordinately hot spices. . . .

Since thus our Redeemer has given to our most illustrious King and Queen, and to their famous kingdoms, this victory in so high a matter, Christendom should take gladness therein and make great festivals, and give solemn thanks to the Holy Trinity for the great exaltation they shall have by the conversion of so many peoples to our holy faith; and next for the temporal benefit which will bring hither refreshment and profit, not only to Spain, to all Christians. This briefly, in accordance with the facts. Dated, on the caravel, off the Canary Islands, the 15 February of the year 1493.

Alvar Núñez Cabeza de Vaca, "Indians of the Rio Grande" (1528-1536)

They are so accustomed to running that, without resting or getting tired, they run from morning till night in pursuit of a deer, and kill a great many, because they follow until the game is worn out, sometimes catching it alive. Their huts are of matting placed over four arches. They carry them on their back and move every two or three days in quest of food; they plant nothing that would be of any use.

They are very merry people, and even when famished do not cease to dance and celebrate their feasts and ceremonials. Their best times are when "tunas" (prickly pears) are ripe, because then they have plenty to eat and spend the time in dancing and eating day and night. As long as these tunas last they squeeze and open them and set them to dry. When dried they are put in baskets like figs and kept to be eaten on the way. The peelings they grind and pulverize.

All over this country there are a great many deer, fowl and other animals which I have before enumerated. Here also they come up with cows; I have seen them thrice and have eaten their meat. They appear to me of the size of those in Spain. Their horns are small, like those of the Moorish cattle; the hair is very long, like fine wool and like a peajacket; some are brownish and others black, and to my taste they have better and more meat than those from here. Of the small hides the Indians make blankets to cover themselves with, and of the taller ones they make shoes and targets. These cows come from the north, across the country further on, to the coast of Florida, and are found all over the land for over four hundred leagues. On this whole stretch, through the valleys by which they come, people who live there descend to subsist upon their flesh. And a great quantity of hides are met with inland.

We remained with the Avavares Indians for eight months, according to our reckoning of the moons. During that time they came for us from many places and said that verily we were children of the sun. Until then Donates and the negro had not made any cures, but we found ourselves so pressed by the Indians coming from all sides, that all of us had to become medicine men. I was the most daring and reckless of all in undertaking cures. We never treated anyone that did not afterwards say he was well, and they had such confidence in our skill as to believe that none of them would die as long as we were among them. . . .

The women brought many mats, with which they built us houses, one for each of us and those attached to him. After this we would order them to boil all the game, and they did it quickly in ovens built by them for the purpose. We partook of everything a little, giving the rest to the principal man among those who had come with us for distribution among all. Every one then came with the share he had received for us to breathe on it and bless it, without which they left it untouched. Often we had with us three to four thousand persons. And it was very tiresome to have to breathe on and make the sign of the cross over every morsel they ate or drank. For many other things which they wanted to do they would come to ask our permission, so that it is easy to realize how greatly we were bothered. The women brought us tunas, spiders, worms, and whatever else they could find, for they would rather starve than partake of anything that had not first passed through our hands .

While traveling with those, we crossed a big river coming from the north and, traversing about thirty leagues of plains, met a number of people that came from afar to meet us on the trail, who treated us like the foregoing ones.

Thence on there was a change in the manner of reception, insofar as those who would meet us on the trail with gifts were no longer robbed by the Indians of our company, but after we had entered their homes they tendered us all they possessed, and the dwellings also. We turned over everything to the principals for distribution. Invariably those who had been deprived of their belongings would follow us, in order to repair their losses, so that our retinue became very large. They would tell them to be careful and not conceal anything of what they owned, as it could not be done without our knowledge, and then we would cause their death. So much did they frighten them that on the first few days after joining us they would be trembling all the time, and would not dare to speak or lift their eyes to Heaven.

Those guided us for more than fifty leagues through a desert of very rugged mountains, and so arid that there was no game. Consequently we suffered much from lack of food, and finally forded a very big river, with its water reaching to our chest. Thence on many of our people began to show the effects of the hunger and hardships they had undergone in those mountains, which were extremely barren and tiresome to travel.

The next morning all those who were strong enough came along, and at the end of three journeys we halted. Alonso del Castillo and Estevanico, the negro, left with the women as guides, and the woman who was a captive took them to a river that flows between mountains where there was a village in which her father lived, and these were the first adobes we saw that were like unto real houses. Castillo and Estevanico went to these and, after holding parley with the Indians, at the end of three days Castillo returned to where he had left us, bringing with him five or six of the Indians. He told how he had found permanent houses, inhabited, the people of which ate beans and squashes, and that he had also seen maize.

Of all things upon earth that caused us the greatest pleasure, and we gave endless thanks to our Lord for this news. Castillo also said that the negro was coming to meet us on the way, near by, with all the people of the houses. For that reason we started, and after going a league and a half met the negro and the people that came to receive us, who gave us beans and many squashes to eat, gourds to carry water in, robes of cowhide, and other things. As those people and the Indians of our company were enemies, and did not understand each other, we took leave of the latter, leaving them all that had been given to us, while we went on with the former and, six leagues beyond, when night was already approaching, reached their houses, where they received us with great ceremonies. Here we remained one day, and left on the next, taking them with us to other permanent houses, where they subsisted on the same food also, and thence on we found a new custom. . . .

Having seen positive traces of Christians and become satisfied they were very near, we gave many thanks to our Lord for redeeming us from our sad and gloomy condition. Anyone can imagine our delight when he reflect how long we had been in that land, and how many dangers and hardships we had suffered. That night I entreated one of my companions to go after the Christians, who were moving through the part of the country pacified and quieted by us, and who were three days ahead of where we were. They did not like my suggestion, and excused themselves from going, on the ground of being tired and worn out, although any of them might have done it far better than I, being younger and stronger.

Seeing their reluctance, in the morning I took with me the negro and eleven Indians and, following the trail, went in search of the Christians. On that day we made ten leagues, passing three places where they slept. The next morning I came upon four Christians on horseback, who, seeing me in such a strange attire, and in company with Indians, were greatly startled. They stared at me for quite awhile, speechless; so great was their surprise that they could not find words to ask me anything. I spoke first, and told them to lead me to their captain, and we went together to Diego de Alcaraz, their commander.

Bartolomé de Las Casas, "Of the Island of Hispaniola" (1542)

God has created all these numberless people to be quite the simplest, without malice or duplicity, most obedient, most faithful to their natural Lords, and to the Christians, whom they serve; the most humble, most patient, most peaceful and calm, without strife nor tumults; not wrangling, nor querulous, as free from uproar, hate and desire of revenge as any in the world. . . .

Among these gentle sheep, gifted by their Maker with the above qualities, the Spaniards entered as soon as soon as they knew them, like wolves, tiger and lions which had been starving for many days, and since forty years they have done nothing else; nor do they afflict, torment, and destroy them with strange and new, and divers kinds of cruelty, never before seen, nor heard of, nor read of. . . . .

The Christians, with their horses and swords and lances, began to slaughter and practice strange cruelty among them. They penetrated into the country and spared neither children nor the aged, nor pregnant women, nor those in child labour, all of whom they ran through the body and lacerated, as though they were assaulting so many lambs herded in their sheepfold.

They made bets as to who would slit a man in two, or cut off his head at one blow: or they opened up his bowels. They tore the babes from their mothers' breast by the feet, and dashed their heads against the rocks. Others they seized by the shoulders and threw into the rivers, laughing and joking, and when they fell into the water they exclaimed: "boil body so and so!" They spitted the bodies of other babes, together with their mothers and all who were before them, on their swords.

They made a gallows just high enough for the feet to nearly touch the ground, and by thirteens, in honour and reverence of our Redeemer and the twelve Apostles, they put wood underneath and, with fire, they burned the Indians alive.

They wrapped the bodies of others entirely in dry straw, binding them in it and setting fire to it; and so they burned them. They cut off the hands of all they wished to take alive, made them carry them fastened on to them, and said: "Go and carry letters": that is; take the news to those who have fled to the mountains.

They generally killed the lords and nobles in the following way. They made wooden gridirons of stakes, bound them upon them, and made a slow fire beneath; thus the victims gave up the spirit by degrees, emitting cries of despair in their torture. . . .

1. How does Christopher Columbus enhance the potential of the New World in his letter? What might be his motivation to "sell" the features of the New World.

2. Compare the Native American perceptions of Christopher Columbus and Cabeza de Vaca. In what ways might these views be different if we had extensive written sources in their own words?

3. Describe the idealized image of the Native American expressed by Bartolomé de las Casas. How does this description reveal a possible split in Spanish opinions of the New World?

4. From the documents what can be inferred regarding differences between the Spanish and the English approaches to exploring the New World?

5. Looking at all three documents, evaluate the role of religion in the European perceptions of the New World.

CHAPTER 2

COMPETING VISIONS: ENGLISH COLONIZATION IN THE SEVENTEENTH CENTURY

SUMMARY

In the seventeenth century, different and sometimes disparate groups of English settlers established several colonies in North America.

Decision To Emigrate

Some Englishmen migrated to the New World for economic reasons, leaving poverty and seeking land. Others came seeking religious freedom.

THE CHESAPEAKE: DREAMS OF WEALTH

In the early to mid-seventeenth century, the English established two successful but diverse colonies around the Chesapeake Bay—Virginia and Maryland.

Entrepreneurs in Virginia

In 1607, the London Company built Jamestown in Virginia. This colony, however, experienced trouble because of a hostile environment and because colonists did not work for the common good.

Saving the Adventurers from Themselves

To save the colony Captain John Smith took over the management of the town and imposed military order. The London Company also restructured the government and sent more people to keep the colony going.

"Stinking Weed"

One key to the eventual success of Virginia was the development by John Rolfe of tobacco as a commercial crop. London Company directors further attracted settlers by giving land grants (headrights), establishing local government (House of Burgesses), and bringing women to the colony. In 1624, King James I declared that Virginia was a royal colony. Nonetheless the economic and social aspects of life there continued much as before.

Deadly Harvest

Disease and battles with the native population made Virginia a dangerous place. These problems, combined with the continued low percentage of women colonists, made establishing a family difficult.

Addressing the Scandal

In 1624, King James I declared that Virginia was a royal colony. Nonetheless, the economic and social aspects of life there continued much as before.

Maryland: The Troubled Sanctuary

In the 1630s, Sir George Calvert and his son Cecilius, the Lords Baltimore, acquired a royal grant to settle a colony north of Virginia, which was named Maryland in honor of the queen. The second Lord Baltimore insisted on religious toleration within the colony, but he still faced much sectarian trouble during the early days.

A "New" England In America

Calvinist religious principles played an important role in the colonization of New England. A small group of Separatists or Pilgrims first went to Holland and then settled the "Plymouth Plantation."

A Godly Commonwealth

A much larger and wealthier group of Puritans, wanting to escape the tyranny of King Charles I, established the Massachusetts Bay Colony. Under the leadership of John Winthrop, they attempted to create a better society in the New World.

"A City on a Hill"

Enjoying a steady stream of new migrants, in the 1630s, the founders of the Massachusetts Bay built rigorous economic and political institutions. Many villages in the colony used democratic town meetings to solve local political problems.

Dissenting Voices

Some of the leaders of the colony disagreed with the laws and theology of the legal authorities, and were expelled from Massachusetts Bay. Two of these, Roger Williams and Anne Hutchinson, were forced to leave the colony. They migrated to what would later become Rhode Island.

Breaking Away

Four colonies—New Hampshire, New Haven, Connecticut, and Rhode Island—were established as a result of people leaving Massachusetts Bay.

Diversity in the Middle Colonies

The key to the Middle Colonies—New York, New Jersey, Pennsylvania, and Delaware—was diversity, both within and among the several colonies.

Anglo-Dutch Rivalry on the Hudson

The Dutch colony of New Netherland had been settled not only by the Dutch but also by Finns, Swedes, Germans, and Africans. England easily wrested the colony from the Dutch and established New York.

Confusion in New Jersey

New Jersey was originally a proprietary colony owned by Lord Berkeley and Sir George Carteret, and was split into two colonies when a group of Quakers bought land there. New Jersey never prospered in the way that New York did, and struggled with much political discord.

Quakers in America

Because they were persecuted in England, the Quakers came to the New World and settled

Pennsylvania.

Penn's "Holy Experiment"
William Penn, a Quaker convert, tried to establish a complex society based on Quaker principles. Although Pennsylvania was successful as a colony, Penn abandoned his experiment in 1701.

Planting the Carolinas
The area south of the Chesapeake known as the Carolinas evolved differently compared with Virginia or Maryland.

Proprietors of the Carolinas
The English settled the land south of Virginia as a result of the restoration of King Charles II. He offered the area as a reward to a few of his followers.

The Barbadian Connection
Success in the Carolinas was largely the result of the work of the Earl of Shaftesbury and the migration of wealthy families from Barbados. In 1729, the land was divided into North and South Carolina and made a royal colony.

The Founding of Georgia
The colony of Georgia resulted from a utopian vision of General James Oglethorpe. He settled the land south of Charleston in order to give hope to the debtors imprisoned in London, and at the same time, occupy land claimed by both England and Spain.

Rugged and Laborious Beginnings
The themes that connect the history of the early colonial development are hard work and diversity.

LEARNING OBJECTIVES

After mastering this chapter, you should be able to:

1. List the problems in England that were motives for emigration.

2. Discuss the corporate problems involved in the settlement of Virginia.

3. Show the importance of tobacco plantations in the social, economic, and political life of the colony of Virginia.

4. Narrate the story of the founding and settlement of Maryland, focusing on its role for Catholics.

5. Describe the impact of the Quakers on the settlement of the Middle Colonies.

6. Describe the type of society William Penn tried to create in his "Holy Experiment."

7. Compare the motives for colonizing Georgia with those for colonizing the other colonies.

8. Discuss the problems of dissent in the Massachusetts Bay Colonies.

GLOSSARY

To build your social science vocabulary, familiarize yourself with the following terms:

1. **duties** taxes or sums required by a government to be paid on the transfer or use of goods. "The duties he collected on tobacco imports began to mount."

2. **indentured servants** servants who are bound or contracted under seal to a period of labor. " . . . most emigrants were single males in their teens or early twenties who came to the New World as indentured servants."

3. **domain** territory or land over which authority or dominion is granted to an individual. " . . . he possessed absolute authority over anyone living in his domain."

4. **ecclesiastical** of or relating to religious matters. "To their enemies . . . the Puritans were a bother, always pointing out civil and ecclesiastical imperfections."

5. **communal** held or owned in common by all members of a group or community. "Many people throughout the ages have espoused such communal rhetoric . . . "

6. **franchise** a right granted or given by a government, such as the right to vote. "This decision greatly expanded the franchise of Massachusetts Bay . . ."

7. **antinomianism** freedom from adherence to moral law. "Even contemporaries found her religious ideas, usually termed Antinomianism, somewhat confusing."

8. **unicameral** having one chamber or house. "Penn signed the Charter of Liberties, a new frame of government that established a unicameral . . . legislature . . ."

9. **mortality** the ratio of death to the population. " . . . high mortality was a major reason that the Chesapeake colonies developed so differently from those of New England."

10. **sovereignty** control or absolute power in a state. " . . . they sparked the English civil war, an event that generated bold new thinking about Republican government and popular sovereignty."

IDENTIFICATION

Briefly identify the meaning and significance of the following terms:

1. Joint-Stock Company

2. Jamestown

3. William Penn

4. Sir Thomas Gates and Sir Thomas Dale

5. "Starving Time"

6. "Plundering Time"

7. William Bradford

8. Robert Browne

9. John Winthrop

10. Thomas Hooker

MATCHING

A. Match the following leaders with the appropriate description:

_____1. Captain John Smith

_____2. Sir Thomas Smith

_____3. John Rolfe

_____4. Sir Edwin Sandys

_____5. John Harvey

a. investor who ousted the original leader of the Virginia Company and instituted colonial reforms

b. governor of Virginia who was sent back to England by the colonists and warned that he would be shot if he ever returned to Virginia

c. adventurer who instituted military discipline and perhaps saved the Virginia colony

d. governor who took over rule of Virginia in 1610

e. wealthy London merchant and original leader of the Virginia Company

f. Virginia settler who married Pocahontas and experimented with growing tobacco in the colony

B.   Match the following individuals with the appropriate description:

_____1. Peter Stuyvesant

_____2. Richard Nicolls

_____3. John, Lord Berkeley

_____4. Sir George Carteret

_____5. William Penn

a. proprietor of New Jersey who sold his claim to a group of Quakers

b. naval officer who was significant in New York and New Jersey's colonial history

c. Quaker who viewed his colony as a "Holy Experiment"

d. English spokesman for the Quaker idea of the "Inner Light"

e. director-general of New Amsterdam

f. proprietor of New Jersey who worked in East Jersey to make a profit

COMPLETION

Answer the question or complete the statement by filling in the blanks with the correct word or words:

1. _____ was the military leader and religious reformer who ruled England after the execution of _____.

2. The Catholic king of England who was exiled by the Glorious Revolution was _____.

3. The original Virginia settlers founded the town of _____ in 1607.

4. Virginia's representative assembly was called the _____.

5. A grant of land to anyone who would pay transportation costs to a colony was known as a _____.

6. A servant bound to a master for a period of time in return for transportation to a colony was an _____ servant.

7. A small annual payment to a proprietor of a colony quitrent in exchange for a grant of land was called a _____.

8. The Puritan who became the most important governor of Massachusetts Bay Colony was _____.

TRUE/FALSE

Mark the following statements either T (True) or F (False):

_____1. The "Great Migration" sent few, if any, immigrants to Massachusetts Bay Colony.

_____2. The form of church government known as Congregationalism let each congregation be independent of outside interference.

_____3. The town meeting was the center of local government in New England.

_____4. Roger Williams was exiled from Massachusetts Bay Colony because he was a radical supporter of John Winthrop.

_____5. Anne Hutchinson was an outspoken critic of Massachusetts Bay orthodoxy.

_____6. Although settled by exiles, Rhode Island did no better than Massachusetts Bay in toleration of heretics.

_____7.   New York, New Jersey, and Pennsylvania had a very homogeneous population.

_____8.   In ruling New York, James, Duke of York, effectively used an assembly.

_____9.   George Fox, the spokesman for the Quaker religion, believed that Christ was in the soul of every man.

_____10. In the seventeenth century, Virginia and Maryland quickly developed a stable society, one especially healthy for families and child rearing.

MULTIPLE CHOICE

Circle the one alternative that *best* completes the statement or answers the question.

1.   In colonizing North America, the English kings
     a. followed a precise plan of geographic development.
     b. wanted to separate the colonies into distinct groups based on economics, politics, religion, and labor system.
     c. negotiated treaties with the Indians.
     d. followed no plan and distributed the land haphazardly, creating overlapping territorial claims.

2.   The flow of immigrants to the English colonies in the seventeenth century
     a. was determined by political upheaval and economic recession.
     b. followed a precise plan of the various monarchs.
     c. followed a precise plan of religious leaders who based the settlement of North America on biblical prophecy.
     d. was determined by North American weather patterns.

3.   The London Company (later the Virginia Company) primarily wanted to
     a. establish a religious haven.
     b. make a profit through the discovery of gold and silver.
     c. experiment with democracy.
     d. establish a military fort to counter the power of the Spanish.

4.   In the early days of the Virginia Colony, the settlers
     a. were about evenly divided between men and women.
     b. were well prepared to plant a colonial outpost.
     c. preferred searching for gold to farming or guarding the settlement.
     d. had few troubles except for the unfriendly Indians.

5. The solution to the economic problems of Virginia was
   a. cultivation of tobacco.
   b. reorganization of the joint-stock company with an infusion of new capital.
   c. a successful agreement with the Native Americans.
   d. trading with Barbados.

6. The Lords Baltimore viewed their colonizing project as
   a. a way to bring the true religion to the Indians.
   b. a profit-seeking joint-stock company.
   c. an outpost to oppose Catholic Spain.
   d. a haven for English Catholics.

7. In the seventeenth century, the colonists in Massachusetts were more successful than Virginias
   a. in relating to the Indians.
   b. in establishing the Anglican Church.
   c. in finding a profitable staple crop.
   d. in adopting a concept of corporate or community welfare.

8. Pilgrims or Separatists left the Anglican Church because they
   a. felt that it was still too Catholic.
   b. could not attend services in Holland.
   c. thought that it was controlled by Calvinists.
   d. maintained loyalty to Archbishop Laud.

9. The lives of Roger Williams and Anne Hutchinson indicate that
   a. Puritans seldom disagreed on matters of theology.
   b. Massachusetts Bay officials insisted on freedom of religious thought and expression.
   c. Massachusetts Bay faced difficulties in creating the perfect society in America.
   d. Massachusetts Bay Colony sent preachers to frontiers as missionaries to the Indians.

10. In Massachusetts the electorate consisted of
    a. the "Elect."
    b. all adult males.
    c. all adult male members of a Congregational Church.
    d. property-holding men and women who were saved.

11. The colony of New York
    a. was originally settled by the Duke of York and then became Dutch.
    b. was originally settled by the Dutch and then taken by force by the English.
    c. was almost completely Dutch, with no African-American population.
    d. had been administered well by Dutch governors.

12. William Penn's Frame of Government for his colony
    a. was based on the ideas of James Harrington.
    b. denied the right of due process.

c. established the Quaker religion in Pennsylvania.
d. granted freedom of conscience to all except Catholics.

13. The government of the Carolinas
    a. was a theocracy.
    b. ignored social and economic factors in granting power.
    c. forbade slavery.
    d. was written by the Earl of Shaftesbury with help from John Locke.

14. The economy of Carolina was
    a. based on slavery and cotton.
    b. as diverse as that of the Middle Colonies.
    c. at first diverse in agriculture and then became dependent on rice as a staple.
    d. not as important as its role as a buffer to Spanish America.

15. The seventeenth-century English colonies
    a. had much in common except for differences over loyalty to the king.
    b. had few common traits other than their loyalty to the monarch.
    c. finally agreed to establish the Anglican Church.
    d. agreed on a crude organization known as a Continental Congress.

THOUGHT QUESTIONS

To check your understanding of the key issues of this period, solve the following problems:

1. Comment on the role Calvinism played in the early history of America.

2. To what extent did environment determine the culture of the colonies?

3. Although seeking religious freedom, the Puritan leaders were religious bigots. Why?

4. What was the role of public relations, promotion, and advertising in the settling of the colonies?

5. What motives explain the development of representative assemblies in the various colonies?

CRITICAL THINKING QUESTIONS

After reading John Smith "The Starving Time" (1624), "The Laws of Virginia" (1610-1611), and John Winthrop "A Model of Christian Charity" (1630), answer the following questions:

John Smith, "The Starving Time" (1624)

It might well be thought, a Countrie so faire (as Virginia is) and a people so tractable, would long ere this have beene quietly possessed to the satisfaction of the adventurers, & the eternizing of the memory of those that effected it. But because all the world doe see a defailement; this following Treatise shall give satisfaction to all indifferent Readers, how the businesse hath bin carried; where no doubt they will easily understand and answer to their question, how it came to passe there was no better speed and successe in those proceedings. . . .

The day before Captain Smith returned for England with the ships, Captain Davis arrived in a small Pinace, with some sixteene proper men more . . . for the Salvages no sooner understood Smith was gone, but they all revolted, and did spoile and murther all they incountered. Now wee were all constrained to live onely on that Smith had onely for his owne Companie, for the rest had consumed their proportions . . . Sicklemore upon the confidence of Powhatan, with about thirtie others as carelesse as himselfe, were all slaine, onely Jeffrey Shortridge escaped, and Pokahontas the Kings daughter saved a boy called Henry Spilman, that lived many yeeres after, by her meanes, amongst the Patawomekes. . . . Now we all found the losse of Captain Smith, yea his greatest maligners could now curse his losse: as for corne, provision and contribution from the Salvages, we had nothing but mortall wounds, with clubs and arrowes; as for our Hogs, Hens, Goats, Sheepe, Horse, or what lived, our commanders, officers & Salvages daily consumed them, some small proportions sometimes we tasted, till all was devoured; then swords, armes, pieces, or any thing, wee traded with the Salvages, whose cruell fingers were so oft imbrewed in our blouds, that what by their crueltie, our Governours indiscretion, and the losse of our ships, of five hundred within six moneths after Captain Smiths departure, there remained not past sixtie men, women and children, most miserable and poore creatures; and those were preserved for the most part, by roots, herbes, acornes, walnuts, berries, now and then a little fish: they that had startch in these extremities, made no small use of it; yea, even the very skinnes of our horses. Nay, so great was our famine, that a Salvage we slew, and buried, the poorer sort tooke him up againe and eat him, and so did divers one another boyled and stewed with roots and herbs: And one amongst the rest did kill his wife, powdered [salted] her, and had eaten part of her before it was knowne, for which hee was executed, as hee well deserved; now whether shee was better roasted, boyled or carbonado'd [grilled], I know not, but of such a dish as powdered wife I never heard of. This was that time, which still to this day we called the starving time; it were too vile to say, and scarce to be beleeved, what we endured.

The Laws of Virginia (1610-1611)

Whereas his Majesty, like himself a most zealous prince, has in his own realms a principal care of true religion and reverence to God and has always strictly commanded his generals and governors, with all his forces wheresoever, to let their ways be, like his ends, for the glory of God.

And forasmuch as no good service can be performed, or were well managed, where military discipline is not observed, and military discipline cannot be kept where the rules or chief parts thereof be not certainly set down and generally know, I have, with the advice and counsel of Sir Thomas Gates, Knight, Lieutenant-General, adhered unto the laws divine and orders politic and martial of his lordship, the same exemplified, as addition of such others as I found either the necessity of the present state of the colony to require or the infancy and weakness of the body thereof as yet able to digest, and do now publish them to all persons in the colony, that they may as well take knowledge of the laws themselves as of the penalty and punishment, which, without partiality, shall be inflicted upon the breakers of the same.

1. First, Since we owe our highest and supreme duty, our greatest,
and all our allegiance to him from whom all power and authority is derived and flows as from the first and only fountain, and being especial soldiers impressed in this sacred cause, we must alone expect our success from him, who is only the blesser of all good attempts, the king of kings, the commander of commanders, and lord of hosts, I do strictly command and charge all captains and officers, of what quality or nature soever, whether commanders in the field or in town or towns, forts or fortresses, to have a care that the Almighty God be duly and daily served and that they call upon their people to hear sermons, as that also they diligently frequent morning and evening prayer themselves by their own exemplar and daily life and duty herein, encouraging others thereunto, and that such who shall often and willfully absent themselves be duly punished according to the martial law in that case provided.

2. That no man speak impiously or maliciously against the holy and
blessed Trinity or any of the three persons, that is to say, against God the Father, God the Son, and God the Holy Ghost, or against the known articles of the Christian faith, upon pain of death.

3. That no man blaspheme God's holy name upon pain of death, or use unlawful oaths, taking the name of God in

vain, curse, or bane upon pain of severe punishment for the first offense so committed and for the second to have a bodkin thrust through his tongue; and if he continue the blaspheming of God's holy name, for the third time so offending, he shall be brought to a martial court and there receive censure of death of his offense.

4.No man shall use any traitorous words against his Majesty's person or royal authority, upon pain of death.

5.No man shall speak any word or do any act which may tend to the derision or despite of God's holy word, upon pain of death; nor shall any man unworthily demean himself unto any preacher or minister of the same, but generally hold them in all reverent regard and dutiful entreaty; otherwise he the offender shall openly be whipped three times and ask public forgiveness in the assembly of the congregation three several Sabbath days.

6.Every man and woman duly, twice a day upon the first tolling of the bell, shall upon the working days repair unto the church to hear divine service upon pain of losing his or her day's allowance for the first omission, for the second to be whipped, and for the third to be condemned to the galleys for six months. Likewise, no man or woman shall dare to violate or break the Sabbath by any gaming, public or private abroad or at home, but duly sanctify and observe the same, both himself and his family, by preparing themselves at home with private prayer that they may be the better fitted for the public, according to the commandments of God and the orders of our church. As also every man and woman shall repair in the morning to the divine service and sermons preached upon the Sabbath day in the afternoon to divine service and catechizing, upon pain for the first fault to lose their provision and allowance for the whole week following, for the second to lose the said allowance and also to be whipped, and for the third to suffer death.

7.All preachers and ministers within this our colony or colonies shall, in the forts where they are resident, after divine service, duly preach every Sabbath day in the forenoon and catechise in the afternoon and weekly say the divine service twice every day and preach every Wednesday. Likewise, every minister where he is resident, within the same fort or fortress, towns or town, shall choose unto him four of the most religious and better disposed as well to inform of the abuses and neglects of the people in their duties and service of God, as also to the due reparation and keeping of the church handsome and fitted with all reverent observances thereunto belonging. Likewise, every minister shall keep a faithful and true record of church book of all christenings, marriages, and deaths of such our people as shall happen within their fort or fortress, towns or town, at any time, upon the burden of a neglectful conscience and upon pain of losing their entertainment.

8.He that, upon pretended malice, shall murder or take away the life of any man, shall be punished with death.

9.No man shall commit the horrible and detestable sins of sodomy, upon pain of death; and he or she that can be lawfully convict of adultery shall be punished with death. No man shall ravish or force any woman, maid or Indian, or other, upon pain of death; and know that he or she that shall commit fornication, and evident proof made thereof, for their first fault shall be whipped, for their second they shall be whipped, and for their third they shall be whipped three times a week for one month and ask public forgiveness in the assembly of the congregation.

10.No man shall be found guilty of sacrilege, which is a trespass as well committed in violating and abusing any sacred ministry, duty, or office of the church irreverently or prophanely, as by being a church robber to filch, steal, or carry away anything out of the church appertaining thereunto or unto any holy and consecrated place to the divine service of God, which no man shall do upon pain of death. Likewise, he that shall rob the store of any commodities therein of what quality soever, whether provisions of victuals, or of arms, trucking stuff, apparel, linen, or woolen, hose or shoes, hats or caps, instruments or tools of steel, iron, etc., or shall rob from his fellow soldier or neighbor anything that is his, victuals, apparel, household stuff, tool, or what necessary else soever, by water or land, out of boat, house, or knapsack, shall be punished with death. . . .

11.Every minister or preacher shall, every Sabbath day before catechising, read all these laws and ordinances publicly in the assembly of the congregation upon pain of his entertainment checked for that week.

John Winthrop, "A Model of Christian Charity" (1630)

God almighty in His most holy and wise providence hath so disposed of the condition of mankind, as in all times some must be rich, some poor, some high and eminent in power and dignity, others mean and in subjection.
Reason: First, to hold conformity with the rest of His works, being delighted to show forth the glory of His

wisdom in the variety and difference of the creatures and the glory of His power, in ordering all these differences for the preservation and good of the whole.

Reason: Secondly, that He might have the more occasion to manifest the work of His spirit. First, upon the wicked in moderating and restraining them, so that the rich and mighty should not eat up the poor, nor the poor and despised rise up against their superiors and shake off their yoke. Secondly, in the regenerate in exercising His graces in them, as in the great ones, their love, mercy, gentleness, temperance, etc., in the poor and inferior sort, their faith, patience, obedience, etc.

Reason: Thirdly, that every man might have need of other, and from hence they might all be knit more nearly together in the bond of brotherly affection. From hence it appears plainly that no man is made more honorable than another, or more wealthy, etc., out of any particular and singular respect to himself, but for the glory of his creator and the common good of the creature, man.

Thus stands the cause between God and us. We are entered into covenant with Him for this work, we have taken out a commission, the Lord hath given us leave to draw our own articles we have professed to enterprise these actions upon these and these ends, we have hereupon besought Him of favor and blessing. Now if the Lord shall please to hear us, and bring us in peace to the place we desire, then hath He ratified this covenant and sealed our commission, [and] will expect a strict performance of the articles contained in it, but if we shall neglect the observations of these articles which are the ends we have propounded, and dissembling with our God, shall fall to embrace this present world and prosecute our carnal intentions seeking great things for ourselves and our posterity, the Lord will surely break out in wrath against us, be revenged of such a perjured people, and make us know the price of the breach of such a covenant.

Now the only way to avoid this shipwreck and to provide for our posterity is to follow the counsel of Micah, to do justly, to love mercy, to walk humbly with our God. For this end we must be knit together in this work as one man, we must entertain each other in brotherly affection, we must be willing to abridge ourselves of our superfluities for the supply of others' necessities, we must uphold a familiar commerce together in all meekness, gentleness, patience, and liberality, we must delight in each other, make others' conditions our own, rejoice together, mourn together, labor and suffer together, always having before our eyes our commission and community in the work, our community as members of the same body So shall we keep the unity of the spirit in the bond of peace. The Lord will be our God and delight in all our ways, so that we shall see much more of His wisdom, power, goodness, and truth than formerly we have been acquainted with. We shall find that the God of Israel is among us, when ten of us shall be able to resist a thousand of our enemies, when He shall make us a praise and glory, that men shall say of succeeding plantations, the Lord make it like that of New England. For we must consider that we shall be as a city upon a hill, the eyes of all people are upon us. So that if we shall deal falsely with our God in this work we have undertaken and so cause Him to withdraw His present help from us, we shall be made a story and byword throughout the world, we shall open the mouths of enemies to speak evil of the ways of God and all professors for God's sake, we shall shame the faces of many of God's worthy servants, and cause their prayers to be turned into curses upon us till we be consumed out of the good land whither we are going. And to shut up this discourse with that exhortation of Moses, that faithful servant of the Lord in His last farewell to Israel, Deut. 30., Beloved there is now set before us life and good, death and evil, in that we are commanded this day to love the Lord our God, and to love one another, to walk in His ways and to keep His commandments and His ordinance, and His laws, and the articles of our covenant with Him that we may live and be multiplied, and that the Lord our God my bless us in the land whither we go to possess it. But if our hearts shall turn away so that we will not obey, but shall be seduced and worship other Gods, our pleasures, our profits, and serve them, it is propounded unto us this day we shall surely perish out of the good land whither we pass over this vast sea to possess it. Therefore let us choose life, that we, and our seed, may live, and by obeying His voice, and cleaving to Him, for He is our life and our prosperity.

1. If you lived in England in the seventeenth century and decided that you wanted to emigrate to the New World, which colony would you have chosen, Virginia or Massachusetts Bay? Why?

2. Discuss possible motivations for John Smith having written "The Starving Time."

3. In what ways do "The Laws of Virginia" differ from today's laws? Why?

4. Does John Winthrop appear to believe that a person of poor or modest means can be an authority in the colony? Which passages from "A Model of Christian Charity" indicate his legal training?

5. What would be the key features of the "city upon a hill" that John Winthrop envisioned?

CHAPTER 3

PUTTING DOWN ROOTS: FAMILIES IN THE ATLANTIC EMPIRE

SUMMARY

The character of the early English settlements varied because of regional factors. A common language and heritage helped pull English American settlers together, however, and by the 1690s, Parliament began to establish a uniform set of rules for an expanding American empire.

Sources of Stability: New England Colonies of The Seventeenth Century

Immigrant Families and New Social Order

In contrast to the early settlers of the Chesapeake colonies who were primarily single males, the early settlers of New England were families, providing a more stable basis for society. The population of New England grew rapidly because of an unprecedented increase in people's longevity. A dispersed population, pure drinking water, and a cool climate helped retard the spread of contagious disease and promoted good health.

Commonwealth of Families

In New England, both town and church were built upon a family foundation. The family was also the basis for educating children. As towns grew, they were required to open schools supported by local taxes. Harvard was the first institution of higher learning founded in the colonies.

Women in Puritan New England

Although women lacked the same economic and political rights afforded men, they worked on family farms alongside their husbands. They tended to join churches in greater numbers than men.

Rank and Status in New England Society

With neither paupers nor noblemen, New England colonials gradually sorted themselves into new social and economic groups, such as provincial gentry, yeomen, and indentured servants. Most northern colonists were yeomen farmers who worked their own land.

The Planters' World

Family Life in a Perilous Environment

Conditions were not as favorable for survival or longevity in the Chesapeake colonies because of contagious diseases and contaminated drinking water. Most colonists came as individuals rather than as members of a family. Family life was much more unstable, and childbearing was extremely dangerous.

Rank and Status in Plantation Society

The cultivation of tobacco shaped Chesapeake society and perpetuated social inequality. Great planters dominated Chesapeake society by controlling large estates and the labor of indentured servants or slaves. Freemen (usually former indentured servants) formed the largest class. Because of the tobacco-based economy, cities and towns were slow to develop, and especially after the 1680s, newcomers discovered that upward social mobility was more difficult to attain than in the northern colonies.

Race And Freedom in British America
Roots of Slavery

Between the sixteenth and nineteenth centuries, almost eleven million blacks were brought to the Americas as slaves. There were almost no objections to enslaving Africans for life because economic considerations required cheap labor, and black Africans were considered by whites to be heathen and barbarous. As the black population expanded, lawmakers drew up ever stricter slave codes. By 1700, slavery was undeniably based on the color of a person's skin.

Constructing African American Identities

Despite the cruelty and alienation of slavery, blacks developed their own unique African American culture in terms of music, art, religion, and language. By the eighteenth century, creole slaves (those born in America) reproduced themselves in greater number than the number of slaves imported from Africa. As slaves, many blacks protested with individual acts of violence or in organized revolts, such as the Stono Uprising of 1739. Others found opportunities for a degree of personal freedom by working, for example, as mariners on colonial sailing vessels.

Politics of Empire

After the restoration of the monarchy in 1660, a British policy of indifference toward the colonies was replaced by one of intervention.

A New Commercial System

England developed a framework of regulatory policies, termed *mercantilism*, to increase exports, decrease imports, and grow richer at the expense of other European states. These policies provided a blueprint for England's first empire and remained in place with only minor adjustments until 1765.

An Empire of Trade

Parliament passed a series of Navigation Acts, which detailed commercial restrictions, and set up the Board of Trade to oversee colonial affairs. Lax enforcement or corruption often impeded the execution of imperial policies, but ultimately the colonists largely obeyed the Navigation Acts because they found it profitable to do so.

Colonial Gentry in Revolt, 1676-1691

In the second half of the seventeenth century, several of the colonies experienced instability as the local gentry split into competing political factions.

Civil War in Virginia: Bacon's Rebellion

In 1676, Virginians suffered from economic depression and political repression. Nathaniel Bacon capitalized on this unrest in leading an unsuccessful rebellion against the government of Lord Berkeley, ostensibly to protect western settlers against Indian raids, but probably because of the governor's monopoly of the fur trade.

The Glorious Revolution in the Bay Colony

In 1675, an Indian uprising known as King Philip's War led England to annul the charter of the Massachusetts Bay Company and merge the colony of Massachusetts into the larger Dominion of New England with the tyrannical Sir Edmund Andros as governor. When James II was deposed during the Glorious Revolution in England, Americans in New England overthrew Governor Andros and the colony of Massachusetts received a new royal charter.

Contagion of Witchcraft

Fear and hysteria resulted in the hanging of nineteen alleged "witches" in Salem, Massachusetts, in 1692. Religious discord and economic tension seem to have been the underlying causes.

The Glorious Revolution in New York and Maryland

News of the Glorious Revolution sparked feuds among the colonial gentry in both New York and Maryland. In New York, Jacob Leisler led an abortive attempt to seize control of the colony from powerful Anglo-Dutch families. In Maryland, John Coode led an anti-Catholic group which successfully petitioned the Crown to transform Maryland into a royal colony.

Common Experiences, Separate Cultures

The creation of a new imperial system did not eliminate the sectional differences in the colonies. It would be a long time before a sense of nationalism would unite the colonies and kindle an American Revolution.

LEARNING OBJECTIVES

After mastering this chapter, you should be able to:

1. Explain the reasons for the growth and social stability of the New England colonies.

2. Discuss the roles, obligations, and rights of colonial women.

3. Explain how conditions in the northern colonies eroded European concepts of social rank and fostered social mobility.

4. Account for the similarities and differences in development between the New England and Chesapeake colonies.

5. Discuss the reasons for the growth of slavery and the slave trade in the English colonies of North America.

6. Discuss the different conditions for slaves in the American colonies and the factors that contributed to the construction of a distinctive African American culture.

7. Explain the reasons for and the results of shifting English colonial policies during the seventeenth century.

8. Explain the historical significance of colonial uprisings in the seventeenth century.

9. Evaluate the causes of the Salem witchcraft hysteria in the 1690s.

GLOSSARY

To build your social science vocabulary, familiarize yourself with the following terms:

1. **patriarch** the father and ruler of a family. "The godly family, at least in theory, was ruled by a patriarch, father to his children, husband to his wife, . . .".

2. **catechize** to teach, especially in the principles of religion, by the method of questions and answers. "the Massachusetts General Court reminded the Bay Colonists of their obligation to catechize their families".

3. **common law** established practices within a society given the consent and authority of law. "Some scholars point out that common law as well as English custom treated women as inferior to men."

4. **hierarchical** characterized by a ranking of persons or things according to class or grade. "According to the prevailing hierarchical view of the structure of society, well-placed individuals were natural rulers.".

5. **demographic conditions** standards for measuring or evaluating population characteristics. "These demographic conditions retarded normal population increase."

6. **aristocrat** one who belongs to a wealthy, usually landholding elite; sometimes with title and political preeminence. "The members of this gentry were not technically aristocrats."

7. **social mobility** the degree to which individuals are capable of moving out of their inherited social rank

32

8. **indigenous** existing, growing, or produced naturally in a region or country. "as the rise of an indigenous ruling elite."

9. **chattel** a movable item of personal property. "English settlers classified some black laborers as slaves for life, as chattel to be bought and sold at the master's will."

10. **mulatto** a person of mixed race, usually black and white. "Mulattoes and pure Africans received the same treatment."

11. **balance of trade** the relationship within a commercial system between exports and imports. "the mother country should establish a more favorable balance of trade."

12. **imperial system** a system organized by a powerful nation, for long-term commercial and economic gain, whose territories or colonies primarily serve the economic interests of that nation. "During the 1660s, the colonists showed little enthusiasm for the new imperial system."

13. **clique** a small, exclusive circle of people. "he probably would have been accepted into the ruling clique."

14. **anarchy** the absence of any noticeable government or source of authority. "Their self-serving policies, coupled with the memory of near anarchy, helped heal divisions. . ."

15. **misogyny** the tendency toward hatred of or discrimination against women. "The underlying misogyny of the entire culture meant that the victims were more often women than men."

IDENTIFICATION

Briefly identify the meaning and significance of the following terms:

1. Charles II _____

_____

2. great migration _____

_____

3. Anthony Johnson _____

_____

4. Royal African Company _____

_____

5. Stono Uprising _____

_____

6. Mercantilist system _____

_____

7. Board of Trade _____

_____

8. Sir William Berkeley _____

_____

9. Glorious Revolution _____

_____

10. "Spectral Evidence" _____

_____

MATCHING

A. Match the following individuals with the appropriate identification:

   1. Nathaniel Bacon   **a.** led a rebellion in Maryland against Catholic authority

   2. Increase Mather   **b.** first governor of Massachusetts Bay Colony

   3. Edmund Andros   **c.** led a rebellion in Virginia against the autocratic
                                    government of Lord Berkeley

   4. Jacob Leisler   **d.** prominent New England clergyman who helped bring
                                    the Salem witchcraft trials to a close

5. John Coode   e. governor of the Dominion of New England who was overthrown in response to the Glorious Revolution

                       f. led an uprising in New York in the name of King William III against the Anglo-Dutch ruling elite

B. Match the following laws or policies with the appropriate description:

1. Sumptuary Law   a. parliamentary law that stated that goods could not be imported into America without first passing through English ports

2. Navigation Act   b. first law passed in Parliament specifically designed to regulate American trade

3. Staple Act   c. law that allowed British to set restrictions on manufacturing

4. Plantation Duty   d. decision that allowed children whose parents could not demonstrate their "election" by God to be baptized into the church

5. Half-Way Covenant   e. law that limited the wearing of fine clothing to the wealthy and prominent

                       f. law requiring money collected in colonial ports to be equal to English customs duties

COMPLETION

Answer the question or complete the statement by filling in the blanks with the correct word or words.

1. In the Chesapeake, an economy based almost entirely on the single commodity of _____ created an insatiable demand for indentured servants and black slaves.

2. Because most colonists to New England migrated as members of _____, the shock of adjusting to a strange environment was lessened.

3. The best-selling book of seventeenth-century New England was Reverend Michael Wigglesworth's _____, a 1662 poem describing in terrifying detail the fate of sinners on Judgment Day.

4. The first institution of higher learning founded in England's mainland colonies was _____.

5. Until the end of the nineteenth century, the creole language _____, which mixed English and African words, was spoken on some of the Sea Islands along the Georgia-South Carolina coast.

6. The term *mercantilist system* was coined by the famous eighteenth-century Scottish economist _____ to describe Great Britain's commercial regulations of her colonies.

7. To establish a more favorable balance of _____, a nation seeks to export more than it imports.

8. American colonists were rankled at the establishment in 1696 by England of _____ courts in America to try offenders of the Navigation Acts because such courts required neither juries nor oral cross-examination, both traditional elements of the common law.

9. In the midst of colonial political troubles, the Wampanoag chief _____ declared war against the colonists in 1675.

10. The village of _____ was plunged into terror in the early 1690s when several adolescent girls began to behave in strange ways and announced they were victims of witches.

TRUE/FALSE

Mark the following statements either T (True) or F (False).

_____1. William and Mary College in Virginia was the first institution of higher learning in the North American colonies.

_____2. Those who came to the Chesapeake region enjoyed longer life expectancy than those in New England.

_____3. The first aristocrats of Virginia were mainly English gentry who emigrated to America.

_____4. There was a significantly greater demand for slave labor in the Chesapeake colonies than in New England by the 1660s.

_____5. By 1700 at the latest, the status of slaves was determined undeniably by skin color.

_____6. After the early 1800s, the increasing number of slaves can be mainly attributed to the importation of slaves from Africa or the West Indies.

_____7. Because of the Navigation Acts, smuggling of goods into America during the eighteenth century increased dramatically.

_____8. Indentured servants formed the largest social class of Chesapeake's society,

_____9. The British *mercantilist system* as it related to its empire was generally well thought out and organized.

_____10. Because of the hysteria and fear they generated, the Salem witchcraft trials have been compared with the McCarthy hearings of the 1950s.

MULTIPLE CHOICE

Circle the one alternative that *best* completes the statement or answers the question.

1. The most plausible explanation for the rapid increase in population in New England was that
   a. colonists there apparently lived much longer than other colonists.
   b. Puritans desired larger families than other colonial groups.
   c. couples in New England married much younger than their counterparts elsewhere.
   d. many more immigrants came to New England than to the southern colonies.

2. Education of the young during the colonial period was primarily a function of the
   a. family.
   b. public schools.
   c. church.
   d. community.

3. In which of the following activities or responsibilities could colonial women most expect to take part?
   a. economic or business transactions
   b. lawmaking
   c. political matters
   d. church activities

4. Most farmers in the northern colonies belonged to which of the following groups?
   a. large-scale planters or aristocrats
   b. indentured servants
   c. yeomen or independent farmers
   d. tenant farmers

5. Most of the settlers of the Chesapeake region emigrated as

a. artisans or craftspeople.
b. families.
c. land-owning aristocrats.
d. indentured servants.

6. Most slaves brought from Africa across the Atlantic by slave traders were sold in which of the following regions?
   a. what is now Mexico
   b. the North American colonies
   c. Central America
   d. Brazil or the Caribbean

7. The mercantilist system was primarily designed by the British for
   a. establishing additional colonies.
   b. reducing political control over the colonies.
   c. supporting the early development of colonial manufacturing.
   d. setting up commercial regulations throughout the empire.

8. The attitude of most New Englanders toward the restrictions of the Navigation Acts was to
   a. ignore them completely.
   b. obey them as much as possible.
   c. refuse to trade any further with Britain.
   d. protest vigorously against them.

9. The issue that prompted Bacon's Rebellion in Virginia was the
   a. inability of the governor to effectively control the Indians on the frontier.
   b. unfair trial of colonial smugglers by British admiralty courts.
   c. decision of Parliament to appoint the governor rather than allow popular elections.
   d. attempt to move the capital from Jamestown to Williamsburg.

10. Which of the following factors did *not* contribute to the hysteria over witchcraft in Salem during the early 1690s?
    a. the refusal of the courts to accept "spectral evidence"
    b. economic tensions
    c. the choice of a minister for the parish
    d. prevalent discrimination against women at the time

11. Until the middle of the seventeenth century, English political leaders
    a. refused to recognize the existence of the American colonies.
    b. largely ignored the American colonies.
    c. established extensive restrictions on American colonists.
    d. petitioned the Crown to forbid Englishmen the right to emigrate to American colonies.

12. The main reason for the lack of development of towns in the Chesapeake region seems to have been the
    a. barrenness or defects of the coastal area.
    b. absence of navigable rivers.
    c. absence of a middle class.
    d. dependence on a one-crop economy.

13. The uprising of Massachusetts Bay colonials in response to the Glorious Revolution was directed against the
    a. customs officials who attempted to enforce the Navigation Acts.
    b. administration of Governor Andros.
    c. large land-holding families.
    d. new rulers of England, William and Mary.

14. The revolts of American colonial gentry during the latter seventeenth century represented
    a. an early rehearsal for the American Revolution.
    b. confrontations between ordinary people and their rulers.
    c. competition among local factions for control of their colonies.
    d. ideological struggles over colonial rights.

15. Regarding Christianity, most slaves in North America
    a. accepted it with no alterations as it was taught to them by whites.
    b. rejected it as an alien faith.
    c. were never exposed to it.
    d. accepted it as their own but with their own cultural variations.

THOUGHT QUESTIONS

To check your understanding of the key issues of this period, solve the following problems:

1. What factors in colonial America contributed to or impeded social mobility and economic opportunity for European settlers?

2. How did family structure and work habits enhance the social stability of Puritan communities? What role did women play in Puritan New England?

3. Contrast economic and demographic conditions in Chesapeake society and that of New England during the seventeenth century.

4. Why, and to what extent, did slavery take root and develop in the North American colonies? How did African Americans adapt to life in North America?

5. Describe the purposes of the English mercantilist system and the laws enacted to enforce it. What were the results for Americans?

CRITICAL THINKING QUESTIONS

Read the following selections: "Bacon's Rebellion: The Declaration" (1676) and "The Examination and Confession of Ann Foster at Salem Village" (1692). Answer the questions following the reading selections.

Bacon's Rebellion: The Declaration (1676)

1. For having, upon specious pretenses of public works, raised great unjust taxes upon the commonalty for the advancement of private favorites and other sinister ends, but no visible effects in any measure adequate; for not having, during this long time of his government, in any measure advanced this hopeful colony either by fortifications, towns, or trade.

2. For having abused and rendered contemptible the magistrates of justice by advancing to places of judicature scandalous and ignorant favorites.

3. For having wronged his Majesty's prerogative and interest by assuming monopoly of the beaver trade and for having in it unjust gain betrayed and sold his Majesty's country and the lives of his loyal subjects to the barbarous heathen.

4. For having protected, favored, and emboldened the Indians against his Majesty's loyal subjects, never contriving, requiring, or appointing any due or proper means of satisfaction for their many invasions, robberies, and murders committed upon us.

5. For having, when the army of English was just upon the track of those Indians, who now in all places burn, spoil, murder and when we might with ease have destroyed them who then were in open hostility, for then having expressly countermanded and sent back our army by passing his word for the peaceable demeanor of the said Indians, who immediately prosecuted their evil intentions, committing horrid murders and robberies in all places, being protected by the said engagement and word past of him the said Sir William Berkeley, having ruined and laid desolate a great part of his Majesty's country, and have now drawn themselves into such obscure and remote places and are by their success so emboldened and confirmed by their confederacy so strengthened that the cries of blood are in all places, and the terror and consternation of the people so great, are now become not only difficult but a very formidable enemy who might at first with ease have been destroyed.

6. And lately, when, upon the loud outcries of blood, the assembly had, with all care, raised and framed an army for the preventing of further mischief and safeguard of this his Majesty's colony.

7. For having, with only the privacy of some few favorites without acquainting the people, only by the alteration of a figure, forged a commission, by we know not what hand, not only without but even against the consent of the people, for the raising and effecting civil war and destruction, which being happily and without bloodshed prevented; for having the second time attempted the same, thereby calling down our forces from the defense of the frontiers and

8. For the prevention of civil mischief and ruin amongst ourselves while the barbarous enemy in all places did invade, murder, and spoil us, his Majesty's most faithful subjects.

Of this and the aforesaid articles we accuse Sir William Berkeley as guilt of each and every one of the same, and as one who has traitorously attempted, violated, and injured his Majesty's interest here by a loss of a great part of this his colony and many of his faithful loyal subjects by him betrayed and in a barbarous and shameful manner exposed to the incursions and murder of the heathen. And we do further declare these the ensuing persons in this list to have been his wicked and pernicious councilors, confederates, aiders, and assisters against the commonalty in these our civil commotions.

Sir Henry Chichley	William Claiburne, Jr.
Richard Whitacre	Ri. Lee
Lt. Col. Christopher	Thomas Hawkins
Wormeley	Thomas Ballard
Nicholas Spencer	William Sherwood
Phillip Ludwell	William Cole
Joseph Bridger	John Page Clerke
Robt. Beverley	John Clauffe Clerk

John West, Hubert Farrell, Thomas Reade, Math. Kempe

And we do further demand that the said Sir William Berkeley with all the persons in this list be forthwith delivered up or surrender themselves within four days after the notice hereof, or otherwise we declare as follows.

That in whatsoever place, house, or ship, any of the said persons shall reside, be hid, or protected, we declare the owners, masters, or inhabitants of the said places to be confederates and traitors to the people and the estates of them is also of all the aforesaid persons to be confiscated. And this we, the commons of Virginia, do declare, desiring a firm union amongst ourselves that we may jointly and with one accord defend ourselves against the common enemy. And let not the faults of the guilty be the reproach of the innocent, or the faults or crimes of the oppressors divide and separate us who have suffered by their oppressions.

These are, therefore, in his Majesty's name, to command you forthwith to seize the persons abovementioned as traitors to the King and country and them to bring to Middle Plantation and there to secure them until further order, and, in case of opposition, if you want any further assistance you are forthwith to demand it in the name of the people in all the counties of Virginia.

Nathaniel Bacon
General by Consent of the people.

William Sherwood

The Examination and Confession of Ann Foster at Salem Village (1692)

After a while Ann ffoster conffesed that the devil apered to her in the shape of a bird at several Times, such a bird as she neuer saw the like before; & that she had had this gift (viz. of striking ye afflicted downe with her eye euer since) & being askt why she thought yt bird was the diuill she answered because he came white & vanished away black & yt the diuill told her yt she should haue this gift & yt she must beliue him & told her she should haue prosperity & she said yt he had apeared to her three times & was always as a bird, and the last time was about half a year since, & sat upon a table had two legs & great eyes & yt it was the second time of his apearance that he promised her prosperity & yt it was Carriers wife about three weeks agoe yt came & perswaded her to hurt these people.

16 July 1692. Ann ffoster Examined confessed yt it was Goody Carrier yt made her a witch yt she came to her in person about Six yeares agoe & told her it she would not be a witch ye diuill should tare her in peices & carry her away at which time she promised to Serve the diuill yt she had bewitched a hog of John Loujoys to death & that she had hurt some persons in Salem Villige, yt goody Carier came to her & would have her bewitch two children of

Andrew Allins & that she had then two popets made & stuck pins in them to bewitch ye said children by which one of them dyed ye other very sick, that she was at the meeting of the witches at Salem Vilige, yt Goody Carier came & told her of the meeting and would haue her goe, so they got upon Sticks & went said Jorny & being there did see Mr. Buroughs ye minister who spake to them all, & this was about two

months agoe that there was then twenty five persons meet together, that she tyed a knot in a Rage & threw it into the fire to hurt Tim. Swan & that she did hurt the rest yt complayned of her by Squesing popets like them & so almost choked them.

18 July 1692. Ann ffoster Examined confessed yt ye deuil in shape of a man apeared to her wth Goody carier about six yeare since when they made her a witch & that she promised to serue the diuill two years, upon which the diuill promised her prosperity and many things but neuer performed it, that she & martha Carier did both ride on a stick or pole when they went to the witch meeting at Salem Village & that the stick broak: as they were caried in the aire aboue the tops of the trees, & they fell but she did hang fast about the neck of Goody Carier & ware presently at the vilage, that she was then much hurt of her Leg, she further saith that she heard some of the witches say there was three hundred & fiue in the whole Country & that they would ruin that place ye Vilige, also said there was present at that meetting two men besides Mr. Burroughs ye minister & one of them had gray haire, she saith yt she formerly frequented the publique metting to worship god. but the diuill had such power ouer her yt she could not profit there & yt was her undoeing: she saith yt about three or foure yeares agoe Martha Carier told her she would bewitch James Hobbs child to death & the child dyed in twenty four hours.

21 July 92. Ann ffoster Examined Owned her former conffesion being read to her and further conffesed that the discourse amongst ye witches at ye meeting at Salem village was that they would afflict there to set up the Diuills Kingdome. This confesion is true as witness my hand.

Ann ffoster Signed & Owned the aboue Examination & Conffesion before me

Salem 10th September 1692.   John Higginson, Just Peace.

1. For what reasons does Nathaniel Bacon demand the surrender of Virginia's Governor Berkeley in 1676?

2. According to the text, what other motives might have prompted Bacon's Rebellion? What were the results? Compare Bacon's Rebellion to other colonial uprisings of the latter seventeenth century.

3. According to the text, what caused the "contagion of witchcraft" in Salem, Massachusetts, during the early 1690s?

4. To what did Ann Foster confess? What evidence substantiated her confession?

5. Give examples of other "witch hunts" that you know have occurred in American history. What lessons do they offer? How might future witch hunts be prevented?

CHAPTER 4

FRONTIERS OF EMPIRE: EIGHTEENTH-CENTURY AMERICA

SUMMARY
Eighteenth-century Americans, living in closer contact than their ancestors with the mother country, were in many ways torn between two cultures—one more sophisticated and traditional, the other more provincial and practical. Few societies in history have expanded in population as rapidly as colonial America of the eighteenth century.

Convicts for America
Between 1715 and 1775, some 50,000 convicts were shipped to America from Britain to be employed as indentured servants.

Cultures of the Backcountry
Voluntary newcomers to America increasingly moved to the backcountry where living conditions were demanding and often violent.

Scotch-Irish and Germans
Non-English colonists, mainly Scotch-Irish and Germans arrived in great numbers throughout the eighteenth century. Many who came were more interested in improving their material lives than in finding religious freedom. Ethnic differences however often spelled disputes with English colonists.

"Middle Ground"
Many Native Americans migrated to the western backcountry and joined existing confederacies of Indian tribes. Rather than isolating themselves from European colonials, the Indians interacted, traded, and compromised with Europeans as much as possible.

Spanish Borderlands of the Eighteenth Century
From the time the Spanish established settlements in North America until the early nineteenth century, they tenuously held onto their northern frontier.

Conquering the Northern Frontier
International rivalries and the lure of gold and silver attracted Spanish settlers to North America. Spanish enthusiasm waned significantly by the eighteenth century.

Peoples of the Spanish Borderlands
Spanish outposts in North America grew very slowly. Spanish colonials exploited and enslaved Native Americans, and their settlements lacked the resources for sustained growth.

British Colonies in an Atlantic World
An urban cosmopolitan culture developed among the more established Atlantic colonies.

Provincial Cities
Urban populations remained small in colonial America. Most American cities were intermediary trading ports where the latest in European ideas and styles were successfully integrated.

Benjamin Franklin
Franklin was the true eighteenth-century American representative of the cosmopolitan, materialistic Atlantic culture. He became the symbol of material progress through human ingenuity.

Economic Transformation
Despite the growth of the population, living standards kept pace, and actually improved. Growing trade with the West Indies, coupled with the ability to purchase cheap manufactured products on credit from England, enriched living standards.

Birth of a Consumer Society
As the British economy picked up significantly after 1690, Americans imported far more commodities than before, and American indebtedness increased dramatically. This influx of British manufactured goods helped to "Anglicize" American culture. The period also witnessed a substantial increase in inter-coastal trade.

Religious Revivals in Provincial Societies
The Great Awakening had a profound impact in colonial America and caused colonists to rethink their basic assumptions about church and state institutions.

The Great Awakening
The Great Awakening brought with it a profound infusion of evangelical exhortations and revival spirit.

Religion of the People
Preachers like George Whitefield and Jonathan Edwards vividly depicted the horrors of hell to captivated audiences in an effort to restore religious vitality. The movement swept the colonies, and although in some cases it bitterly polarized communities, it brought Americans closer together, gave them an awareness of a larger religious community, and enhanced their optimism.

Clash of Political Cultures
Political theorists often revered the British form of government and its "unwritten" constitution.

The English Constitution
In concept at least, political power was divided among the monarchy and his council of advisors, the two-chamber Parliament, and various local governments. Each group provided a check on the ambitions of the others.

The Reality of British Politics
In practice, however, this system was vulnerable to corruption and idleness. Some protesters such as the "Commonwealthmen" observed that many of England's rulers were corrupt and that the institutions of the "mixed" constitution were no longer in balance.

Governing the Colonies: The American Experience
Although colonial leaders attempted in many ways to recreate British-style institutions, government in America was decidedly different. Legislative assemblies, which helped to offset the ineptitude of royal governors appointed by the Board of Trade in England to oversee colonial affairs, rose to prominence in the colonies.

Colonial Assemblies
Often aggressive in asserting rights and powers, the colonial assemblies viewed their mission as preserving the rights of the American colonists.

Century of Imperial War
A number of wars, the results of the imperial ambitions of Britain and France, were engaged for mastery of North America.

King William's and Queen Anne's Wars
Although these wars resulted in little change in territorial control, both sides realized the enormous stakes in their rivalry for control in North America.

King George's War and Its Aftermath
This war revealed the capability of American colonial forces in waging war against the French, as well as the colonial desire to gain complete control of the West. The imperial struggle spread to the Ohio Valley by the 1750s.

Albany Congress and Braddock's Defeat
Although the colonial assemblies failed to accept it, Benjamin Franklin proposed a most ambitious plan for common colonial defense and western expansion. The British general, Braddock, led an unorganized and failing attempt to seize control of the Ohio Valley by attempting to take Fort Duquesne from the French.

Seven Years' War
Finally, between 1756 and 1760, the showdown for North American supremacy was staged. The British were overwhelmingly triumphant, largely owing to the efforts of William Pitt in London and their strength of numbers in America. The war left Britain with an empire that expanded

around the globe.

Perceptions of War
The American colonists became aware of their part in a great empire, but also in an intimate sense of what America had become.

Rule Britannia?
Colonial Americans enthusiastically identified with and in so many ways supported the British Empire. Most Americans rejoiced at being "equal partners" in this great imperial enterprise.

LEARNING OBJECTIVES

After mastering this chapter, you should be able to:

1. Assess the reasons behind the phenomenal population growth of the colonies.

2. Discuss reasons for colonial economic expansion and patterns of settlement.

3. Explain the differences and importance of Scotch-Irish and German settlement.

4. Determine the nature of and problems relating to the Spanish North American empire.

5. Describe the influence of the Great Awakening on American religion, common interest, and "nationality."

6. Explain the rise of the colonial assemblies and the governing problems they faced.

7. Discuss the different advantages and disadvantages of the British American colonists and the French in the wars for mastery of the North American continent.

8. Determine Pitt's (British) overall plan and strategy for victory in the Seven Years' War.

9. Summarize the "fruits of victory" for the British and also possible seeds of discontent and distrust in Britain's relationship with the colonies.

GLOSSARY

To build your social science vocabulary, familiarize yourself with the following terms:

1. **demography** the study or measurement of people from an economic or societal perspective. " . . . one of the first persons to bring scientific rigor to the study of demography."

2. **ethnic diversity** the appearance of differences amongst ethnic groups. "Non-English colonists poured into American ports throughout the eighteenth century, creating rich ethnic diversity . . . "

3. **confederacies** loose political organizations usually established for economic or territorial advantages. "The goal of the Indian confederacies was rather to maintain a strong independent voice . . . "

4. **millennium** in Christian belief, the thousand-year reign and triumph of Christ prior to the end of human civilization. "God must be preparing Americans, his chosen people, for the millennium."

5. **sects** in a religious sense, differing, sometimes less than organized groups of like believers. " . . . that shattered the old harmony among Protestant sects."

6. **revivalists** those who participate in a religious awakening for the primary purpose of calling others to God. "How could the revivalists be certain that God had sparked the Great Awakening?"

7. **anti-intellectualism** opposition to seeking truth through observation or reason. " . . . attacks on formal learning invited the crude anti-intellectualism of such fanatics . . ."

8. **patronage** a system of appointing persons to positions with no regard to experience or qualifications, but rather based on personal considerations. "The patronage posts did not generate income . . ."

9. **anglicize** to make more English. ". . . the language, of the law became increasingly anglicized."

10. **balance of power** to maintain (primarily in European history) a relative balance or equilibrium between the major expansionist nations. "The major concern was preserving a balance of power among the European states."

IDENTIFICATION

Briefly identify the meaning and significance of the following terms:

1. Scotch-Irish_____

_____.

2. Middle Ground _____

_____.

3. Backcountry _____

_____.

4. Great Awakening _____

_____.

5. Balanced Constitution _____

_____.

6. Benjamin Franklin's
   Autobiography _____

_____.

7. Fort Duquesne _____

_____.

8. King George's War _____

_____.

9. Albany Plan _____

_____.

10. Peace of Paris_____

_____ .

MATCHING

A. Match the following individuals with the appropriate identification:

1.	George Whitefield	**a**.	Puritan theologian and leader of the Great Awakening in New England
2.	Jonathan Edwards	**b**.	Organizer of first Spanish settlement north of the Rio Grande
3.	Gilbert Tennent	**c**.	founder of the Methodist Church in England
4.	James Davenport	**d**.	revivalist who launched the New Light movement during the Great Awakening with his sermon, "on the Danger of an Unconverted Ministry"
5.	Juan de Onate	**e**.	fanatical New Light preacher who attacked the formally educated through crude emotionalism
		f.	itinerant evangelist from England who inspired thousands of Americans during the Great Awakening

B. Match the following publications or documents with the appropriate description:

1.	*Cato's Letters*	**a**.	British scholarly journal that spread enlightened philosophical views
2.	*Independent Reflector*	**b**.	series of essays by Trenchard and Gordon denouncing political corruption in England
3.	*New England Courant*	**c**.	New York weekly journal that actively supported civil and religious virtues and freedoms
4.	*The Spectator*	**d**.	a weekly newspaper founded by Franklin that satirized Boston's political and religious leaders
5.	Albany Plan	**e**.	Franklin's association for the promotion of "useful knowledge"

f. system calling for colonial unity

COMPLETION

Answer the questions or complete the statement by filling in the blanks with the correct word or words.

1. _____ was most responsible for the rapid expansion of American population during the eighteenth century.

2. Most of the produce carried along backcountry roads of western Pennsylvania and the Shenandoah Valley was transported in _____.

3. According to the principles of the Enlightenment, individuals were to make certain that public institutions such as government were constructed or developed according to _____ or _____.

4. In the search for useful knowledge and inventions, Enlightenment scientists utilized _____.

5. A major source of political information vigorously put forth, especially in New York and Massachusetts, to exercise vigilance against the spread of "privileged power" was the _____.

6. During the war known as _____, American colonists captured the French fortress, Louisburg, only to have to return it to the French by the Treaty of Aix-la-Chapelle.

7. The center of colonial government were the local _____.

8. The climax to the Seven Years' War was British General Wolfe's successful assault on _____.

TRUE/FALSE

Mark the following statements either T (True) or F (False).

_____1. During the late colonial period, approximately one half of the population at any time was under sixteen years of age.

_____2. A much larger percentage of the colonial population lived in cities in 1775 than fifty years earlier.

_____3. Although popular among New England Puritans, the Great Awakening failed to attract much support from other denominations.

_____4. As the names imply, the Houses of Commons and Lords represented people of distinctly different socioeconomic groups in England.

_____5. The Constitution of the United States is very similar in composition and purpose to the British Constitution.

_____6. Although most colonists assumed that their colonial governments were modeled after Britain's, there were in reality very few similarities.

_____7. The royal governors serving in the colonies possessed no real powers other than those given to them by the colonial assemblies.

_____8. Because of the rapid increase in colonial population, the economy could not keep pace and there was a noticeable decline in per capita income throughout the 1700s.

_____9. One basic assumption shared by most Enlightenment philosophers was that humans by nature were weak and easily corruptible.

MULTIPLE CHOICE

Circle the one alternative that *best* completes the statement or answers the question.

1. Artifacts taken from northwestern Massachusetts indicate that the colonists in those parts in the mid-eighteenth century
    a. were crude frontiersmen dressed in primitive garb.
    b. were culturally very similar to the English; they dressed in like fashion, and used many of the same utensils.
    c. lived very much as did the Indians who inhabited the same region.
    d. had very little in common with their counterparts in Britain.

2. Most Scotch-Irish immigrants to America settled in
    a. Pennsylvania.
    b. New Jersey.
    c. New York.
    d. Massachusetts.

3. The German Lutherans who settled in the Middle Colonies came to America primarily in search of

a. religious freedom.
b. improved material lives.
c. Indian converts.
d. animal furs to trap and trade.

4. The balance of trade between England and the colonies turned so much to England's favor by the mid-eighteenth century chiefly because
   a. of the decline in trade between the colonies and the West Indies.
   b. the English were willing to buy greater quantities of American raw materials
   c. industrialization allowed England to sell a greater quantity of certain goods at cheaper prices to American buyers.
   d. of stricter enforcement of the Navigation Acts.

5. Enlightenment philosophers claimed that
   a. humans could achieve perfection in this world through the appeal to reason.
   b. knowledge was of little use when confined to speculation.
   c. religion was no longer to be tolerated in any form.
   d. all absolutist forms of government must be replaced by representative republican governments.

6. As a product of the Enlightenment, Benjamin Franklin
   a. turned to organized religion for meaning and sustenance.
   b. devoted himself to European ideas and sought to model American concepts after them.
   c. rejected the practical pursuits of life in favor of contemplation and intellectual inquiry.
   d. constantly pursued his numerous curiosities until they yielded new and practical ideas that were quite different than many European ideas.

7. Jonathan Edwards preached that
   a. a combination of good deeds and steadfast faith could bring salvation.
   b. salvation would come through repentance only.
   c. God was omnipotent and the eternal fate of helpless individuals was determined at birth
   d. Old Light spokesmen were the only true representatives of the Almighty.

8. Royal governors were usually
   a. elected by the colonial assembly.
   b. elected by popular vote within the colony.
   c. appointed by the Parliamentary Board of Trade.
   d. appointed by the king.

9. Members of colonial assemblies perceived their most important duty to be to
   a. maintain the balance between the various branches of government.
   b. strive for new privileges and powers at the expense of the governor.
   c. cooperate with the governor as much as possible.

d. preserve colonial liberties against any attack or intrusion.

10. Franklin's purpose with the Albany Plan was to
   a. organize a council of delegates from the separate colonies to coordinate common defense and western expansion.
   b. propose the dredging of a canal connecting Albany with Lake Erie.
   c. set up a system of common taxes and tariffs throughout the colonies.
   d. draft a constitution freeing the colonies from British control.

11. Colonial Americans of the eighteenth century
   a. still confronted the "howling wilderness" which previous generations had encountered.
   b. still lived in geographic isolation as in the seventeenth century.
   c. could not escape the economic and cultural influence of Britain.
   d. came in search of religious freedom more so than any other reason.

12. Colonial commerce by the mid-eighteenth century
   a. diminished along inter-coastal routes.
   b. was hampered by a decline in credit offered from England.
   c. maintained strict regional and sectional differences keeping colonists isolated and provincial.
   d. helped to "anglicize" American culture by exposing colonists to large amounts of British product.

13. Native Americans of the middle ground
   a. maintained a strong independent role in commercial exchange with European Americans.
   b. sought to isolate themselves completely from European contact.
   c. sought military confrontation before economic cooperation.
   d. continued to war against each other rather than to establish intertribal confederacies.

14. The Peace of Paris in 1763
   a. maintained essentially the same borders of British and French holdings in North America.
   b. left the French-speaking Canadians under French control.
   c. gave Britain title to Canada, Florida, and all the land east of the Mississippi River.
   d. provided only a temporary cease-fire between British and French forces in North America.

15. The English constitution
   a. was a cumulative body of laws, statutes, and court decisions.
   b. was a formal document similar to the later U.S. Constitution.
   c. gave essential sovereignty to the monarch.
   d. had not been alerted since it had been first conceived during the Middle Ages.

THOUGHT QUESTIONS

To check your understanding of the key issues of this period, solve the following problems:

1. Why were Americans of the eighteenth century caught between two cultures? What economic and social differences by this time distinguished them from the British?

2. What factors made America ripe for a religious reawakening in the 1740s?

3. Discuss the differences between the developing political systems in the American colonies and the British form of government.

4. What was at stake in the bitter showdown for supremacy in North America between the British and the French?

5. What was the genius behind Franklin's Albany Plan?

CRITICAL THINKING QUESTIONS

After reading Benjamin Franklin from *The Autobiography of Benjamin Franklin* (1771), Jonathan Edwards from "Sinners in the Hands of an Angry God," (1741), and Jonathan Edwards from "Some Thoughts Concerning the Present Revival of Religion in New England," (1742), answer the following questions:

Benjamin Franklin, from The Autobiography of Benjamin Franklin (1771)

In 1739 arriv'd among us from England the Rev. Mr. Whitefield, who had made himself remarkable there as an itinerant preacher. . . . The Multitudes of all Sects and Denominations that attended his Sermons were enormous, and it was matter of Speculation to me who was one of the Number, to observe the extraordinary Influence of his Oratory on his Hearers, and how much they admir'd & respected him, notwithstanding his common Abuse of them, by assuring them they were naturally half Beasts and half Devils. It was wonderful to see the Change soon made in the Manners of our Inhabitants; from being thoughtless or indifferent about Religion, it seem'd as if all the World were growing Religious; so that one could not walk thro' the Town in an Evening without Hearing Psalms sung in different Families of every Street. . . . Mr. Whitefield, in leaving us, went preaching all the Way thro' the Colonies to Georgia. The Settlement of that Province had lately been begun; but instead of being made with hardy industrious Husbandmen accustomed to Labor, the only People fit for such an Enterprise, it was with Families of broken Shopkeepers and other insolvent Debtors, many of indolent & idle habits, taken out of the Gaols, who being set down in the Woods, unqualified for clearing Land, & unable to endure the Hardships of a new Settlement, perished in Numbers, leaving many helpless Children unprovided for. The Sight of their miserable Situation inspired the benevolent Heart of Mr. Whitefield with the idea of building an Orphan House there. . . . Returning northward he preached up this Charity, & made large Collections; for his Eloquence had a wonderful Power over the Hearts and Purses of his Hearers, of which I myself was an Instance. I did not disapprove of the Design, but as Georgia was then destitute of Materials & Workmen, and it was propos'd to send them from Philadelphia at a great Expense, I thought it would have been better to have built the House here & Brought the Children to it. This I advis'd, but he was resolute in his first Project, and rejected my Counsel, and I thereupon refus'd to contribute. I happened soon after on one of his Sermons, in the Course of which I perceived he intended to finish with a Collection, & I silently resolved he should get nothing from me. I had in my Pocket a Handful of Copper Money, three or four silver Dollars, and five Pistoles in gold. As he proceeded I began to soften, and concluded to give the Coppers. Another Stroke of his

Oratory made me asham'd of that, and determin'd me to give the Silver & he finished so admirably, that I empty'd my Pocket wholly into the Collector's Dish, Gold and all. At this Sermon there was also one of our Club, who being of my Sentiments respecting the Building in Georgia, and suspecting a Collection might be intended, had by Precaution emptied his Pockets before he came from home; towards the Conclusion of the Discourse, however, he felt a strong Desire to give, and apply'd to a Neighbor who stood near him to borrow some Money for the Purpose.

Jonathan Edwards, from "Sinners in the Hands of an Angry God" (1741)

. . . This that you have heard is the case of every one of you that are out of Christ. That world of misery, that lake of burning brimstone, is extended abroad under you. There is the dreadful pit of the glowing flames of the wrath of God; there is hell's wide gaping mouth open; and you have nothing to stand upon, nor any thing to take hold of; there is nothing between you and hell but the air; 'tis only the power and mere pleasure of God that holds you up.

    You probably are not sensible of this; you find you are kept out of hell, but don't see the hand of God in it, but look at other things, as the good state of your bodily constitution, your care of your own life, and the means you use for your own preservation. But indeed these things are nothing; if God should withdraw his hand, they would avail no more to keep you from falling, than the thin air to hold up a person that is suspended in it.

    Your wickedness makes you as it were heavy as lead, and to tend downwards with great weight and pressure towards hell; and, if God should let you go, you would immediately sink, and swiftly descend and plunge into the bottomless gulf; and your healthy constitution, and your own care and prudence, and best contrivance, and all your righteousness, would have no more influence to uphold you and keep you out of hell, than a spider's web would have to stop a falling rock. . . .

    The God that holds you over the pit of hell, much as one holds a spider or some loathsome insect over the fire, abhors you, and is dreadfully provoked. His wrath towards you burns like fire; he looks upon you as worthy of nothing else but to be cast into the fire. He is of purer eyes than to bear you in his sight; you are ten thousand times as abominable in his eyes as the most hateful, venomous serpent is in ours. You have offended him infinitely more than ever a stubborn rebel did his prince, and yet 'tis nothing but his hand that holds you from falling into the fire every moment. . . .

    O sinner! Consider the fearful danger you are in! 'Tis a great furnace of wrath, a wide and bottomless pit, full of fire and of wrath that you are held over in the hand of that God whose wrath is provoked and incensed as much against you as against many of the damned in hell. You hang by a slender thread, with the flames of Divine wrath flashing about it, and ready every moment to singe it and burn it asunder. . . .

    It would be dreadful to suffer this fierceness and wrath of Almighty God one moment; but you must suffer it to all eternity. There will be no end to this exquisite, horrible, misery. . . .

    How dreadful is the state of those that are daily and hourly in danger of this great wrath and infinite misery! But this is the dismal case of every soul in this congregation that has not been born again, however moral and strict, sober and religious, they may otherwise be. Oh! that you would consider it, whether you be young or old!

Jonathan Edwards, from "Some Thoughts Concerning the Present Revival of Religion in New England" (1742)

God has made as it were two worlds here below, the old and the new (according to the names they are now called by), two great habitable continents, far separated one from the other; the latter is but newly discovered, . . . it has been, until of late, wholly the possession of Satan, the church of God having never been in it, as it has been in the other continent, from the beginning of the world. This new world is probably now discovered, that the new and most glorious state of God's church on earth might commence there; that God might in it begin a new world in a spiritual respect, when he creates the new heavens and new earth. . . .

    The old continent has been the source and original of mankind, in several respects. The first parents of mankind dwelt there; and there dwelt Noah and his sons; and there the second Adam was born, and was crucified and rose again; and it is probable that, in some measure to balance these things, the most glorious renovation of the world shall originate from the new continent, and the church of God in that respect be from hence. And so it is probable that that will come to pass in spirituals, that has in temporals, with respect to America; that whereas till of late, the world was supplied with its silver and gold and earthly treasures from the old continent, now it is supplied chiefly from the new, so the course of things in spiritual respects will be in like manner turned.

    And it is worthy to be noted that America was discovered about the time of the reformation, or but little before: which reformation was the first thing that God did towards the glorious renovation of the world, after it had sunk into the depths of darkness and ruin, under the great antichristian apostasy. So that as soon as this new world is (as it were) created, and stands forth in view, God presently goes about doing some great thing to make way for the introduction of the church's latter day glory, that is to have its first seat in, and is to take its rise from that new world. . .

I observed before, that when God is about to do some great work for his church, his manner is to begin at the lower end; so when he is about to renew the whole habitable earth, it is probable that he will begin in this utmost, meanest, youngest and weakest part of it, where the church of God has been planted last of all; and so the first shall be last, and the last first. . . .

1. In what ways does Benjamin Franklin betray an apparent conflict between his intellect and his emotion?
2. What elements of the excerpt from *The Autobiography of Benjamin Franklin* indicate some inter-colonial conflict?
3. What was "Sinners in the Hands of an Angry God" an effective sermon? What was the basis of its appeal?
4. In "Some Thoughts Concerning the Present Revival of Religion in New England" how does Jonathon Edwards emphasize the differences between the Old World and the New? How accurate was his assessment?
5. What are the elements of the Great Awakening revealed in the sermons of Whitefield and Edwards?

CHAPTER 5

THE AMERICAN REVOLUTION:
FROM GENTRY PROTEST TO POPULAR REVOLT, 1763-1783

SUMMARY

Between 1763 and 1783, Americans increasingly rebelled against English rule, declared independence, and finally won the military struggle against the British.

EQUALITY WITHIN

At the end of the Seven Years' War, American society, on the whole optimistic and prosperous, looked to the future with considerable political and economic expectation.

Fear of Betrayal

Through the mounting conflict to 1776, King George III, his ministers, and Parliament based their views on inaccurate information on the colonies while stubbornly defending Parliament's "sovereign supreme power over every part of the dominions of state."

The American Perspective: No Taxation Without Representation

The postwar conflict forced the Americans to define their views on the power of colonial assemblies, representative government, and freedom from England's revenue taxation.

Politics of Virtue

The American ideology also contained a heavy emphasis on religious and moral components based on various sources from the Great Awakening and John Locke to the Commonwealth men. The American variant found power dangerous unless contained by virtue; to believers political error resulted from corruption and sin.

Eroding the Bonds of Empire: Challenge and Resistance

After the war with the French, the British maintained a large military presence in the colonies, which Americans opposed for two reasons: British troops failed to protect the thousands of Americans who died during uprisings by the Native Americans of the backcountry; and after the Proclamation of 1763 was issued, British troops obstructed western settlement. When Grenville insisted that Americans help pay for those troops with new taxes on trade, well-to-do Americans involved in commerce quickly protested.

Popular Mobilization

The protests of gentlemen grew to a mass movement with opposition to Britain's Stamp Act. Americans resisted in colonial assemblies, in a "congress" in the streets, and in a boycott effected by the Sons of Liberty and by newly mobilized colonial women.

Damage Control

A new English government repealed the law while maintaining the principle of parliamentary supremacy, including the right to revenue taxation, but the crisis had reduced American respect and loyalty for Britain's imperial officeholders.

Townshend's Boast: Tea and Sovereignty

Townshend's new ministry tried new taxes on American imports and new enforcement mechanisms including customs commissioners supported by admiralty courts. Americans resisted with a boycott, "rituals of non-consumption," and a circular letter suggesting ways to thwart the acts.

The Boston Massacre Heightens Tensions

A British transfer of troops to Boston heightened tensions ever more, and patriots again resisted. One confrontation with British troops resulted in the "Boston Massacre." Parliament, now led by Lord North, dropped all of the Townshend duties except that on tea, a symbol of Parliament's sovereignty.

An Interlude of Order, 1770-1773

A brief period of calm and apparent reconciliation followed. But the actions of corrupt imperial officials and the continued agitation of radicals led by Sam Adams brought about a renewal of tensions.

The Final Provocation: The Boston Tea Party

The Boston Tea Party, a colonial response to new English regulations, led to the Coercive Acts and American rebellion.

Decision for Independence

With the fighting begun, fifty-five American delegates from twelve of the colonies met in a Continental Congress which Adams soon led into a radical stance.

Shots Heard Around the World

Before the Continental Congress reconvened, the first blows of the American Revolution fell at Lexington and Concord.

The Second Continental Congress Directs the War Effort

The fighting led to a Second Continental Congress which slowly took control of the American war effort but only discussed independence until British actions and Tom Paine's arguments pushed it to a declaration.

War for Independence

English military and economic power might have prevailed had it not been for Britain's logistical problems and the American commitment to independence. The Americans maintained a regular army to symbolize the new country's independence and to attract foreign support. At the same time colonial militia controlled large areas of the country and compelled support for the patriots' war effort. Thousands more took up arms for the British, hoping in either case to gain "unalienable rights."

Early Disasters Test the American Will
Washington's army suffered several serious defeats in New York and New Jersey and was "on the run" by late 1776.

"Times That Try Men's Souls"
In 1777 the Americans captured Burgoyne's army at Saratoga but then lost a series of battles in an unsuccessful attempt to prevent Howe from reaching Philadelphia, lost again at Germantown, then dug in at Valley Forge.

Victory in a Year of Defeat
The American victory at Saratoga persuaded the French to offer an alliance, founded on their desire for revenge and Franklin's brilliant diplomacy--that turned the American rebellion into a much wider war.

The French Alliance
Exploiting the protracted hostility between the British and the French, American diplomacy, led brilliantly by Benjamin Franklin, turned the American rebellion into a much wider war.

The Final Campaign
The final British "southern strategy" let loose a fury. Americans, more determined than ever, dug in and won a final victory at Yorktown.

The Loyalist Dilemma
Many Americans remained loyal to the Crown, often because they feared independence would bring social disorder, which would threaten the very liberties for which their American patriot opponents fought. American hatred and British distrust forced almost one hundred thousand loyalists into bitter flight from their homeland.

Winning the Peace
A highly talented American peace delegation, Benjamin Franklin, John Adams and John Jay, negotiated a very successful treaty with the British, gaining not only independence but also very favorable boundaries and important fishing rights.

Republican Challenge
Having won the war for independence, the Americans still faced many difficulties in shaping a new republican government, having closed "but the first act of the great drama."

LEARNING OBJECTIVES

After mastering this chapter, you should be able to:

1. Explain why both the American gentry and the common folk supported the American Revolution.

2. Describe the "expectant" nature of American society in the 1760s.

3. Assess and explain the responsibility of George III and Parliament for the loss of their American colonies.

4. Describe each of the fundamental principles and the "politics of virtue" of the American perspective on imperial politics.

5. Analyze both the motivation for Grenville's regulations and the popular mass movement that formed in resistance to them.

6. Trace the Townshend duties from their origins through the American resistance to their repeal.

7. Trace the growing conflict between the colonists and the North ministry from the Tea Act through the fighting at Lexington and Concord.

8. Analyze the American decision to declare independence from the convening of the Second Continental Congress to the Declaration of Independence.

9. Compare and contrast the military assets and liabilities of both the British and American forces in the Revolutionary War.

10. Describe the role of African Americans in the fighting of the American Revolution.

11. Describe both the British and American victories in New York and New Jersey through the winter of 1776-1777.

12. Explain the significance of the American victory at Saratoga in 1777.

13. Trace the American diplomacy leading to the treaties with the French in February 1778.

14. Analyze the British southern strategy from their victory at Charleston to Cornwallis's defeat

at Yorketown.

15. Explain how American Loyalists were the greatest losers in the American Revolution.

16. Analyze the role of diplomacy in the success of the American Revolution.

17. Describe and explain the role of colonial religious values in promoting the revolutionary ferment and patriotism of the common folk in the American Revolution.

GLOSSARY

To build your social science vocabulary, familiarize yourself with the following terms:

1. **deference**   yielding to the authority or judgment of another. "they had not shown Randolph proper deference."

2. **gentry**   well-born people of the class just below aristocracy. "The initial stimulus for rebellion came from the gentry . . ."

3. **Whigs**   an eighteenth- and nineteenth-century major British political party of liberal principles. " 'Whigs' had set policy . . ."

4. **patronage**   the power to grant government positions and favors. " 'Whigs' had . . . controlled patronage . . ."

5. **sovereignty**   the final supreme authority to rule. ". . . they clung doggedly to the principle of parliamentary sovereignty . . ."

6. **chancellor of the exchequer**   the British official in charge of the treasury. ". . . chancellor of the exchequer who replaced Bute in 1763 . . ."

7. **vice-admiralty courts**   British naval courts. "The new act expanded the jurisdiction of vice-admiralty courts over commerce . . ."

8. **committees of correspondence**   area patriot committees organized to communicate issues, positions, and events throughout the colonies. "Adams suggested the formation of a committee of correspondence to communicate grievances . . ."

9. **logistics**   the procurement, maintenance, and movement of military supply and equipment. "The British had to transport supplies across the Atlantic, a logistic challenge of unprecedented complexity."

10. **strategy**   a military commander's overall plan of large military operations. "This thinking shaped Washington's wartime strategy..."

11. **militia**   a fighting body of citizens, as opposed to professional soldiers. ". . . he failed to comprehend the importance of the militia."

12. **republican**   characterizing a government where sovereignty rests in an electorate (a body of voters) that chooses representatives to govern. "not so much because the French monarchy favored the republican cause"

13. **guerrilla**   a type of warfare carried out by small, irregular, independent bands of soldiers. "The southern strategy turned the war into a bitter guerrilla conflict"

14. **banditti**   bandits or outlaws. "The British had unleashed a horde of banditti across South Carolina."

15. **morality play**   medieval drama that illustrated morality with personification of virtues and vices. "For ordinary men and women, the American Revolution may have seemed a kind of morality play"

IDENTIFICATION

Briefly identify the meaning and significance of the following terms:

1. George III _____

_____

2. Earl of Bute _____

_____

3. Pontiac _____

_____

4. Patrick Henry_____

_____

5. Lord Rockingham _____

_____

6. Samuel Adams _____

_____

7. First Continental Congress (1774) _____

_____

8. Second Continental Congress (1775) _____

_____

9. Thomas Paine _____

_____

10. Benjamin Franklin _____

_____

MATCHING

A. Match the following battles with the appropriate description:

____ 1. Trenton

____ 2. Saratoga

____ 3. Charleston

____ 4. King's Mountain

____ 5. Yorktown

a. Clinton and Cornwallis tried to take the South with the capture of a city and six thousand American troops

b. Washington surprised sleeping Hessians at a British outpost

c. American backwoodsmen defeated British regulars and Loyalist raiders

d. Washington defeated Cornwallis in the last major battle

e. Washington's inexperienced troops lost a major battle to Howe's British forces

f. Americans convinced the French of the patriots' power and resolve

B. Match the following acts of Parliament with the appropriate description.

____ 1. Revenue Act of 1764

    a. second of Grenville's revenue measures; it led to the Virginia resolve and a colonial congress

____ 2. Stamp Act

    b. duties on paper, glass, paint, and tea; it hurt English manufacturers as well as American consumers

____ 3. Declaratory Act

    c. North's attempt to punish Americans for the "Tea Party"; it closed the Boston port

____ 4. Townshend Revenue Act

    d. not a revenue measure; it permitted an English company to sell a product in America through its own agents

____ 5. Coercive Acts

    e. known as the Sugar Act; it represented a major break with the Navigation Acts and redefined the relationship between the colonies and England

    f. a defense of Parliament's sovereignty over the colonies; it was passed to compensate for the repeal of the Stamp Act

COMPLETION

Answer the question or complete the statement by filling in the blanks with the correct word or words.

1. In the period preceding the American Revolution, colonial women assisted the resistance to the British by helping to enforce _____.

2. Samuel Adams hoped to create in America a _____ —an ideal commonwealth of virtuous citizens.

3. Patrick Henry introduced the _____ _____, which held that Virginians could be taxed only by their own representatives in the colonial assembly.

4. In 1772, Rhode Islanders destroyed a British customs vessel, the _____.

5. Parliament passed the Tea Act to save the _____.

6. The _____ established a civil government for a Canadian province that included land as far south as the Ohio River.

7. The first blows of the American Revolution came at _____ and _____.

8. The British march on Concord led to the mobilization of special Massachusetts militia forces called _____.

9. In December 1775 Parliament passed the _____ to cut off all American trade.

10. The American Congress sent _____, _____, and _____ to negotiate peace with Britain.

TRUE/FALSE

Mark the following statements either T (True) or F (False):

___ 1. George III's indifference to colonial and other governmental affairs angered his American subjects.

___ 2. The imperial crisis that followed the French and Indian War forced Americans to define and develop their principles of representative government.

___ 3. Americans accepted the expense of the British army because it protected them from the Indians.

___ 4. After street violence flared in response to the Stamp Act, colonial leaders avoided giving the lower classes any role in the struggle against the British.

___ 5. Many colonial leaders believed that only virtue could protect liberty from power, and that Americans were more virtuous than the English.

___ 6. Customs commissioners appointed by Townshend taxed common Americans but permitted wealthy colonials to escape payment of duties.

___ 7. The Second Continental Congress insisted on a Declaration of Independence before assuming control of the American war effort.

___ 8. The British underestimated American commitment to political ideals.

___ 9. The colonists won most early battles because their "minutemen" militia was well trained and disciplined.

___ 10. By the end of the revolutionary fighting, the Americans had adopted, implemented, and exercised their republican form of government.

MULTIPLE CHOICE

Circle the one alternative that *best* completes the statement or answers the question.

1. After the gentry initiated the American rebellion, the common folk
   a. followed the lead of their "betters."
   b. lost rights gained during the colonial period.
   c. took for themselves a greater role in public affairs.
   d. fought a social-economic revolution against all gentry.

2. In disputes with the colonies, the Parliament demonstrated
   a. a willingness to compromise.
   b. a consistent and creative policy.
   c. ignorance and misunderstanding of American conditions.
   d. unwillingness to defend its right to govern the Americans.

3. The American religious perspective on government originated in
   a. existing British political practices.
   b. the Great Awakening and the Commonwealth traditions.
   c. the political theory of the Earl of Bute.
   d. the political theory of George III.

4. When the British left troops in America following the Seven Years' War, colonists
   a. supported the redcoats as protection against the French.
   b. supported the redcoats as protection against the Indians.
   c. opposed the redcoats for enforcing all of the old Navigation Acts.
   d. opposed the redcoats for obstructing economic development.

5. The Sugar Act differed from earlier regulations such as the Navigation Acts in which of the following ways?
   a. It forced the colonists to trade in sugar only with England.
   b. It taxed sugar far more than any other product had ever been taxed.
   c. It taxed sugar for the specific benefit of the East India Company.
   d. It taxed for the purpose of collecting revenue from the Americans.

6. Which of the following did not occur as part of the Stamp Act crisis?
   a. Patrick Henry denounced British taxation with his Virginia Resolves.
   b. A Stamp Act Congress drew together colonial leaders from different regions.
   c. Resistance drew many common folk into significant political action, including street violence.
   d. Massachusetts reacted so bitterly that the British imposed the Coercive or Intolerable Acts.

7. While repealing the Townshend duties, the North ministry retained a tax on tea to
   a. regulate trade in that commodity.
   b. punish American tea smugglers.
   c. punish John Hancock, Samuel Adams, and the Sons of Liberty.
   d. symbolize Parliament's power to tax Americans.

8. Which list places events in a correct chronological order?
   a. Townshend duties, Boston Tea Party, Boston Massacre, Coercive Acts
   b. Townshend duties, Boston Massacre, Boston Tea Party, Coercive Acts
   c. Boston Tea Party, Coercive Acts, Boston Massacre, Townshend duties
   d. Coercive Acts, Boston Tea Party, Boston Massacre, Townshend duties

9. The Continental Congress called in response to the Coercive Acts established the Association to
   a. cut off all trade with Great Britain.
   b. begin the formation of an intercolonial government.
   c. begin training an American army.
   d. improve communication among the colonies.

10. With *Common Sense,* Thomas Paine persuaded many Americans to
    a. avoid a final break with England.
    b. seek above all else a peaceful resolution to their dispute with the "parent country."
    c. end their ties with the British.
    d. denounce Parliament while maintaining ties to the king.

11. Which was **not** an important military problem for the British?
    a. poorly disciplined and inadequately trained troops
    b. distance for transport of troops and supplies
    c. the vast size of America
    d. American determination and commitment

12. Washington's wartime strategy was shaped by his decision to
    a. maintain a regular, well-trained army.
    b. emphasize the use of guerrilla bands.

c. win an early, spectacular victory to sap the British will to fight.

d. emphasize the role of militia units in direct combat with British armies.

13. The British southern strategy set off a ferocious conflict between
    a. the British and French navies.
    b. American troops and Tory raiders.
    c. American and Hessian troops.
    d. American and British regulars.

14. Many of the American loyalists fled their homeland to settle in London where
    a. they were treated as second-class citizens.
    b. they were all denied any monetary compensation for their sacrifices.
    c. they were treated the same as the native-born English.
    d. many of their leaders became important members of the ruling ministry.

15. In negotiating the Treaty of Paris (1783) the American delegation
    a. proved ineffective and gained independence only with strong support of both the French and the Spanish.
    b. proved effective, but gained nothing except independence.
    c. proved ineffective, but won independence because of Spain's fear of Britain's American ambitions.
    d. proved effective, and gained much more than independence.

THOUGHT QUESTIONS

To check your understanding of the key issues of this period, solve the following problems:

1. How revolutionary was the American war for independence? Did it bring enough change to warrant the name "Revolution"?

2. Did Americans' political principles and behavior justify their assumption of public virtue?

3. Would republicanism have developed as quickly and thoroughly if the Americans had not fought for independence?

4. To what extent does the American Revolution resemble a modern war? Was it the first "people's war"? An early "world war"?

5. How did the American Revolution appear to a Loyalist? To a law-abiding, tax paying Londoner

CRITICAL THINKING EXERCISES

Using the material in Chapter 5 and the Primary Sources listed below, please answer the following questions:

Benjamin Franklin, "Testimony Against the Stamp Act"
Phillis Wheatley, "Our Modern Egyptians"

Benjamin Franklin, Testimony Against the Stamp Act (1766)

Q. What is your name, and place of abode?

A. Franklin, of Philadelphia.

Q. Do the Americans pay any considerable taxes among themselves?

A. Certainly many, and very heavy taxes.

Q. What are the present taxes in Pennsylvania, laid by the laws of the colony?

A. There are taxes on all estates, real and personal; a poll tax; a tax on all offices, professions, trades, and businesses, according to their profits; an excise on all wine, rum, and other spirit; and a duty of ten pounds per head on all Negroes imported, with some other duties.

Q. For what purposes are those taxes laid?

A. For the support of the civil and military establishments of the country, and to discharge the heavy debt contracted in the last [Seven Years'] war. . . .

Q. Are not all the people very able to pay those taxes?

A. No. The frontier counties, all along the continent, have been frequently ravaged by the enemy and greatly impoverished, are able to pay very little tax. . . .

Q. Are not the colonies, from their circumstances, very able to pay the stamp duty?

A. In my opinion there is not gold and silver enough in the colonies to pay the stamp duty for one year.

Q. Don't you know that the money arising from the stamps was all to be laid out in America?

A. I know it is appropriated by the act to the American service; but it will be spent in the conquered colonies, where the soldiers are, not in the colonies that pay it. . . .

Q. Do you think it right that America should be protected by this country and pay no part of the expense?

A. That is not the case. The colonies raised, clothed, and paid, during the last war, near 25,000 men, and spent many millions.

Q. Where you not reimbursed by Parliament?

A. We were only reimbursed what, in your opinion, we had advanced beyond our proportion, or beyond what might reasonably be expected from us; and it was a very small part of what we spent. Pennsylvania, in particular, disbursed about 500,000 pounds, and the reimbursements, in the whole, did not exceed 60,000 pounds. . . .

Q. Do you think the people of America would submit to pay the stamp duty, if it was moderated?

A. No, never, unless compelled by force of arms. . . .

Q. What was the temper of America towards Great Britain before the year1763?

A. The best in the world. They submitted willingly to the government of the Crown, and paid, in all their courts, obedience to acts of Parliament. . . .

Q. What is your opinion of a future tax, imposed on the same principle with that of the Stamp Act? How would the Americans receive it?

A. Just as they do this. They would not pay it.

Q. Have not you heard of the resolutions of this House, and of the House of Lords, asserting the right of Parliament relating to America, including a power to tax the people there?

A. Yes, I have heard of such resolutions.

Q. What will be the opinion of the Americans on those resolutions?

A. They will think them unconstitutional and unjust.

Q. Was it an opinion in America before 1763 that the Parliament had no right to lay taxes and duties there?

A. I never heard any objection to the right of laying duties to regulate commerce; but a right to lay internal taxes was never supposed to be in Parliament, as we are not represented there. . . .

Q. Did the Americans ever dispute the controlling power of Parliament to regulate the commerce?

A. No.

Q. Can anything less than a military force carry the Stamp Act into execution?

A. I do not see how a military force can be applied to that purpose.

Q. Why may it not?

A. Suppose a military force sent into America; they will find nobody in arms; what are they then to do? They cannot force a man to take stamps who chooses to do without them. They will not find a rebellion; they may indeed make one.

Q. If the act is not repealed, what do you think will be the consequences?

A. A total loss of the respect and affection the people of America bear to this country, and of all the commerce that depends on that respect and affection.

Q. How can the commerce be affected?

A. You will find that, if the act is not repealed, they will take very little of your manufactures in a short time.

Q. Is it in their power to do without them?

A. I think they may very well do without them.

Q. Is it their interest not to take them?

A. The goods they take from Britain are either necessaries, mere conveniences, or superfluities. The first, as cloth, etc., with a little industry they can make at home; the second they can do without till they are able to provide them among themselves; and the last, which are mere articles of fashion, purchased and consumed because the fashion in a respected country; but will now be detested and rejected. The people have already struck off, by general agreement, the use of all goods fashionable in mourning. . . .

Q. If the Stamp Act should be repealed, would it induce the assemblies of America to acknowledge the right of Parliament to tax them, and would they erase their resolutions [against the Stamp Act]?

A. No, never.

Q. Is there no means of obliging them to erase those resolutions?

A. None that I know of; they will never do it, unless compelled by force of arms.

Q. Is there a power on earth that can force them to erase them?

A. No power, how great soever, can force men to change their opinions. . . .

Q. What used to be the pride of the Americans?

A. To indulge in the fashions and manufactures of Great Britain.

Q. What is now their pride?

A. To wear their old clothes over again, till they can make new ones.

Phillis Wheatley, "Our Modern Egyptians"

February 11, 1774

Rev'd and honor'd Sir,

    I have this Day received your obliging kind Epistle, and am greatly satisfied with your Reasons respecting the Negroes, and think highly reasonable what you offer in Vindication of their natural Rights. Those that invade them cannot be insensible that the divine Light is chasing away the thick Darkness which broods over the Land of Africa; and the Chaos which has reign'd so long, is converting into beautiful Order, and reveals more and more clearly, the glorious Dispensation of civil and religious Liberty, which are so inseparably united, that there is little or no Enjoyment of one without the other. Otherwise, perhaps, the Israelites had been less solicitous for their Freedom from Egyptian Slavery; I don't say they would have been contented without it. By no Means, for in every human Breast, God has implanted a Principle, which we call Love of Freedom; it is impatient of Oppression, and pants for Deliverance. And by the leave of our modern Egyptians, I will assert that the same principle lives in us. God grant Deliverance in his own Way and Time, and get him honor upon all those whose Avarice impels them to countenance and help forward the Calamities of their fellow Creatures. This I desire not for their Hurt, but to convince them of the strange Absurdity of their Conduct whose Words and Actions are so diametrically opposite. How well the cry for Liberty, and the reverse Disposition for the exercise of oppressive Power over others agree, I humbly think it does not require the Penetration of a Philosopher to determine.

    Phillis   Wheatley

1. Is Franklin's description of colonial opposition to the Stamp Act consistent with your text's emphasis on gentry protest to popular revolt?

2. What was Washington's principal military contribution to the success of that revolt?

3. What was the principal contribution of the colonial militaries?

4. Was the American ideology of resistance and revolt consistent with Phillis Wheatley's view of the revolution?

5. How would an American planter have responded to Wheatley's argument? How would he have reconciled his argument with revolutionary rhetoric?

CHAPTER 6

THE REPUBLICAN EXPERIMENT

SUMMARY

After the Revolution, Americans tried to construct practicing governments based on republican principles.

THE REPUBLICAN CHALLENGE

In the 1780s, many Americans feared their Revolution could still fail if not grounded in a virtuous republican government, but ordinary folk, influenced by evangelicalism, expected God-given progress founded on "goodness and not wealth." They expected the Revolution to bring them greater liberty, a voice in government, and an end to special privilege. Others, fearing liberty led to democratic excesses, emphasized the need for order.

THE PEOPLE'S GOVERNMENT

Although less wrenching than the great social upheavals of modern times, the Revolution caused Americans to consider the role of equality in their society.

Social and Political Reform

Fearful of privilege, republicans insisted on the appearance of equality and some social and political reforms. They abolished remnants of aristocratic privilege, changed electoral patterns, and moved toward separation of church and state.

African Americans in the New Republic

Some republicans noted the contradiction between their ideals of virtue and the evils of slavery, and many African Americans issued claims for equality based on that glaring inconsistency and the achievements of their people, including, for example, Benjamin Banneker and Phillis Wheatley. Northerners attacked and abolished the institution, but refused to accept freedmen as their equals; many Southerners questioned the morality of slavery; none defended it as a "positive good."

The Scandal of Women's Rights

By the 1870s, few accepted the earlier view of unlimited power for patriarchs; thus some women began to demand more of their husbands and society, and to claim special responsibility for nurturing in their children the virtues essential to republican government. Although women made some gains in education and law, society still defined them exclusively as homemakers, wives, and mothers.

Postponing Liberty

Republicans of the era made few concrete achievements of equality, but established ideals and assumptions that would influence later generations.

THE STATES: THE LESSONS OF REPUBLICANISM
After 1776, Americans wrote new provisional, sometimes experimental, state constitutions, which reflected their social and regional differences.

Blueprints for State Government
Political change resulted in new written state constitutions that reflected the American distrust of power that followed the revolution against the British government.

Natural Rights and the State Constitutions
The new constitutions tended to emphasize fundamental freedoms, especially those of religion, speech, and press, and to grant great power to legislatures, little to governors.

Power to the People
Massachusetts set an important precedent by drafting its constitution in a special convention called for that purpose. In all states, more of "the People's men" appeared in government.

CREATING A NEW NATIONAL GOVERNMENT
During the military crisis of the Revolution, the Second Continental Congress assumed national authority, but independence would result in the creation of greater central authority.

Articles of Confederacy
Americans created a weak national Congress because they trusted state power more than central power, but most felt only apathy for their new government.

Western Lands: Key to the First Constitution
The major point of dispute for the new government was the ownership of western lands claimed by some of the new states, territory which other states felt should be shared by all with ownership granted to the new confederation government.

The Confederation's Major Achievement
The new national government did acquire these lands, and provided for their orderly survey, sale, and governance, which prevented the chaotic conditions of earlier settlement in the southwest of the new country.

FEAR OF ANARCHY
Complaints about the Articles of Confederation abounded, most of them reflecting economic frustrations.

The Nationalist Critique
The national government lacked the power to do much about some important national problems, the economy floundered but Congress could not regulate trade; the government owed money but

could not tax--leading a group of "nationalists" to call for major constitutional reforms.

Diplomatic Humiliation
In foreign affairs, Congress claimed lands occupied by the Spanish and the English but did not have the power to contest the Europeans for control of the land.

"HAVE WE FOUGHT FOR THIS?"
Most Americans still feared centralized power, but many prosperous republicans had come to fear that ordinary citizens lacked republican virtue and threatened order and that the weakness of the Confederation threatened commercial prosperity. Only a strong central government, they argued, could solve both problems.

The Genius of James Madison
Madison provided these anxious nationalists with a theory to sustain their hope for a large republic with a strong government, reversing Montesquieu's argument that republics would work in only a small area, holding that a large republic would prosper as a variety of interests would develop, check one another, and leave government in the hands of able and virtuous men.

Moment of Decision
The nationalist movement grew stronger because of fears aroused by Shays's Rebellion and culminated in the constitutional convention.

The Philadelphia Convention
The fifty-five men who were to write the constitution were mostly young, practical, and prominent nationalists.

Inventing a Federal Republic
They based their work on Madison's Virginia Plan, which called for a strong central government "consisting of a supreme Legislature, Executive, and Judiciary."

Compromise Saves the Constitution
The delegates compromised, especially on the issues of representation and of counting slaves as population, but retained the essentials of the Virginia Plan.

A Republic with Slaves
The slavery issue threaten to disrupt the convention, but the delegates compromised repeatedly in order to complete what most of them saw as the most important responsibility, the establishment of a strong national government.

The Last Details
In a last review of their work the delegates created a stronger executive, a president independent of Congress and selected by an electoral college.

We, the People

To bypass serious difficulties for ratification of their handiwork, the delegates called for approval by special state conventions, with the Constitution going into effect when approved by nine states.

Whose Constitution? The Struggle for Ratification
The delegates sent their handiwork to the Confederation Congress, which submitted it to the states to consider for ratification.

Federalists and Antifederalists
Federalists were better organized, financed, and led than their opponents, but Antifederalist views, especially their aversion to centralized power, had wide appeal. The Federalists won the struggle for ratification but Antifederalist views would remain influential throughout American history.

Adding the Bill of Rights
Antifederalists had also protested the Constitution's lack of guarantees for individual rights. To overcome those objections, the Federalists agreed to add the Bill of Rights, the first ten amendments to the Constitution.

A New Beginning
The American people had won their sovereignty and accepted the resulting responsibility, and created a new, stronger government based on the Constitution. Yet no one really knew whether this republican experiment would work.

LEARNING OBJECTIVES

After mastering this chapter, you should be able to:

1. Explain the principles that led Sam Adams and other republicans to vehemently oppose the "Sans Souci Club."

2. Describe the conflict among American republicans of the 1780s over the relative importance of liberty as opposed to order.

3. Delineate the types and extent of the social and political changes brought by the American Revolution.

4. Describe the post-revolutionary positions on slavery of both the North and the South.

5. Specify the post-revolutionary changes in the expectations, rights, and roles of American women.

6. Describe the major sources and principles of the earliest American constitutions.

7. Identify the major problems of western settlement and evaluate the Confederation Congress's responses to those problems.

8. Identify the major domestic and foreign-policy problems of the Confederation Congress and the nationalists' critique of the congressional responses.

9. Explain how republican ideology contributed to the ills confronting the country in the 1780s, and how Madison proposed to deal with those problems.

10. Trace the development of the movement for a new constitution from the Annapolis convention through Shays's Rebellion to the Philadelphia convention of 1787.

11. Identify the major differences between the Virginia and New Jersey Plans, then describe the compromise of the issue by the delegates at the convention.

12. Describe the conflict over slavery and its resolution by the delegates to the Philadelphia convention.

13. Identify the major issues separating the Federalists and Antifederalists. Describe and evaluate the positions taken by each.

14. Trace the ratification process from the organization of the opposing sides to June 1788.

15. Describe and explain the major contribution of the Antifederalists to the Constitution.

16. Explain why and how the new government protected the people from themselves.

GLOSSARY

To build your social science vocabulary, familiarize yourself with the following terms:

1. **primogeniture** the right of inheritance by the elder son. ". . . states abolished laws of primogeniture . . ."

2. **entail** to limit inheritance to an unalterable line of heirs. "states abolished laws of entail"

3. **muse** a poet or one possessing the powers and talents of a poet. "Phllis Wheatley Boston's celebrated 'African muse'"

4. **natural rights** inalienable individual rights derived from nature. ". . . possessed natural

rights over which government exercised no control . . ." (p. 167)

5. **equity** quality of being just, impartial, and fair. "Virginians scoffed at these pleas for equity."

6. **ordinance** a public regulation or statute. "Jefferson . . . drafted an ordinance . . ."

7. **nationalist** an advocate of centralized national power. ". . . nationalists regarded their opponents as . . . naive."

8. **confederation** a union of nations or states in which sovereignty is retained by each member. ". . . to divide the United States into separate confederations . . ."

9. **quorum** required minimum number of members present for legal transaction of business. ". . . postponed for a lack of a quorum.

10. **anarchy** social and political confusion due to absence of governmental authority. ". . . unrestrained individualism that led to anarchy . . ."

11 **veto** one governmental branch's rejection of a bill passed by another branch. ". . . armed the chief executive with a veto power . . ."

12 **ratification** formal sanction to make valid. "ratification would not be easy."

13. **obstructionist** one who deliberately hinders or blocks. "Their cause seem[ed] far more obstructionist than it was"

14. **demagogue** one who obtains power by arousing emotions and prejudices of others. " little demagogue of a petty parish . . . "

IDENTIFICATION

Briefly identify the meaning and significance of the following terms:

1. State constitutions _____

_____

2. Articles of Confederation _____

_____

3. Land Ordinance of 1785 _____

4. Northwest Ordinance of 1787 _____

_____

5. The Federalist Number 10 _____

_____

6. Shays's Rebellion _____

_____

7. Virginia Plan _____

_____

8. New Jersey Plan _____

_____

9. Antifederalists _____

_____

10. Bill of Rights _____

_____

MATCHING

A. Match the following political leaders of the Confederation period with the appropriate description:

1. Thomas Jefferson
   a. negotiated a treaty with the Spanish that aroused southern and western hostility

2. Robert Morris
   b. countered Montesquieu's argument against a large republic

3. John Jay
   c. proposed a national bank and other controversial financial measures

79

4. George Washington   **d**. drafted important ordinance of 1784 that served as basis for later land and northwestern ordinances

5. James Madison   **e**. confronted frustrated army officers to prevent a potential rebellion

      f. persuaded Congress to sell southeastern Ohio lands to his company

B. Match the following delegates with the role they played at the Constitutional Convention in 1787:

1. Patrick Henry   **a**. drafted the plan to replace the Confederation with a new federal system

2. James Madison   **b**. stayed away because he "smelled a rat"

3. William Paterson   **c**. polished the final wording of the Constitution

4. Benjamin Franklin   **d**. proposed a plan that would have retained much of the Articles of Confederation

5. Gouverneur Morris   **e**. presented the "Virginia Plan" to the convention

      f. chaired a "grand committee" that arranged some of the convention's important compromises

COMPLETION

Answer the question or complete the statement by filling in the blanks with the correct word or words.

1. Bostonian Republicans regarded the social gathering known as the _____ as too foolish and profligate for Americans.

2. The officers' organization called _____ provoked a similar protest of the against aristocratic pretension.

3. Women gained some changes in _____ laws in post-Revolution period.

4. In a significant change from English tradition, Americans would insist on _____ constitutions.

5. The Articles concentrated power in the _____ branch of government.

6. Scotch-Irish frontiersmen called the _____ protested Pennsylvania's inadequate military defense.

7. The Confederation's land ordinance provided for the survey unit of six miles square, the _____.

8. The argument that a republic could survive only in a small territory was stated by _____.

9. Virginian _____ wrote the most influential of the Declaration of Rights of the period's constitutions.

10. _____ was the most famous of the settlers who moved through the Cumberland Gap to Kentucky.

TRUE/FALSE

Mark the following statements either T (True) or F (False):

____ 1. When Northerners criticized slavery in the period after the Revolution, southern planters united in almost unanimous defense of the institution.

____ 2. The Revolution raised the expectations of American women because republican ideology assigned them new professional and political roles.

____ 3. The Confederation Congress proved ineffective in foreign affairs but effective in regulating the domestic economy.

____ 4. Western settlement south of the Ohio was much more orderly than that of the Northwest Territory.

____ 5. Although twelve states supported a 1781 tariff amendment to the Articles, Rhode Island's single opposing vote killed the plan.

____ 6. The Massachusetts adoption of a state constitution in 1780 set a precedent that the definition of fundamental rights should not be left to ordinary officeholders.

____ 7. Madison believed that competing "interest groups" would neutralize one another, leaving the power to govern with the able and virtuous.

____ 8. Angry agrarians joined Shays's Rebellion to protest the Confederation Congress's inability to provide the use of the Mississippi as an outlet for farm products.

____ 9. In return for a prohibition against interference with the slave trade until 1808, Virginians backed down on their demand for a constitutional requirement of a two-thirds vote on trade measures passed by Congress.

____ 10. Alexander Hamilton opposed New York Antifederalists with a threat to lead New York City to secede from the state unless it ratified the Constitution.

MULTIPLE CHOICE

Circle the one alternative that best completes the statement or answers the question.

1. Which best describes the extent of revolutionary-era reforms?
   a. full equality for all white Americans
   b. full equality for all white male Americans
   c. some substantive reforms and an expectation of more to come
   d. no reforms of any consequence

2. In spite of republican misgivings, southern slavery survived the post-revolutionary era because
   a. the South had developed a theory of slavery as a "positive social good."
   b. whites feared the political power of freed blacks.
   c. planters resented the "meddling" of northern abolitionists.
   d. there were powerful economic incentives to forced labor.

3. On the whole, authors of the state constitutions supported
   a. the value of the English precedent for a flexible, unwritten constitution.
   b. the need to spell out fundamental or "natural" rights.
   c. the need for a powerful executive to check the power of the legislature.
   d. the need for stable and powerful governments to balance the potential excesses of liberty.

4. During the Confederation era, western lands became a hotly debated topic because
   a. no state wanted national control of western settlement.
   b. the cost of removing the Native Americans would be astronomical.
   c. the sections disagreed over the expansion of slavery.
   d. all states wanted a share of the expected bounty of land sales.

5. The assumption underlying both the weakness of the Confederation government and opposition to a stronger government was that
   a. only the gentry could govern well.
   b. only the common folk could govern well.

c. any concentration of power was dangerous.

d. only elected officials could be trusted with power.

6. Montesquieu proposed that republican government would work best in
    a. a small territory.
    b. a large territory.
    c. a society with social equality.
    d. a primitive society close to a "state of nature."

7. The most divisive difference between the Virginia and New Jersey Plans involved
    a. the counting of slaves as population for both representation and taxation purposes.
    b. providing constitutional guarantees for fundamental liberties.
    c. the method of representation in the legislative branch.
    d. the continuation of the slave trade.

8. Those Antifederalists who drew much of their republican thought from the "Commonwealth men" feared the Constitution would lead to
    a. representation by powerful men out of touch with constituents.
    b. a national government that would not be strong enough to control majority tyranny.
    c. excessive factionalism that would destroy republicanism.
    d. the same problems suffered by the Articles of Confederation Congress.

9. When compared to their Antifederalist opponents, the supporters of the Constitution were more likely to be
    a. state government officials.
    b. subsistence or noncommercial farmers.
    c. residents of commercialized areas.
    d. residents of rural, noncommercial areas.

10. In support of a Bill of Rights, Madison argued that the greatest threat to popular liberties came from
    a. the majority.
    b. public apathy.
    c. a powerful minority.
    d. a corrupted gentry.

11. The Articles government's greatest achievement was its
    a. success against the British and Spanish in the West.
    b. legislation of a system for orderly settlement of the West.
    c. management of the postwar prosperity.
    d. establishment of sound public finance.

12. John Jay's treaty with Spain (1785) outraged southern delegates to the Articles of Confederation Congress because it

a. gave up use of the Mississippi River for twenty-five years.
b. lost all trade privileges with Spain.
c. failed to remove Spanish forts from the West.
d. lost Georgia's boundary dispute with Spanish Florida.

13. Madison's principal nationalist theory held that uniting the states in a larger republic would
a. defeat the country's foreign enemies.
b. keep government closer to the people.
c. create a variety of interests to check one another.
d. put Montesquieu's theory into practice.

14. The advantages enjoyed by supporters of ratification of the Constitution *did not* include
a. the name "Federalist."
b. the support of most newspapers.
c. support in *The Federalist* essays.
d. popular suspicion of political power.

15. A judge knowledgeable about American history would look to which of the following to discover the "original intent" of the Constitution's framers?
a. the *Journal, Acts and Proceedings of the Convention Assembled at Philadelphia,* recorded by the Convention secretary
b. the *Secret Proceedings and Debates of the Convention Assembled at Philadelphia,* recorded by Robert Yates and edited by Citizen Genet
c. the *Notes of Debates in the Federal Convention of 1787,* recorded by James Madison
d. the records and notes of the various state ratification conventions

THOUGHT QUESTIONS

To check your understanding of the key issues of this period, solve the following problems:

1. Most Americans of the 1780s wanted the kind of government provided by the Articles of Confederation, with all its weaknesses. True or false? Explain your answer.

2. Was it necessary to replace the Articles of Confederation? Could they have been modified to provide Americans with a successful, democratic, and, perhaps, parliamentary government?

3. Was the nationalist movement for a stronger central government a reaction to excesses following the Revolution?

4. Madison proposed that a large republic would balance and check competing factions (interests) and thus permit able and virtuous men to attain power to govern for the common

good. Has the system worked as he hoped?

5.	Antifederalists argued that a strong national government, in a distant capital, would escape the political control of the people. Has the system worked as they feared?

CRITICAL THINKING EXERCISES

Using material in Chapter 6 of the text and the Primary Sources provided below, please answer the questions which follow the Documents.

"The Virginia, or Randolph, Plan"
"Federalist Paper #10"

The Virginia, or Randolph, Plan (1787)

1.	Resolved that the Articles of Confederation ought to be so corrected and enlarged as to accomplish the objects proposed by their institution; namely "common defence, security of liberty and general welfare."

2.	Resolved therefore that the rights of suffrage in the National Legislature ought to be proportioned to the Quotas of contribution, or to the number of free inhabitants, as the one or the other rule may seem best in different cases.

3.	Resolved that the National Legislature ought to consist of two branches.

4.	Resolved that the members of the first branch of the National Legislature ought to be elected by the people of the several States. . . . to receive liberal stipends by which they may be compensated for the devotion of their time to public service, to be ineligible to any office established by a particular State, or under the authority of the United States, except those peculiarly belonging to the functions of the first branch, during the term of service, and for the space of after its expiration; to be incapable of reelection for the space of after the expiration of their term of service, and to be subject to recall.

5.	Resolved that the members of the second branch of the National Legislature ought to be elected by those of the first, out of a proper number of persons nominated by the individual Legislatures, to be of the age of years at least; to hold their offices for a term sufficient to ensure their independency; to receive liberal stipends, by which they may be compensated for the devotion of their time to public service; and to be ineligible to any office established by a particular State, or under the authority of the United States, except those peculiarly belonging to the functions of the second branch, during the term of service, and for the space of after the expiration thereof.

6.	Resolved that each branch ought to possess the right of originating Acts; that the National Legislature ought to be impowered to enjoy the Legislative Rights vested in Congress by the Confederation and moreover to legislate in all cases to which the separate States are incompetent, or in which the harmony of the United States may be interrupted by the exercise of individual Legislation; to negative all laws passed by the several States, contravening in the opinion of the national Legislature the articles of Union; and to call forth the force of the Union against any member of the Union failing in its duty under the articles thereof.

7.	Resolved that a National Executive be instituted; [to be chosen by the National Legislature for the terms of years; to be chosen by the National Legislature for the terms of years;] to receive punctually, at stated times, a fixed compensation for the services rendered, in which no increase or diminution shall be made so as to affect the Magistracy, existing at the time of the increase of diminution, and to be ineligible a second time; and that besides a general authority to execute the National laws, it ought to enjoy the Executive rights vested in Congress by the Confederation.

8.	Resolved that the Executive and a convenient number of the national Judiciary, ought to compose a

Council of revision with authority to examine every act of the National Legislature before it shall operate, and every act of a particular Legislature before a Negative thereon shall be final; and that the dissent of the said Council shall amount to a rejection, unless the Act of the National Legislature be passed again, or what of a particular Legislature be again negatived by the members of each branch.

9.   Resolved that National Judiciary be established to consist of one or more supreme tribunals, and of inferior tribunals to be chosen by the National Legislature, to hold their offices during good behaviour; and to receive punctually at stated times fixed compensation for their services, in which no increase or diminution shall be made so as to affect the persons actually in office at the time of such increase or diminution. That the jurisdiction of the inferior tribunals shall be to hear and determine in the dernier resort, all piracies and felonies on the high seas, captures from an enemy; cases in which foreigners or citizens of other States applying to such jurisdictions may be interested, or which respect the collection of the National revenue; impeachments of any National officers, and questions which may involve the national peace and harmony.

10.   Resolved that provision ought to be made for the admission of States Lawfully arising within the limits of the United States, whether from a voluntary junction of Government and Territory or otherwise, with the consent of a number of voices in the National legislature less than the whole.

11.   Resolved that a Republican Government and the territory of each State, except in the instance of a voluntary junction of Government and territory, ought to be guaranteed by the United States to each State.

12.   Resolved that provision ought to be made for the continuance of Congress and their authorities and privileges, until a given day after the reform of the articles of Union shall be adopted, and for the completion of all their engagements.

13.   Resolved that provision ought to be made for the amendment of the Articles of Union whensoever it shall seem necessary, and that the assent of the National Legislature ought not to be required thereto.

14.   Resolved that the Legislative Executive and Judiciary powers within the several States ought to be bound by oath to support the articles of Union.

15.   Resolved that the amendments which shall be offered to the Confederation, by the Convention ought at a proper time, or times, after the approbation of Congress to be submitted to an assembly or assemblies of Representatives, recommended by the several Legislatures to be expressly chosen by the people, to consider and decide thereon.

Publius (James Madison), Federalist Paper #10 (1788)

. . . [I]t may be concluded that a pure democracy, by which I mean a society, consisting of a small number of citizens, who assemble and administer the government in person, can admit of no cure for the mischiefs of faction. A common passion or interest will, in almost every case, be felt by a majority of the whole; a communication and concert results from the form of government itself; and there is nothing to check the inducements to sacrifice the weaker party, or an obnoxious individual. Hence it is, that such democracies have ever been spectacles of turbulence and contention; have ever been found incompatible with personal security, or the rights of property; and have in general been short in their lives, as they have been violent in their deaths. Theoretic politicians, who have patronized this species of government, have erroneously supposed, that by reducing mankind to a perfect equality in their political rights, they would, at the same time, be perfectly equalized, and assimilated in their possessions, their opinions, and their passions.

A republic, by which I mean a government in which the scheme of representation takes place, opens a different prospect, and promises the cure for which we are seeking. Let us examine the points in which it varies from pure democracy, and we shall comprehend both the nature of the cure, and the efficacy which it must derive from the union.

The two great points of difference between a democracy and a republic, are first, the delegation of the government, in the latter, to a small number of citizens elected by the rest; secondly, the greater number of citizens, and greater sphere of country, over which the latter may be extended.

The effect of the first difference is, on the one hand, to refine and enlarge the public views, by passing them through the medium of a chosen body of citizens, whose wisdom may best discern the true interest of their country, and whose patriotism and love of justice, will be least likely to sacrifice it to temporary or partial considerations. Under such a regulation, it may well happen that the public voice pronounced by the representatives of the people, will be more consonant to the public good, than if pronounced by the people themselves convened for the purpose. On the other hand, the effect may be inverted. Men of factious tempers, of local prejudices, or of sinister designs, may by intrigue, by corruption, or by other means, first obtain the suffrages, and then betray the interests of the people. The question resulting is, whether small or extensive republics are most favourable to the election of proper guardians of the public wealth; and it is clearly decided in favour of the latter by two obvious considerations.

In the first place it is to be remarked, that however small the republic may be, the representatives must be raised to a certain number, in order to guard against the cabals of a few; and that however large it may be, they must be limited to a certain number, in order to guard against the confusion of a multitude. Hence the number of representatives in the two cases not being in proportion to that of the constituents, and being proportionally greatest in the small republic, it follows, that if the proportion of fit characters be not less in the large than in the small republic, the former will present a greater opinion, and consequently a greater probability of a fit choice.

In the next place, as each representative will be chosen by a greater number of citizens in the large than in the small republic, it will be more difficult for unworthy candidates to practise with success the vicious arts, by which elections are too often carried; and the suffrages of the people being more free, will be more likely to centre on men who possess the most attractive merit, and the most diffusive and established characters.

It must be confessed, that in this, as in most other cases, there is a mean, on both sides of which inconveniences will be found to lie. By enlarging too much the number of electors, you render the representative too little acquainted with all their local circumstances and lesser interests; as by reducing it too much, you render him unduly attached to these, and too little fit to comprehend and pursue great and national objects. The federal constitution forms a happy combination in this respect; the great and aggregate interests being referred to the national, the local and particular to the state legislatures.

The other point of difference is, the greater number of citizens and extent of territory which may be brought within the compass of republican, than of democratic government; and it is this circumstance principally which renders factious combinations less to be dreaded in the former, than in the latter. The smaller the society the fewer probably will be the distinct parties and interests composing it; the fewer the distinct parties and interests, the more frequently will a majority be found of the same party; and the smaller the number of individuals composing a majority, and the smaller the compass within which they are placed, the more easily will they concert and execute their plans of oppression. Extend the sphere, and you take in a greater variety of parties and interests; you make it less probable that a majority of the whole will have a common motive to invade the rights of other citizens; or if such a common motive exists, it will be more difficult for all who feel it to discover their own strength, and to act in unison with each other. Besides other impediments, it may be remarked, that where there is a consciousness of unjust dishonourable purposes, communication is always checked by distrust, in proportion to the number whose concurrence is necessary.

Hence it clearly appears, that the same advantage, which a republic has over a democracy, in controlling the effects of faction, is enjoyed by a large over a small republic-is enjoyed by the union over the states composing it. Does this advantage consist in the substitution of representatives, whose enlightened views and virtuous sentiments render them superior to local prejudices and to schemes of injustice? It will not be denied, that the representation of the union will be most likely to possess these requisite endowments. Does it consist in the greater security afforded by a greater variety of parties, against the event of any one party being able to outnumber or oppress the rest? In an equal degree does the encreased variety of parties, comprised within the union, encrease this security. Does it, in fine, consist in the greater obstacles opposed to the concert and accomplishment of the secret wishes of an unjust and interested majority? Here, again, the extent of the union gives it the most palpable advantage.

The influence of factious leaders may kindle a flame within their particular states, but will be unable to spread a general conflagration through the other states: A religious sect, may degenerate into a political faction in a part of the confederacy; but the variety of sects dispersed over the entire face of it, must secure the national councils against any danger from that source: A range of paper money, for an abolition of debts, for an equal division of property, or for any other improper or wicked project, will be less apt to pervade the whole body of the union, than a particular member of it; in the sample proportion as such a malady is more likely to taint a particular county or district, than an entire sate.

In the extent an proper structure of the union, therefore, we behold a republican remedy for the diseases most incident to republican government. And according to the degree of pleasure and pride, we feel in being republicans, ought to be our zeal in cherishing the spirit, and supporting the character of federalists.

Publius.

1. The text asserts that "Following the war, Americans aggressively ferreted out and, with republican fervor, denounced any races of aristocratic presence." What evidence does the author present to support this assertion?

2. Despite the Declaration of Independence's claim of equality for all, women and African Americans in the new republic were clearly treated as less equal. Using the text, describe the efforts made by each group in the post-Revolution period to improve their position in the society of the new nation.

3. Despite differences over details, early state constitutions revealed many similarities. Using the text, describe the ways in which these state constitutions were most similar.

4. Read "The Virginia, or Randolph, Plan" and discuss how this plan would have acted to provide the larger states with more power in the proposed new constitution. Why would the smaller states have opposed it?

5. In "Federalist Paper #10", why does James Madison indicate that "faction" is one of the major dangers facing the new nation? How does he propose to reduce that danger?

C H A P T E R 7

DEMOCRACY IN DISTRESS:
THE VIOLENCE OF PARTY POLITICS, 1788-1800

SUMMARY

A debate in the first United States Senate in 1789 over what title to use when addressing George Washington as president revealed the range of political questions to be considered by early politicians and perhaps foreshadowed later attitudes adopted by rival groups over the proper roles and powers of the new government.

Force of Public Opinion
The Constitution transferred control of the national government from the states to the people. As ordinary American voters became keenly interested in political issues and debates, elected officials learned that public opinion, not just the leadership of a social elite, would play a major role in guiding the country's future.

Establishing Government
In 1789, George Washington began his career as president, an office he managed successfully and with popular approval. Congress refined the machinery of government with the creation of executive departments and a federal court system and provided revenue with passage of a tariff act.

Jefferson and Hamilton
In spite of Washington's disdain for political squabbling, Americans began to divide into two camps: the Federalists, led by Secretary of the Treasury Alexander Hamilton, and the Republicans, led by Secretary of State Thomas Jefferson. The factions developed differing conceptions about the nature of government and society, economic policy, foreign affiliations, and interpretation of the Constitution.

Hamilton's Grand Design
Hamilton argued for a strong national government and central economic planning in the hands of the monied elite to ensure order in political and economic affairs. Jefferson feared such a government would become oppressive, threatening states' rights and infringing upon individual liberty. Hamilton wished to transform the United States into a self-sufficient industrial power, while Jefferson hoped the nation would remain one of small, independent farmers.

Funding and Assumption
To signal national solvency and to attract investment capital, Hamilton argued that the national government must fund (repay) the national debt as well as assume any outstanding state debts.

Critics argued that the scheme enriched current money speculators at the expense of original investors.

The Controversial Bank of the United States

Hamilton urged creation of a national bank, owned primarily by private stockholders, to administer the country's finances and supervise its currency. While opponents complained that such a bank was unconstitutional, Hamilton argued that the Constitution should be loosely interpreted to expand the powers of the national government whenever "necessary and proper."

Setback for Hamilton

Although Congress had passed Hamilton's earlier financial plans, Madison and Jefferson rallied opponents with a variety of political and moral objections to defeat Hamilton's call for governmental promotion of manufacturing.

Foreign Affairs: Honest Policy or Political Treason?

Jefferson admired the French and hoped that the outbreak of their revolution in 1789 indicated a worldwide republican assault on absolute monarchy and aristocratic privilege. Hamilton cautioned against the anarchic results of excessive democracy and urged closer American ties to Britain.

The Peril of Neutrality

Warfare between Britain and France in 1793 complicated American politics. Britain continued to maintain forts in the Northwest Territory while seizing American ships and impressing American sailors on the high seas. The efforts of French minister Edmond Genet to solicit private American aid for the French cause spurred an official Proclamation of Neutrality from President Washington.

Jay's Treaty and the Hint of Civil War

Washington sent Chief Justice John Jay to London to negotiate a settlement of America's grievances. Secretly forewarned by Hamilton that the Americans would compromise on most issues, the British remained firm. While the resultant Jay's Treaty maintained peace, Republican critics denounced it as a "sellout" of American rights.

Securing the West

The Federalists regained some popularity with other treaties that extracted major concessions in the West. Indian resistance in the Northwest Territory was crushed and Spain agreed to favorable American terms in Pinckney's Treaty.

Popular Political Culture

Partisan Newspapers and Political Clubs

Newspapers and political clubs emerged to champion either the Republican or Federalist cause. The journals were fiercely partisan, presenting rumor or opinion as fact, while the purpose of the clubs was clearly political indoctrination. Political debates were bitter as each faction became convinced of its choices and increasingly suspicious of the other's wisdom and motives.

Whiskey Rebellion Linked to Republican Conspiracy

The Federalists branded the civil unrest caused by the Whiskey Rebellion as Republican agitation. Jefferson felt the Federalists used the episode as an excuse to create an army for the purpose of intimidating Republicans.

Washington's Farewell

Washington's "Farewell Address" of 1796 warned Americans to avoid political factions and entangling foreign alliances. Written largely by Hamilton, the address sought to serve the Federalist cause in the forthcoming election.

The Adams Presidency

Hamilton's attempt to manipulate the election of 1796 backfired, angering newly elected president John Adams and heightening tensions within the Federalist party.

The XYZ Affair and Domestic Politics

During the first years of Adams's presidency, the relations between the United States and France steadily deteriorated. This period of increasing hostility became known as the Quasi-War. An American commission sent by Adams to pursue a peaceful settlement was met by French officials who arrogantly demanded a bribe as the price for negotiations. This so-called XYZ Affair humiliated and infuriated Americans.

Crushing Political Dissent

The Federalists used the outpouring of anti-French sentiment in America as an excuse to increase the nation's military defenses, a move intended to stifle internal political opposition as well as thwart French aggression.

Silencing Political Opposition: The Alien and Sedition Acts

Purportedly measures to protect American security, the Alien and Sedition Acts were, in reality, Federalist measures designed to harass Republican spokespersons by disallowing criticism of the government. These blatantly political attempts to silence opposition ultimately proved counterproductive.

The Republicans Appeal to the States

Jefferson and Madison drafted separate protests known as the Virginia and Kentucky Resolutions asserting that the individual states had the right to interpret federal law, while labeling the Alien and Sedition Acts as unconstitutional.

Adams's Finest Hour

Having refused to ask Congress for a formal declaration of war against France, Adams pursued peaceful negotiations. The Convention of Mortefontaine ended the Quasi-War and restored good relations between France and the United States.

The Peaceful Revolution: The Election of 1800

The Federalists lost office in 1800 partly as a result of internal party disputes, but more importantly, as a result of losing touch with public opinion.

Lessons from Political Extremism

The election of 1800 is perhaps most noteworthy for the peaceful transition of government leadership from one political party to that of the opposition, demonstrating that such a process could be accomplished without widespread confusion, villainy, or violence. As Americans would often learn, political extremists are often more interested in private rather than public interests.

LEARNING OBJECTIVES

After mastering this chapter, you should be able to:

1. Discuss the impact of public opinion on national leaders in setting the agenda from 1788 to 1800.

2. Evaluate George Washington's strengths and weaknesses as president.

3. Compare and contrast the political and economic philosophies advocated by Alexander Hamilton with those of Thomas Jefferson.

4. Explain how foreign affairs acted as a catalyst in the development of American political parties.

5. Evaluate the strengths and weaknesses of John Adams as president.

6. Describe the XYZ Affair and its impact on domestic politics, specifically explaining the intent and results of the Alien and Sedition Acts as well as the Kentucky and Virginia Resolutions.

7. Discuss the terms and results of the Convention of Mortefontaine.

8. Summarize the accomplishments of the Federalists while they were in power.

9. Explain the factors which contributed to the downfall and demise of the Federalist party.

10. Explain the description of the election of 1800 as a "peaceful revolution."

GLOSSARY

To build your social science vocabulary, familiarize yourself with the following terms:

1. **dialectic** the art of arriving at the truth by revealing the contradictions in an opponent's argument and overcoming them. "this dialectic had almost spun out of control. . ."

2. **partisan** strongly supportive of one side, party, or person, often unreasonably so. "The 'public' followed the great debates in hundreds of highly partisan newspapers and magazines."

3. **monarchist** one who favors government by an absolute ruler. "Hamilton was publicly accused of being a secret monarchist . . ."

4. **anarchy** a condition of lawlessness and disorder due to a lack of governmental authority. Hamilton "assumed that in a republican society, the gravest threat to political stability was anarchy . . ."

5. **funding** a plan for repayment of the principle and interest of a debt. "Madison . . . attacked the funding scheme . . ."

6. **assumption** taking over the debt(s) of another. "Hamilton's assumption proposal threatened to destroy . . . the supply of cut-rate securities."

7. **"loose construction"** a broad interpretation of the Constitution expanding the implied powers of Congress. "Hamilton's loose construction carried the day . . ."

8. **reciprocity** a mutual exchange of privileges between countries. "Great Britain . . . refused to grant the United States full commercial reciprocity . . ."

9. **ideologue** one who strongly advocates certain ideas. "militant republicans, ideologues eager to liberate all Europe. . ."

10. **asylum** shelter against arrest and extradition granted to political refugees by a nation. "Genet . . . requested asylum, . . . and spent the remainder of his life residing in New York."

11. **contraband** materials whose trade is forbidden. "The Royal Navy would continue to search American vessels on the high seas for contraband . . ."

12. **credo** a statement or set of fundamental beliefs. Washington's Farewell Address " . . . became the credo of later American isolationists . . ."

13. **sedition** conduct inciting resistance to or against lawful authority. "The Sedition Law . . . defined criticism of the United States government as criminal libel."

14. **debacle** a sudden, disastrous turn of events. "Following the XYZ debacle . . . Talleyrand changed his tune."

15. **lame duck** an elected officeholder or assembly continuing in office from the period of

an election to the inauguration of a successor. ". . . the House of Representatives, a 'lame duck' body still controlled by members of the Federalist party."

IDENTIFICATION

Briefly identify the meaning and significance of the following terms:

1. Judiciary Act of 1789 _____

_____

2. Hamilton's *Report on Public Credit* _____

_____

3. Report on Manufactures _____

_____

4. Jay's Treaty _____

_____

5. Whiskey Rebellion _____

_____

6. XYZ Affair _____

_____

7. Quasi-War _____

_____

8. Alien and Sedition Acts _____

_____

9. Virginia and Kentucky Resolutions _____

_____

10. Election of 1800 _____

_____

MATCHING

A. Match the following treaties with the appropriate result:

1. Proclamation of Neutrality

2. Jay's Treaty

3. Treaty of Greenville

4. Treaty of San Lorenzo

5. Convention of
   Mortefontaine

a. avoidance of war between the United States and Britain

b. concessions by Spain to the United States in hopes of preventing an Anglo-American alliance

c. avoidance of active U.S. entanglement in the British-French war of 1793

d. agreement between France and the United (Pinckney's Treaty) States nullifying the alliance of 1778

e. cession of lands to the United States by Native Americans of the Northwest Territory

f. removal of all trade restrictions against the United States by Britain

B. Match the following public figures with the appropriate description:

1. James Madison

2. John Marshall

3. Charles C. Pinckney

4. Matthew Lyon

a. Republican Congressman convicted of sedition for his criticism of President Adams

b. "midnight judge" appointed as chief justice by President Adams

c. editor of the Republican newspaper, *National Gazette*

d. Hamilton's collaborator on *The Federalist,* but opponent of his financial schemes

5. Philip Freneau

   e. U.S. representative to France outraged by the XYZ Affair; Federalist candidate for vice president in 1800

   f. secretary of war during Washington's administration

COMPLETION

Answer the question or complete the statement by filling in the blanks with the correct word or words.

1. In 1789, Congress created the Departments of _____, _____, and _____.

2. The first chief justice of the Supreme Court and a leading figure in New York politics was _____.

3. Alexander Hamilton defended the constitutionality of the national bank on the basis of the _____ powers of Congress.

4. The minister who precipitated a major diplomatic crisis by seeking American aid for France in its war against Britain was _____.

5. The United States had little chance of securing a successful negotiation of its problems with Britain because a secret message relaying America's willingness to compromise was sent to British officials by _____.

6. General Anthony Wayne led an American army to victory over Indians in the Northwest Territory at the Battle of _____.

7. John Fenno established a newspaper strongly supporting Federalist philosophy and policies, the _____.

8. In 1794, farmers in western Pennsylvania rebelled against the levy of a federal excise tax on _____.

9. "Millions for defense, but not one cent for tribute" was the reaction of Federalist John Marshall to the _____ _____.

10. A recurrence of the tie that resulted in the election of 1800 was prevented by the ratification of the _____ Amendment.

TRUE/FALSE

Mark the following statements either T (True) or F (False).

_____ 1. Politics in the United States from 1788 to 1800 was marked by a high degree of consensus, that is, agreement among Americans on public policy.

_____ 2. George Washington is the only president to have received a unanimous vote of the electoral college.

_____ 3. Southern planters urged adoption of high protective tariffs to discourage European imports.

_____ 4. Hamilton perceived little or no conflict between private greed and public good.

_____ 5. As president, George Washington felt he should defer to Congress in the shaping of foreign policy.

_____ 6. Spain offered favorable terms to the United States in Pinckney's Treaty because she feared a potential Anglo-American alliance aimed at her possessions in North America.

_____ 7. The Whiskey Rebellion of 1794 in western Pennsylvania, resulting in significant property damage and loss of life, necessitated the dispatch of a large federal army to put down the disturbance.

_____ 8. In the election of 1796, Hamilton urged Federalist electors to "throw away" their votes for John Adams, a candidate he deemed too independent.

_____ 9. The tie that resulted from the election of 1800 was resolved when Aaron Burr agreed to withdraw and allow the election of Thomas Jefferson.

_____ 10. The Kentucky and Virginia resolutions demanded southern secession as a protest against the Alien and Sedition Acts.

MULTIPLE CHOICE

Circle the one alternative that *best* completes the statement or answers the questions.

1. American newspapers in the 1790s
   a. offered a powerful tool for popular political mobilization.
   b. catered to a provincial culture that prized politeness.
   c. rarely criticized public figures.
   d. had difficulty remaining solvent.

2. In its first session, Congress
   a. levied a strongly protective tariff of 30 percent on imports.
   b. provided for the establishment of a federal court system.
   c. established the Department of Navy.
   d. prohibited the president from dismissing cabinet level appointees without Senate approval.

3. Thomas Jefferson maintained that the economic well-being of the United States required a(n)
   a. dependence on the monied classes.
   b. development of manufacturing.
   c. emphasis on agricultural productivity.
   d. reduced reliance on the international market.

4. Alexander Hamilton's financial plans for the United States included
   a. funding of the national debt.
   b. repudiation of the states' debts.
   c. establishment of state banks.
   d. all of the above.

5. Hamilton argued that his credit system would
   a. reduce the influence of individual states in shaping national economic policy.
   b. signal to investors around the world that U.S. bonds represented a good risk.
   c. encourage American investment capital to remain in this country.
   d. all of the above.

6. Hamilton overcame opposition to his credit system by promising to
   a. reward those states that had already paid their debts.
   b. grant partial payment to original as well as current bondholders.
   c. grant huge tracts of vacant western lands to state bondholders.
   d. support the location of the new federal capital on the Potomac River.

7. Britain threatened American neutrality during Washington's administration by refusing to
   a. vacate military forts in the Northwest Territory.
   b. allow the sale of British goods in America.
   c. negotiate a settlement of differences.
   d. accept American currency in payment of past debts.

8. In Pinckney's Treaty, the United States gained from Spain
   a. an opening of the Mississippi River to American commerce.
   b. a secure southern boundary on the thirty-first parallel.
   c. a promise to stay out of Indian affairs.
   d. all of the above.

9. The Republicans tended to favor

a. strict interpretation of the Constitution to defend states' rights.

b. central economic planning, particularly the establishment of a national bank.

c. an affiliation with the British in foreign affairs.

d. maintenance of the public order, even if that meant calling out federal troops.

10. According to George Washington, the Whiskey Rebellion represented a(n)
    a. minor protest by a few disgruntled farmers.
    b. Republican effort to undermine the authority of the federal government.
    c. Federalist attempt to intimidate Republicans.
    d. predictable reaction to excessive state taxes.

11. In his Farewell Address, George Washington warned Americans to avoid
    a. one-party domestic politics.
    b. Hamilton's financial schemes.
    c. entangling alliances with foreign nations.
    d. all of the above.

12. As president, John Adams
    a. received consistent public and private support from Alexander Hamilton and the High Federalists.
    b. consulted throughout his term with Vice President Thomas Jefferson on all major issues.
    c. dismissed members of Washington's old cabinet whom he felt were unqualified or disloyal.
    d. refused to ask Congress for a formal declaration of war against France in response to the diplomatic humiliation of the XYZ Affair.

13. The Alien and Sedition Acts were designed to
    a. promote freedom of speech and of the press.
    b. encourage foreign immigration.
    c. harass and suppress Republican spokespersons.
    d. promote friendship between the United States and France.

14. The Virginia and Kentucky Resolutions of 1798
    a. called for rigid enforcement of the Alien and Sedition Acts.
    b. labeled Jefferson and Madison as traitors.
    c. argued for the states' right of resisting "unconstitutional" national laws.
    d. urged unqualified support for President Adams.

15. In the election of 1800,
    a. the House of Representatives elected Thomas Jefferson.
    b. the Supreme Court decided the disputed election.
    c. John Adams received enthusiastic support from Alexander Hamilton.
    d. Aaron Burr withdrew any claims to the presidency.

THOUGHT QUESTIONS

To check your understanding of the key issues of this period, answer the following questions:

1. Washington is often touted by historians as one of our best presidents. Explain why. What qualities and policies make for a "good" or a "bad" president? Who would you characterize as America's greatest presidents?

2. What precedents established by Washington influenced later American politics and politicians? Which of these precedents do we or should we still follow?

3. Who had the better plan for the nation's future, Alexander Hamilton or Thomas Jefferson? Explain.

4. Washington argued that the president could withhold information from the public in the interest of national security. Explain why you agree or disagree with this view.

5. An obvious restriction of free speech, the Sedition Act outlawed criticism of the government. Is such a restriction ever a wise policy?

CRITICAL THINKING QUESTIONS

Read Chapter 7 of the text and the following selections: Benjamin Banneker's letter to Thomas Jefferson, Molly Wallace's "Valedictory Oration," and Samuel Cornish's "An Independent Press." Answer the questions following the reading selections.

Benjamin Banneker, Letter to Thomas Jefferson (1791)

Sir, I am fully sensible of the greatness of that freedom which I take with you on the present occasion; a liberty which Seemed to me Scarcely allowable, when I reflected on that distibguished, and dignifying station in which you Stand; and the almost general prejudice and prepossession which is so previlent in the world against those of my complexion. . . .

Sir I freely and Chearfully acknoweldge, that I am of the African race, and, in that colour which is natural to them of the deepest dye:† and it is under a Sense of the most profound gratitude to the Supreme Ruler of the universe, that I do now confess to you, that I am not under that State of tyrannical thralldom, and inhuman capivity, to which too many of my bretheren are doomed; but that I have abundantly tasted of the fruition of those bessings which proceed from that free and unequalled liberty with which you are favoured and which I hope you will willingly allow you have received from the immediate Hand of that Being from whom proceedeth every good and perfect gift.

Sir, Suffer me to recall to your mind that time in which the Arms and tyranny of the British Crown were exerted with powerful effort, in order to reduce you to a State of Servitude; look back I entreat you on the variety of dangers to which you were exposed, reflect on that time in which every human aid appeared unavailable, and in which even hope and fortitude wore the greatful Sense of your miraculous and providential preservation; You cannot but acknowledge, that the present freedom and tranquility
which you enjoy you have mercifully received, and that it is the peculiar blessing of Heaven.

This, Sir, was a time in whch you clearly saw into the injustice of a State of Slavery, and in which you have Just apprehension of the horrors of its condition, it was now Sir, that you abhorrence thereof was so excited, that you publickly held forth this true and invaluable doctrine, which is worthy to be recorded and remembered in all

Succeeding ages. "We hold these truths to be Self evident, that all men are created equal, and that they are endowed by their creator with certain inalienable rights, that amongst them are life, liberty, and the persuit of happiness." . . .

Sir, I suppose that your knowledge of the situation of my brethren is too extensive to need a recital here; neither shall I presume to prescribe methods by which they may be relieved, otherwise than by recommending to you, and all others, to wean yourselves from those narrow prejudices which you have imbibed with respect to them, and as Job proposed to his friends, "Put your Souls in their Souls' stead," thus shall your hearts be enlarged with kindness and benevolence towards them, and thus shall you need neither the direction of myself or others in what manner to proceed herein.

And now, Sir, altho my Sympathy and affection for my brethren hath caused my enlargement thus far, I ardently hope that your candour and generosity will plead with you in my behalf, when I make known to you, that it was not originally my design; but that having taken up my pen in order to direct to you as a present, a copy of an Almanack which I have calculated for the Succeeding year, I was unexpectedly and unavoidably led thereto. . . .

Molly Wallace, Valedictory Oration (1792)

The silent and solemn attention of a respectable audience, has often, at the beginning of discourses intimidated, even veterans, in the art of public elocution. What then must my situation be, when my sex, my youth and inexperience all conspire to make me tremble at the talk which I have undertaken? . . . With some, however, it has been made a question, whether we ought ever to appear in so public a manner. Our natural timidity, the domestic situation to which by nature and custom we seem destined, are, urged as arguments against what I have now undertaken:-Many sarcastical observations have been handed out against female oratory: But to what do they amount? Do they not plainly inform us, that, because we are females, we ought therefore to be deprived of what is perhaps the most effectual means of acquiring a just, natural and graceful delivery? No one will pretend to deny, that we should be taught to read in the best manner. And if to read, why not to speak? . . . But yet it might be asked, what, has a female character to do with declamation? That she should harangue at the head of an Army, in the Senate, or before a popular Assembly, is not pretended, neither is it requested that she ought to be an adept in the stormy and contentious eloquence of the bar, or in the abstract and subtle reasoning of the Senate; -we look not for female Pitt, Cicero, or Demosthenes.

There are more humble and milder scenes than those which I have mentioned, in which a woman may display her elocution. There are numerous topics, on which she may discourse without impropriety, in the discussion of which, she may instruct and please others, and in which she may exercise and improve her own understanding. After all, we do not expect women should become perfect orators. Why then should they be taught to speak in public? This question may possibly be answered by asking several others.

Why is a boy diligently and carefully taught the Latin, the Greek, or the Hebrew language, in which he will seldom have occasion, either to write or to converse? Why is he taught to demonstrate the propositions of Euclid, when during his whole life, he will not perhaps make use of one of them? Are we taught to dance merely for the sake of becoming dancers? No, certainly. These things are commonly studied, more on account of the habits, which the learning of them establishes, than on account of any important advantages which the mere knowledge of them can afford. So a young lady, from the exercise of speaking before a properly selected audience, may acquire some valuable habits, which, otherwise she can obtain from no examples, and that no precept can give. But, this exercise can with propriety be performed only before a select audience: a promiscuous and indiscriminate one, for obvious reasons, would be absolutely unsuitable, and should always be carefully avoided. . . .

Samuel Cornish, An Independent Press

The noble objects which we have in view by the publication of this Journal . . . encourage us to come boldly before an enlightened publick. . . . We should advertise to the world our motives by which we are actuated, and the objects which we contemplate.

We wish to plead our own cause. Too long have others spoken for us. Too long has the publick been deceived by misrepresentations, in things which concern us dearly, though in the estimation of some mere trifles; for though there are many in society who exercise towards us benevolent feelings; still (with sorrow we confess it) there are those who make it their business to enlarge upon the least trifle, which tends to the discredit of any person of colour; and pronounce anathemas and denounce our whole body for the misconduct of this guilty one. We are aware that there are many instances of vice among us, but we avow that it is because no one has taught its subjects to be virtuous; many instances of poverty, because no sufficient efforts accommodated to minds contracted by slavery, and deprived of early education have been made, to teach them how to husband their hard earnings, and to secure to themselves comfort.

Education being an object of the highest importance to the welfare of society, we shall endeavour to present just and adequate views of it, and to urge upon our brethren the necessity and expediency of training their children, while young, to habits of industry, and thus forming them for becoming useful members of society. It is surely time that we should awake from this lethargy of years, and make a concentrated effort for the education of our youth. We form a spoke in the human wheel and it is necessary that we should understand our [de]pendence on the different parts, and theirs on us, in order to perform our part with propriety.

Though not desiring of dictating, we shall feel it our incumbent duty to dwell occasionally upon the general principles and rules of economy. The world has grown too enlightened, to estimate any man's character by his personal appearance. Though all men acknowledge the excellency of Franklin's maxims, yet comparatively few practise upon them. We may deplore when it is too late, the neglect of these self-evidents truths, but it avails little to mourn. Ours will be the task of admonishing our brethren on these points.

The civil rights of a people being of the greatest value, it shall ever be our duty to vindicate our brethren, when oppressed; and to lay the case before the publick. We shall also urge upon our brethren (who are qualified by the laws of the various states), the expendiency of using their elective franchise; and of making independent use of the same. We wish them not to become the tools of party.

And as much time is frequently lost, and wrong principles instilled, by the perusal of works of trivial importance, we shall consider it a part of our duty to recommend to our young readers, such authors as will not only enlarge their stock of useful knowledge, but such as will also serve to stimulate them to higher attainments in science.

We trust also, that through the columns of the FREEDOM'S JOURNAL, many practical pieces, having for their bases, the improvement of our brethren, will be presented to them, from the pens of many of our respected friends, who have kindly promised their assistance.

It is our earnest wish to make our Journal a medium of intercourse between our brethren in the different states of this great confederacy: that through its columns an expression of our sentiments, on many interesting subjects which concern us, may be offered to the publick: that plans which apparently are beneficial may be candidly discussed and properly weighed; if worthy, receive our cordial approbation; if not, our marked disapprobation.

Useful knowledge of every kind, and everything that relates to Africa, shall find a ready admission in our columns; and as that vast continent becomes daily more known, we trust that many things will come to light, proving that the natives of it are neither so ignorant nor stupid as they have generally supposed to be.

And while these important subjects shall occupy the columns of the FREEDOM'S JOURNAL, we would not be unmindful of our brethren who are still in the iron fetters of bondage. They are our kindred by all the times of nature; and though but little can be effected by us, still let our sympathies be poured forth, and our prayers in their behalf, ascend to Him who is able to succour them.

From the press and the pulpit we have suffered much by being incorrectly represented. Men whom we equally love and admire have not hesitated to represent us disadvantageously, without becoming personally acquainted with the true state of things, nor discerning between virtue and vice among us. The virtuous part of our people feel themselves sorely aggrieved under the existing state of things—they are not appreciated.

Our vices and our degradation are ever arrayed against us, but our virtues are passed by unnoticed. And what is still more lamentable, our friends, to whom we concede all the principles of humanity and religion, from these very causes seem to have fallen into the current of popular feeling and are imperceptibly floating on the stream—actually living in the practice of prejudice, while they abjure it in theory, and feel it not in their hearts. Is it not very desirable that such should know more of our actual condition; and of our efforts and feelings, that in forming or advocating plans for our amelioration, they may do it more understandingly? In the spirit of candor and humility we intend by a simple representation of facts to lay our case before the publick, with a view to arrest the progress of prejudice, and to shield ourselves against the consequent evils. We wish to conciliate all and to irritate none, yet we must be firm and unwavering in our principles, and perservering in our efforts.

1. The text author contends that "accelerated changes in information technology often spark fierce public debate." Why is this so?

2. Is there ever justification for censorship of news or information? Using the text, how would critics of American newspapers in the 1790s have answered that question? How are their arguments similar to or different from the arguments of critics today who say that access to the Internet/World Wide Web in schools and colleges should be restricted or monitored?

3. Would Benjamin Banneker's letter to Thomas Jefferson and Molly Wallace's "Valedictory Oration" have been printed by American newspapers in the 1790s? Explain why or why not for each.

4. What were the purposes and objectives of Samuel Cornish's newspaper, *Freedom's Journal*? Who might have wished restriction of this newspaper and for what reasons?

5. What does the text author mean when he says that modern Americans must constantly relearn the lessons from political extremism?   What acts of political extremism are discussed in Chapter 7 and what "lessons" do they offer us? Does the news media ever go "too far" in its coverage of people and events? Explain.

CHAPTER 8

JEFFERSONIAN ASCENDANCY: THEORY AND PRACTICE OF GOVERNMENT

SUMMARY

In theory, advocates of Jeffersonian democracy declared their passion for liberty and equality. In practice, however, they lived in a society whose members accepted slavery and sought to remove Native Americans from the path of the white man's progress. In theory, Jeffersonians had insisted upon a strict interpretation of the constitution, peaceful foreign relations, and reduction of the size and powers of the federal government. As president, however, Jefferson interpreted the Constitution broadly to accommodate the Louisiana Purchase; increased federal power to enforce the embargo of 1807; and led the country to the brink of war. While some Americans praised Jefferson's pragmatism, others felt betrayed.

Developing Regional Identities

Substantial population growth, improved transportation links within the various sections, and attacks on the institution of slavery, contributed to a growing sense of regionalism in the new nation. Powerful sectional loyalties had already begun to undermine national unity.

Expansion and Conquest

The trans-Appalachian West-with its rich soil and developing system of water transportation-experienced substantial growth after 1790. Native Americans offered some resistance but were pushed aside by the onrushing settlers.

Commercial Capitalism

Economic growth in the United States before 1820 was built on agriculture and commerce. The success of the "carrying trade" diverted investment from more risky manufacturing ventures — although some innovations, especially in the textile industry, did appear. American workers reacted to new machines with ambivalence, fearful of reduced wages and loss of independence and status.

Republican Ascendancy

Although a shy and introspective man, Thomas Jefferson proved to be a capable and pragmatic president. The Federalists would fail to recapture power because of their reluctance to adopt popular campaigning techniques, their resistance to territorial expansion, and their opposition to the War of 1812.

Jeffersonian Reforms

An astute and successful politician, Jefferson accomplished most of his early goals with reduction of the federal bureaucracy, taxes, and military spending. He regarded a large federal deficit as dangerous to republican institutions and a large military presence as liable to provoke hostilities.

Louisiana Purchase

Due to a fortuitous chain of international events, Jefferson managed to double the territory of the United States for only $15 million in 1803 with the Louisiana Purchase from France. Although initially concerned that such an action might be unconstitutional, Jefferson recognized a good deal and quickly presented the treaty for Senate ratification.

Lewis and Clark Expedition

In the midst of the Louisiana controversy, Jefferson authorized the highly successful Lewis and Clark expedition for western exploration.

Conflict with the Barbary States

Jefferson also dispatched an American fleet to battle the Barbary Pirates rather than submit to their demands for tribute. Concluding his first term on a wave of popularity, Jefferson enjoyed an overwhelming reelection in 1804.

Sources of Political Dissension
Attack on the Judges

Angered at the Federalists' attempt to entrench their political power in the national government by the Judiciary Act of 1801, the Republicans repealed the law and then proceeded with their own attempts to remove some and prevent other Federalist judges from obtaining office. While proclaiming victory in *Marbury* v. *Madison* (1803), few Republicans realized that the Supreme Court's decision established the precedent of judicial review of federal statutes.

Politics of Desperation

As Federalist power declined, Republicans fell to squabbling amongst themselves. One radical faction, labeled the "Tertium Quids" or "no accounts" by the newspapers, argued that Jefferson's pragmatic policies sacrificed the purity of Republican principles.

The Burr Conspiracy

Vice-President Aaron Burr schemed with dissident Federalists, quarreled with and shot Alexander Hamilton in a duel, and launched a potentially treasonous expedition against the United States. During Burr's subsequent trial, Chief Justice John Marshall's disallowal of circumstantial evidence helped earn Burr an acquittal and ensure that in the future, treason could not be charged lightly or for purely political purposes.

The Slave Trade

Acting upon the charge of the constitutional convention, Congress considered and passed a bill prohibiting the importation of slaves beginning in 1808. Lax American enforcement, however, especially in the South, resulted in continued, illegal operations of slave smugglers.

Failure of Foreign Policy

During Jefferson's second term, a military stalemate in the resumed warfare between Britain and France forced the belligerents into an economic struggle. Owing to its naval superiority, Britain was more successful at this, not only seizing American ships, but also impressing American sailors. The British attack on the American warship *Chesapeake* in 1807 for its refusal to submit to a British search infuriated Americans.

Embargo Divides the Nation

Jefferson's recommendation for an embargo of American goods in 1807 failed to win foreign respect for American neutrality. His policy of "peaceable coercion" succeeded only in depressing the economy and angering northern merchants and was repealed in 1809.

A New Administration Goes to War

Although James Madison won the election of 1808, he proved to be an ineffective president. Poorly designed Republican policies failed to keep us out of war. General William Henry Harrison defeated an Indian army at Tippecanoe but drove the Indian leader Tecumseh into the arms of the British.

Fumbling Toward Conflict

Aggressive "War Hawks" in the United States were convinced that war against Britain would restore national honor, remove British aid to western Indians, and open Canada to American expansion.

The Strange War of 1812

In spite of early optimism, American war efforts were marred by poor preparation, ineffective leadership, and an ill-designed strategy. Although momentarily preoccupied with Napoleon, Britain appeared no better in executing offensive operations once its full attention could be directed at the United States.

Hartford Convention: Demise of the Federalists

In late 1814, disgruntled Federalists gathered at Hartford to protest the war and recommend constitutional changes designed to protect the minority interests of New England. The demands, presented In Washington just as news broke concerning what seemed a successful conclusion to war, made the Federalists appear foolish if not treacherous, hastening their demise as a political force.

Treaty of Ghent Ends the War

The Treaty of Ghent, signed on Christmas Eve 1814, ended the deadlock of war with no major concessions granted by either side. A belated American victory at the Battle of New Orleans led to a widespread conception that the United States had won the War of 1812.

Republican Legacy

The early Republican presidents championed a democratic, egalitarian society in which virtuous, independent citizens might pursue their own economic interests. The Republicans, however, had failed to dismantle slavery and incorporate African Americans into their republican scheme.

LEARNING OBJECTIVES

After mastering this chapter, you should be able to:

1. Describe the condition and advances of the American economy in this era.

2. List the goals of Jefferson as president and evaluate his success in accomplishing them.

3. Explain the circumstances and consequences of the Louisiana Purchase.

4. Describe the background, results, and significance of the *Marbury* v. *Madison* decision (1803).

5. List and explain the sources of political dissension with which Jefferson had to contend.

6. Evaluate the success of American efforts to end the slave trade.

7. Explain the reasons for the failure of American foreign policy in preventing the War of 1812.

8. Analyze the causes, conduct, and outcome of the War of 1812.

9. Account for James Madison's ineffectiveness as president.

10. Discuss the reasons for the ultimate demise of the Federalist party during this era.

GLOSSARY

To build your social science vocabulary, familiarize yourself with the following terms:

1. **disingenuousness** a condition lacking in candor. "the Federalist Party accused the Republicans . . . of disingenuousness."

2. **pragmatism** a practical approach to problems or affairs. "Some Americans praised the president's pragmatism; others felt betrayed."

3. **sycophants** ones who attempt to win favor or advancement by flattering persons of influence. "It is a cursed delusion, adopted by traitors, and recommended by sycophants."

4. **staple crops** crops produced regularly and in great quantities for markets. "Southerners concentrated on staple crops, tobacco, rice, and cotton . . ."

5. **despotism** government in which the ruler has unlimited authority. ". . . the bill 'establishes a complete despotism' . . ."

6. **extortion** act of obtaining money or information from another by coercion or intimidation.   "In 1801, .

7. **stalwarts** ones who actively support an organization or cause. ". . . Adams quickly filled these positions with stalwarts of the Federalist party."

8. **opportunist** one who takes advantage of opportunities, especially with little regard for   principles

9. **subterfuge** deception in order to conceal or evade. ". . . the British did little to halt this   obvious su

10. **impressment** forcible drafting into service "The document . . said nothing about   impressm

11. **embargo** a governmental order prohibiting the departure of commercial ships from its   ports. "Th

12. **coercion** an act of compelling by force or threat. "'Peaceable coercion' turned into a Jeffersonian nightmare."

13. **chauvinism** excessive or unthinking loyalty. "New Englanders . . . ridiculed such chauvinism."

14. **blockade** a war measure designed to obstruct the commerce and communication of the enemy. "the Royal Navy did not bother to blockade the major northern ports."

15. **flotilla** a fleet of ships. "Captain Thomas MacDonough turned back a British flotilla . . ."

IDENTIFICATION

Briefly identify the meaning and significance of the following terms.

1. Tecumseh_____

_____

2. Albert Gallatin_____

_____

3. Louisiana Purchase_____

_____

4. Lewis and Clark Expedition_____

_____

5. Barbary States_____

_____

6. *Marbury* v. *Madison* (1803)_____

_____

7. John Randolph_____

_____

8. Aaron Burr_____

_____

9. "War Hawks"_____

_____

10. Treaty of Ghent_____

_____

MATCHING

A. Match the following judges with the appropriate description:

| 1. John Jay | **a.** Chief Justice of the Supreme Court appointed in 1801 by President Adams |

2. John Marshall   **b.** Republican Judge presiding over the impeachment proceedings of Federalist judges

3. William Marbury   **c.** an alcoholic and insane Federalist judge impeached and convicted

4. John Pickering   **d.** Federalist judge impeached, but not convicted, because of seditious speech

5. Samuel Chase   **e.** Federalist spokesman retiring from national affairs after Adams's defeat

    f. "midnight judge" who lost his case for appointment in a celebrated decision

B.   Match the following military leaders with the appropriate action:

1. Andrew Jackson   **a.** commanded American forces to victory over western Indians at the Battle of Tippecanoe

2. William Henry Harrison   **b.** captured control of Lake Erie by defeating a British fleet at Put-in-Bay

3. Oliver Hazard Perry   **c.** led American forces to victory over the British at the Battle of New Orleans

4. William Hull   **d.** resisted a British naval attack on Lake Champlain

5. Edward Pakenham   **e.** ordered a British attack against well-defended American positions at New Orleans

    f. surrendered an entire American army to a smaller British force at Detroit

COMPLETION

Answer the question or complete the statement by filling in the blanks with the correct word or words.

1. The influence of New England was apparent in the settlement of the Western Reserve, a narrow strip of land along Lake Erie in northern _____.

2. Andrew Jackson led his Tennessee militia to a crushing victory over the Creek Indians at the Battle of _____.

3. Although suspicious of standing armies, Jefferson ensured professional leadership for American forces in battle by creating the military academy at _____ in 1802.

4. Napoleon lost interest in a plan to reestablish a French empire in America when his troops were unable to recapture control of the island of _____.

5. The faction of extreme Republicans who opposed many of Jefferson's policies were called _____ _____.

6. Initially, Aaron Burr was aided in his conspiracy by the commander of the United States Army in the Mississippi Valley, _____.

7. In 1806 the British government issued a series of trade restrictions known as the _____.

8. In 1807 the United States suffered humiliation when a British ship fired on the American warship _____ for its refusal to submit to a search.

9. Successor to Thomas Jefferson as president, _____ lacked the personal qualities necessary for effective leadership.

10. Francis Scott Key was inspired to write "The Star-Spangled Banner" upon witnessing the survival of Fort _____ against a heavy British assault in September 1814.

TRUE/FALSE

Mark the following statements either T (True) or F (False).

_____ 1. Thomas Jefferson was inflexible as president, refusing to veer from pure Republican philosophy.

_____ 2. Regional identifications among Americans in commerce and politics in the early nineteenth century might be explained partly by a defensiveness to outside criticism.

_____ 3. Jefferson felt the Indians could be "civilized" by converting them to yeoman farmers.

_____ 4. As evidence of his political guile and skills, Thomas Jefferson never vetoed one act of Congress in his two terms as president.

_____5. Jefferson argued that disarmament promoted peace rather than invited aggression.

_____6. Jefferson dismissed all Federalist government workers, demanding the complete loyalty of the federal bureaucracy.

_____7. Illegal slaves smuggled into the United States after 1808 were to be set free if apprehended by federal authorities.

_____8. Eyewitness testimony helped convict Aaron Burr of treason for his private expedition of 1806.

MULTIPLE CHOICE

Circle the one alternative that best completes the statements or answers the question.

1. Which of the following statements about the economy of Jeffersonian America is true?
   a. The prosperity of the United States depended primarily upon industry.
   b. American cities functioned primarily as deports for international trade.
   c. About 25 percent of the population lived and worked in urban centers.
   d. Population increases were fueled primarily by increased immigration.

2. Which of the following was *not* a commercial innovation of this period?
   a. introduction of the agricultural fair.
   b. expansion of the merchant marine.
   c. construction of the Erie Canal.
   d. introduction of the textile industry in New England.

3. As president, Thomas Jefferson
   a. insisted on a great deal of formal ceremony.
   b. maintained close ties with congressional leaders.
   c. delivered public speeches in a dynamic manner.
   d. lacked charm and grace in personal conversations.

4. Which of the following actions by the Jefferson administration coincided with the Republican belief in strict interpretation of the constitution?
   a. negotiation of a treaty for the purchase of Louisiana.
   b. waging of war against the Barbary Pirates.
   c. attempted removal of Federalist judges for seditious speeches.
   d. repeal of all direct taxes, including the controversial Whiskey Tax.

5. Which of the following statements about the Louisiana Purchase is true?
   a. No one questioned the constitutionality of the arrangement.
   b. Strict borders for the purchase were not specified.

c. Louisiana residents were immediately granted representative government.

d. Most Americans objected to the outrageous price demanded by France.

6. In the decision of *Fletcher* v. *Peck* (1810), the Supreme Court
   a. established the precedent for judicial review of federal statutes.
   b. invalidated the sale of the Yazoo claims because of fraud.
   c. ordered the breakup of the Tertium Quids.
   d. upheld its authority to rule on the constitutionality of state laws.

7. Aaron Burr
   a. planned a potentially treasonous expedition.
   b. served as vice president under John Adams.
   c. shot and killed Thomas Jefferson in a duel.
   d. received the support of Hamilton in his bid to become governor of New York.

8. The law prohibiting the importation of African slaves into the United States was
   a. overturned in 1808 because of constitutional provision.
   b. supported by virtually all Americans.
   c. rigidly enforced by American officials.
   d. complemented by a similar British law of 1807.

9. The Embargo Act of 1807
   a. failed to protect American neutrality.
   b. forbade the purchase of British or French goods.
   c. earned the approval and support of northern merchants.
   d. seriously damaged the British and French economies.

10. As a result of Macon's Bill Number 2,
    a. the United States restored trade with all countries except Britain and France.
    b. British minister David M. Erskine relayed his nation's willingness to rescind the Orders in Council.
    c. Napoleon offered, although never intended to keep, a promise to respect American neutrality.
    d. President Madison relieved international tensions and delayed agitation for war.

11. Americans favored war against Britain in 1812 because of
    a. British seizure of American ships and impressment of American sailors.
    b. perceived British provocation of Indian attacks against western settlers.
    c. American hopes to conquer Canada.
    d. all of the above.

12. The Battle of New Orleans was militarily significant in that it
    a. helped convince the British to negotiate an end to the war.

b. established General William Henry Harrison as a military hero and a potential presidential candidate.

c. prevented British occupation of a strategic city they would have been reluctant to surrender.

d. demonstrated the effectiveness of a frontal assault in dislodging an inferior force.

13. Which of the following changes in the Constitution was recommended by New Englanders at the Hartford Convention?

a. congressional representation for slaves.

b. limitation on the president to a single term in office.

c. increased power of the president to declare and wage war.

d. easing of restrictions for the entry of new states.

14. Which of the following was *not* among the results of the War of 1812?

a. rejuvenated American nationalism.

b. victory over the western Indians.

c. rebirth of the Federalist party.

d. nationwide acclaim for Andrew Jackson.

15. American craftspeople resisted the introduction of mechanization because they feared it would

a. lead to increased reliance by American industry upon foreign investors.

b. threaten American workers with loss of wages and autonomy.

c. reduce the available number of work hours.

d. require broader worker skills and tasks in the manufacturing process.

THOUGHT QUESTIONS

To check your understanding of the key issues of this period, solve the following problems:

1. Describe the attitudes and policies which guided white American leaders of the early nineteenth century in their dealings with Native Americans.

2. Characterize Thomas Jefferson as president. Did Jefferson defend or betray Republican policies once in office?

3. Analyze the success of political dissension during Jefferson's administration.

4. What were the causes of the War of 1812? How did the United States attempt to avoid war? Why were these attempts unsuccessful?

5. Who were the winners and who were the losers in the War of 1812? Explain your answer.

CRITICAL THINKING QUESTIONS

Read Chapter 8 of the text and the following selections: *State* v. *Boon* (1801) and *Marbury* v. *Madison* (1803). Answer the questions following the reading selections.

State v. Boon (1801)

HALL, J. The prisoner has been found guilty of the offence charged in the indictment [Boon was indicted and convicted under the third section of the act of 1791 for killing a slave belonging to another]; whether any, or what punishment, can be inflicted upon him in consequence thereof, is not to be decided. . .

We must consider the words of the enacting clause, without regard to the preamble. . . . If any person hereafter shall be guilty of killing a slave &c. such offender shall be adjudged guilty of murder &c. and shall suffer the same punishment, as if he had killed a free man. In case the person had killed a free man what punishment would the law have inflicted upon him? Before this question can be solved another must be asked; because upon that, the solution of the first depends. What sort of a killing was it? Or what circumstances of aggravation or mitigation attended it? . . . That to which the Legislature referred us for the purpose of ascertaining the punishment, proper to be inflicted is, in itself, so doubtful and uncertain that I think no punishment whatever can be inflicted; without using a
discretion and indulging a latitude, which in criminal cases, ought never to be allowed a Judge.
. . . Much latitude of construction ought not to be permitted to operate against life; if it operate at all, it should be in favor of it. Punishments ought to be plainly defined and easy to be understood; they ought not to depend upon construction or arbitrary discretion. . . .
But it has been also contended, on behalf of the state, that the offense with which the prisoner is charged, is a felony at common law, and that having been found guilty by the jury, he ought to be punished, independently of any Act of Assembly on the subject. . . .
Slaves in this country possess no such rights; their condition is . . . abject;
. . . they are not parties to our constitution; it was not made for them.
. . . it is doubtful whether the offense with which he is charged is a felony at common law or not. It is doubtful whether he ought to be punished or not, that, certainly, is a sufficient reason for discharging him . . . I cannot hesitate to say, that he ought to be discharged.

JOHNSTON, J. The murder of a slave, appears to me, a crime of the most atrocious and barbarous nature; much more so than killing a person who is free, and on an equal footing. It is an evidence of a most depraved and cruel disposition, to murder one, so much in your power, that he is incapable of making resistance, even in his own defence . . . and had there been nothing in our acts of Assembly, I should not hesitate on this occasion to have pronounced sentence of death on the prisoner.
. . . From the context, and taking every part of the section [of the act of 1791] under consideration, there remains no doubt in my mind respecting the intention of the Legislature; but the judges in this country . . . have laid down, and invariably adhered to, very strict rules in the construction of penal statutes in favor of life . . .
. . . judgment in this case should be arrested.

TAYLOR, JR. . . . But when the court is called upon, under an act of Assembly, to pronounce the highest punishment known to the law, they must be satisfied that the language used is clear and explicit to the object intended . . . I think no judgment can be pronounced.

Marbury v. Madison (1803)

[Chief Justice Marshall delivered the opinion of the Court.]

In the order in which the Court has viewed this subject, the following questions have been considered and decided: 1st. Has the applicant a right to the commission he demands? 2d. If he has a right, and that right has been violated, do the laws of this country afford him a remedy? 3d. If they do afford him a remedy, is it a mandamus issuing from this court? . . .

It is . . . the opinion of the Court: 1st. That by signing the commission of Mr. Marbury, the President of the United States appointed him a justice of the peace for the county of Washington, in the District of Columbia; and that the seal of the United States, affixed thereto by the secretary of state, is conclusive testimony of the verity of the signature, and of the completion of the appointment; and that the appointment conferred on him a legal right to the office for the space of five years. 2d. That, having this legal title to the office, he has a consequent right to the commission; a refusal to deliver which is a plain violation of that right, for which the laws of his country afford him a remedy. 3d. It remains to be inquired whether he is entitled to the remedy for which he applies?. . .

This . . . is a plain case for a mandamus, either to deliver the commission, or a copy of it from the record; and it only remains to be inquired, whether it can issue from this court?

The act to establish the judicial courts of the United States authorizes the Supreme Court, "to issue writs of mandamus, in cases warranted by the principles and usages of law, to any courts appointed or persons holding office, under the authority of the United States." The secretary of state, being a person holding an office under the authority of the United States, is precisely within the letter of this description; and if this court is not authorized to issue a writ of mandamus to such an officer, it must be because the law is unconstitutional . . .

The Constitution vests the whole judicial power of the United States in one Supreme Court, and such inferior courts as Congress shall, from time to time, ordain and establish....

In the distribution of this power, it is declared that "the Supreme Court shall have original jurisdiction in all cases affecting ambassadors, other public ministers and consuls, and those in which a state shall be a party. In all other cases, the Supreme Court shall have appellate jurisdiction." . . .

If it had been intended to leave it in the discretion of the legislature to apportion the judicial power between the supreme and inferior courts according to the will of that body, it would certainly have been useless to have proceeded further than to have defined the judicial power, and the tribunals in which it should be vested. The subsequent part of the section is mere surplusage, is entirely without meaning, . . .

It cannot be presumed that any clause in the Constitution is intended to be without effect . . .

To enable this court, then, to issue a mandamus, it must be shown to be an exercise of appellate jurisdiction...

The authority, therefore, given to the Supreme Court, by the Act establishing the judicial courts of the United States, to issue writs of mandamus to public officers, appears not to be warranted by the Constitution . . .

1.   Why did some English observers view Jeffersonian Republicans as hypocritical?

2.   What progress had seemingly been achieved from 1741 and 1791 in North Carolina law regarding the murder of slaves? How did the law of 1791 prove insufficient, as revealed in the decision of *State* v. *Boon* (1801)?

3.   What accounts for the deep-rooted ambivalence by Americans toward industrialization that the text author notes has persisted into the modern age? Give modern-day examples of such ambivalence.

4.   In *Marbury* v. *Madison* (1803), how did Marshall deflect possible opposition while establishing an important precedent?

5.   Using the following three cases as discussed in the reading and the text, explain how Chief Justice John Marshall helped establish the independence of the Supreme Court from purely political interests:

a.   *Marbury* v. *Madison* (1803).
b.   *Fletcher* v. *Peck* (1810).
c.   the trial of Aaron Burr (1807).

CHAPTER 9

NATIONALISM AND NATION-BUILDING

SUMMARY

A great surge of westward expansion and economic development, accompanied by soaring nationalist fervor, characterized the United States after the War of 1812.

Expansion and Migration
Before the abundant potential wealth of the Mississippi Valley could be realized, a dramatic westward surge had to be encouraged.

Extending the Boundaries
When John Quincy Adams hammered out the Transcontinental Treaty of 1819 with Spain, he was confirming the belief of most Americans in a continental destiny. Interest in the West grew as john Jacob Astor carried the fur trade to the Pacific Northwest, and the legends of "mountain men" were popularized.

Settlement to the Mississippi
Pushing the Indian tribes before them, settlers surged westward into the trans-Appalachian West. Most of the land originally passed through the hands of speculators, who purchased it at a feverish rate, to squatters who could eventually gain title through preemption rights. Local marketing centers (developed to meet the needs of the farmers) quickly arose. Many rapidly became cities.

The People and Culture of the Frontier
Most western settlers moved in family units and carried the elements of their "civilized" eastern existence with them. Communal cooperation eventually accomplished most of the work that had previously required self-reliance. Attracted by more land to the west, many settlers pulled up stakes after only a few years. The novelist James Fenimore Cooper popularized the "Leatherstocking" western hero and the western romantic myth.

Transportation and the Market Economy
Political leaders realized the importance of linking these distant citizens with the rest of the nation through a viable transportation network.

A Revolution in Transportation: Roads and Steamboats
The National (or Cumberland) Road was the first of the overland toll roads. Chartered by the states, these "turnpikes" failed for the most part to meet the popular demands for cheap transportation over great distances. America's river network proved to be its greatest transportation system, and the Ohio-Mississippi system beckoned first the flatboat trade and, after Robert Fulton's invention in 1807, the steamboat.

The Canal Boom

In addition to rivers and roads, a system of canals was needed to link the Great Lakes, the Ohio, and the Mississippi with the coastal states. In 1825, the Erie Canal was finished, signaling the birth of the "canal boom," which lasted until the late 1830s.

Emergence of a Market Economy

Increasing farm productivity promoted the transition from low-profit diversification farming to high-profit staple farming in regional concentrations. The availability of good farmland, increasing demand for cotton, the invention of the cotton gin, and slave labor made the South the world's greatest cotton producer.

Commerce and Banking

The extension of credit by local merchants and manufacturers was crucial—it insured profits, the expansion of capital, and the need for banking. This demand for money after the War of 1812 caused the number of state and private banks to proliferate.

Early Industrialism

The surge of a market economy encouraged new industrial development. The factory system was first applied to textile manufacturing. The development of infant industries before the 1840s, however, was less dramatic here than in some parts of Europe, and as late as 1840 only 8.8 percent of the nation's population was employed in factories.

The Politics of Nation-building After the War of 1812

Awakening nationalism provided the dominant theme for public policies after the War of 1812.

The Republicans in Power

As the nation was emerging economically, the federal government responded supportively. Henry Clay called for an "American System" of protective tariffs and financed internal improvements. A second Bank of the United States was chartered in 1816 to promote the nation's financial stability.

Monroe as President

James Monroe projected the image of a high-principled, disinterested statesman. Congress responded weakly to the economic crisis which began in 1819, and Monroe had no program of his own. He insisted that he was not responsible for the drastic economic downturn. He prized national harmony over economic prosperity.

The Missouri Compromise

Congress narrowly averted a national calamity with the Missouri Compromise in 1820, which settled the most serious sectional issue yet to challenge the federal government. Although Jefferson called the decision "a fire bell in the night," it seemed that for the moment nationalism was triumphant.

Postwar Nationalism and the Supreme Court

With strong national leadership by Federalist John Marshall, the Supreme Court made great contributions to nationalism and the expansive powers of the federal government. In such decisions as *McCulloch* v. *Maryland* and *Gibbons* v. *Ogden,* the Supreme Court supported economic nationalism at the expense of certain state powers. Under Marshall, the Court played a powerful role in supporting the growth of a prosperous nationwide, capitalist economy.

Nationalism in Foreign Policy: The Monroe Doctrine

Recognizing the threat of a European Grand Alliance, and concerned with the collapsing Spanish empire in Latin America, and with the possibility of European re-colonization in the Western Hemisphere, President Monroe and Secretary of State John Quincy Adams issued the Monroe Doctrine, which was delivered as a warning to European powers that the United States opposed further colonization and political interference in the Americas.

Adams and the End of the Era of Good Feelings

Quincy Adams was the supreme spokesman for nonpartisan and scientific achievement, but his leadership could not survive the growing sectional and economic divisions in the nation.

LEARNING OBJECTIVES

After mastering this chapter, you should be able to:

1. Analyze the factors that contributed to the rise of nationalism after the War of 1812.

2. Describe the process by which western lands were organized and sold.

3. Understand why families moved westward and the living conditions they faced.

4. Explain the development of a national transportation network and its contribution to a market economy.

5. List and explain the reasons why the South became the world's greatest cotton producer.

6. Describe how new economic activities brought forth the early factory system.

7. Discuss the steps taken by Congress to encourage industry and enterprise.

8. Develop the main issues of sectional disturbance that accompanied the Missouri Compromise.

9. Analyze the role played in economic and political matters by the Supreme Court under Chief Justice Marshall.

10. Explain the perceived international conditions which led to the Monroe Doctrine as well as the specific intent of this statement.

GLOSSARY

To build your social science vocabulary, familiarize yourself with the following terms:

1. **nationalism** loyalty or allegiance to a nation and its accomplishments. "Nationalism was more than pious rhetoric during an era when foundations were being laid for economic growth."

2. **assimilated** to be incorporated into a group or made similar. "They often married Indian women and assimilated much of the culture and technology of the Native Americans."

3. **speculation** the purchase of property with the intention of selling later at a profit. ". . . speculation in public lands proceeded at a massive and feverish rate."

4. **squatter** one who lives on and works the land without having clear title. "In some areas squatters arrived before the official survey . . ."

5. **solidarity** the coming together of interests and needs within an identifiable group. "These communal events represented a creative response to the shortage of labor and . . . provided a source for communal solidarity."

6. **retrenchment** retreat from active or progressive policy. "State credit had been overextended, and the panic . . . forced retrenchment."

7. **specie** coined money—a legal unit of exchange. " . . . banking institutions filled the void by issuing bank notes, promises to redeem their paper in *specie* . . ."

8. **market economy** a system identified by the distribution of large amounts of goods to a large consumer audience. "The growth of a market economy of national scope—still based mainly on agriculture . . ."

9. **protective tariff** a tax on imported products that is designed to protect domestic manufacturers from outside competition. ". . . President Madison proposed to Congress that it consider such measures as . . . a protective tariff . . ."

10. **implied powers** the doctrine that the general powers of the federal government extend beyond the specific wording of the Constitution and can be consulted for the expansion of the powers of Congress over the states. "In response to the first question, Marshall set forth his doctrine of 'implied powers'."

IDENTIFICATION

Briefly identify the meaning and significance of the following terms:

1. Adams-Onís Treaty _____

_____

2. Claims Associations _____

_____

3. "Preemption" Rights _____

_____

4. National Road _____

_____

5. Erie Canal _____

_____

6. Cotton Gin _____

_____

7. "Putting-Out" System _____

_____

8. "American System" _____

_____

9. "Era of Good Feeling" _____

_____

10. *McCulloch* v. *Maryland* _____

_____

MATCHING

A. Match the following inventors/capitalists with the appropriate description:

_____1. John Jacob Astor

a. governor of New York who was mainly responsible for the planning and financing of the Erie Canal

_____2. De Witt Clinton

b. New Englander who invented the cotton gin

_____3. Robert Fulton

c. New York merchant who founded a fur trading outpost on the Columbia River

_____4. Francis Cabot Lowell

d. inventor of the power loom for textile factories

_____5. Eli Whitney

e. first to demonstrate successfully the steamboat, which solved upstream navigation

f. one of the founding partners of the first successful cotton mills, heralding the beginnings of the factory age in New England

B. Match the following political leaders with the appropriate description:

_____1. John C. Calhoun

a. president who was reelected by a landslide despite a deepening economic depression

_____2. John Marshall

b. congressman who in 1815 envisioned a transportation revolution based on roads and canals

_____3. John Quincy Adams

c. proponent of the "American System" to make the United States economically self-sufficient

_____4. Henry Clay

d. president of the United States during the War of 1812

_____5. James Monroe

e. Federalist Supreme Court Chief Justice who dominated the court during the formative years of the republic

f. author of most of the Monroe Doctrine, warning European powers not to extend their imperial systems to the Western Hemisphere

123

COMPLETION

Answer the question or complete the statement by filling in the blanks with the correct word or words.

1. The treaty that secured Florida for the United States and drew a dividing line between Spanish territory in the Southwest and U.S.-held Northwest Territory was the _____.

2. The main focus of westward agrarian expansion after 1815 was the land between the _____ and the _____.

3. Sac and Fox Indian leader _____ attempted unsuccessfully to recapture lands east of the Mississippi in the 1830s.

4. Although roads and canals were few by 1815, the United States had a superb natural transportation system in its _____.

5. Before the coming of the steamboat, almost all river cargo was carried on small vessels called _____.

6. The completion of the Erie Canal helped make _____ the unrivaled commercial capital of the United States.

7. The serious threat to national harmony during the Monroe administration involved the question of admitting _____ to the nation as a slave state.

8. The Supreme Court decision in *Dartmouth College* v. _____ determined that any charter granted by a state was a legal and inviolable contract and strengthened the position of business enterprises against the states.

TRUE/FALSE

Mark the following statements either T (True) or F (False):

_____1. The congressional branch of the federal government took a more active role in national economic development than did either of the other two branches.

_____2. The most dramatic and important movement of westward expansion after 1815 involved the migration of settlers to the western Rocky Mountain region.

_____3. Typical agricultural pioneers of this period were proponents of innovation, progress, and

124

social change.

_____ 4. Because of its extensive navigable river system, the South had less need than the other regions of the country for internal transportation improvements.

_____ 5. Because it was a labor-saving device, the cotton gin diminished the need for slave labor in the South.

_____ 6. The canal boom ended because most states had overextended credit and the waterways were no longer profitable.

_____ 7. By 1815, most manufacturing had moved from the households and small shops of the skilled artisans to the large factories.

_____ 8. The Supreme Court decision in *McCulloch v. Maryland* strengthened the power of Congress over interstate commerce.

_____ 9. That any state charter granted to a private corporation was protected as a valid contract was determined in the Supreme Court case *Dartmouth College* v. *Woodward*.

_____ 10. John Q. Adams believed American interests would best be served by avoiding all foreign entanglements including an Anglo-American alliance.

MULTIPLE CHOICE

Circle the one alternative that *best* completes the statement or answers the question.

1. The view which most whites had toward Indian society after 1815 was that
   a. their culture was radically inferior and was doomed to extinction.
   b. certain Indian tribes were fairly advanced and thus could continue to exist east of the Mississippi.
   c. "civilized Indians" should develop reservations based upon private property ownership.
   d. Indians should be prepared for citizenship and integration into American society.

2. Preemption rights dealt with
   a. preference given to commercial developers over private farmers and businesspeople.
   b. encouragement given to speculators to drive up the price of land.
   c. the right of a state government to tax all property within its borders.
   d. the right of squatters to obtain legal title to land they have farmed at the prevailing minimum price.

3. Most settlers moved westward to
    a. escape the overcrowded East.
    b. settle on cheaper, more fertile land.
    c. repudiate the settled, civilized way of life in the East.
    d. hunt and trap for furs.

4. One of the most significant reasons for the country's rapid economic development was the
    a. success of the early toll roads.
    b. ascendancy of the factory system over small scale "cottage" manufacturing.
    c. natural transportation systems afforded by navigable rivers.
    d. system of protective tariffs to limit competition with foreign manufacturers.

5. The main idea presented by historian Frederick Jackson Turner was that
    a. American character and institutions were shaped most strongly by the frontier experience.
    b. American colonists had the privilege of trying to improve their way of life beyond the constraints of European civilization.
    c. social evolution passed from the stage of savagery directly to civilization.
    d. the outstanding models for civilized life were the advance societies of western Europe

6. For most Americans of the early nineteenth century, the reality of the frontier was
    a. one of difficulty and deprivation to be endured until civilized standards took hold.
    b. overly glamorized and idolized.
    c. such that modern society should be abandoned in favor of a more primitive life.
    d. the solitary hunter facing insurmountable odds in the wilderness.

7. The dominant theme reflected in public policies during the Monroe administration was
   a. renewed conflict between the federal government and the separate state governments.
   b. awakening nationalism.
   c. sectionalism, the rivalry between the various regions of the country.
   d. the spread of slavery.

8. The "American System" reflected the nation's need for
   a. economic progress and self-sufficiency.
   b. dis-entanglement from European affairs.
   c. an update of the Federalist model for government.
   d. a transportation network throughout the country.

9. Because of the absence of a two-party system after the War of 1812
   a. no legislation issued forth and the federal government was completely immobilized.
   b. public accountability and the need for popular support diminished considerably.
   c. greater political dialogue resulted along with expansion of issued legislation and ideologies.
   d. the president had greater authority over legislation.

10. Regarding the issue of political parties in the United States after 1815, which of the following is true?
    a. The Federalists replaced the Republicans as the majority party in Congress.
    b. The Republicans retained majorities in Congress, but the Federalists provided strong opposition.
    c. The two-party system was disrupted, leaving only an unorganized Republican Party.
    d. Several smaller political parties developed to rival the two major parties.

11. Which of the following was not included in the final passage of the Missouri Annexation Bill and its amendments?
    a. the Tallmadge amendment
    b. the 36° 30' line to divide free and slave territory in the Louisiana Purchase
    c. admission of Maine as a free state
    d. upholding of the practice of admitting one slave state with one free state

12. In major decisions rendered between 1819 and 1824, the Marshall Court
    a. strengthened the federal government by supporting a broad interpretation of its constitutional powers.
    b. left the relative positions of state versus national authority uninterrupted.
    c. supported the strict constructionist views of the Jeffersonians, leaving the states with greater powers than before.
    d. decided that charters issued by the states did not constitute legal contracts.

13. Under Chief Justice Marshall, the doctrine of "implied powers" meant that

a. states could stretch their powers if in so doing their economic interests were served.

b. if no specific authorization could be found in the Constitution, it was possible for Congress to act on the basis of more general powers implied.

c. a state could tax a federal institution only if that institution served the interests of that state exclusively.

d. the Supreme Court has the "implied power" to rule on the constitutionality of issues or laws emanating from the separate states.

14. The assumed purpose of the European Grand Alliance was to

a. confront Napoleon's armies during their retreat from Russia.

b. oppose Britain's mastery of the seas.

c. Threaten Britain and the United States with Hapsburg and Bourbon hegemony in Europe as well as possibly in the Western Hemisphere.

d. replace France's Continental System.

15. The Monroe Doctrine was primarily aimed at

a. Britain.

b. France.

c. the Grand Alliance.

d. Germany.

THOUGHT QUESTIONS

To check your understanding of the key issues of this period, solve the following problems:

1. Why was the desire to acquire new territories and settle the western lands such a strong national impulse after 1815?

2. Much of the lore of the West describes life as romantic, heroic, and idyllic. Is this an accurate portrayal? Why or why not?

3. America was relatively slow to industrialize, but because of the early development of a market economy, there always seemed to be an abundance of goods flowing throughout the country. What factors contributed to this major economic accomplishment?

4. As nationalism seemed to emerge triumphant, stronger sectional rivalries developed between North and South. Why did sectionalism develop, and how did the debate over Missouri reflect these differences?

5. How was nationalism reflected in foreign policy from the Adams-Onís Treaty through the Monroe Doctrine?

CRITICAL THINKING QUESTIONS

After reading *The Harbinger Female Workers of Lowell* (1836), Letters to the *Voice of Industry* (1846), and Harriet Hanson Robinson *Lowell Textile Workers* (1898), answer the following questions:

The Harbinger, Female Workers of Lowell (1836)

We have lately visited the cities of Lowell [Mass.] and Manchester [N.H.] and have had an opportunity of examining the factory system more closely than before. We had distrusted the accounts which we had heard from persons engaged in the labor reform now beginning to agitate New England. We could scarcely credit the statements made in relation to the exhausting nature of the labor in the mills, and to the manner in which the young women-the operatives-lived in their boardinghouses, six sleeping in a room, poorly ventilated.

We went through many of the mills, talked particularly to a large number of the operatives, and ate at their boardinghouses, on purpose to ascertain by personal inspection the facts of the case. We assure our readers that very little information is possessed, and no correct judgments formed, by the public at large, of our factory system, which is the first germ of the industrial or commercial feudalism that is to spread over our land. . . .

In Lowell live between seven and eight thousand young women, who are generally daughters of farmers of the different states of New England. Some of them are members of families that were rich in the generation before. . . .

The operatives work thirteen hours a day in the summer time, and from daylight to dark in the winter. At half past four in the morning the factory bell rings, and at five the girls must be in the mills. A clerk, placed as a watch, observes those who are a few minutes behind the time, and effectual means are taken to stimulate to punctuality. This is the morning commencement of the industrial discipline (should we not rather say industrial tyranny?) which is established in these associations of this moral and Christian community.

At seven the girls are allowed thirty minutes for breakfast, and at noon thirty minutes more for dinner, except during the first quarter of the year, when the time is extended to forty-five minutes. But within this time they must hurry to their boardinghouses and return to the factory, and that through the hot sun or the rain or the cold. A meal eaten under such circumstances must be quite unfavorable to digestion and health, as any medical man will inform us. After seven o'clock in the evening the factory bell sounds the close of the day's work.

Thus thirteen hours per day of close attention and monotonous labor are extracted from the young women in these manufactories. . . . So fatigued-we should say, exhausted and worn out, but we wish to speak of the system in the simplest language-are numbers of girls that they go to bed soon after their evening meal, and endeavor by a comparatively long sleep to resuscitate their weakened frames for the toil of the coming day.

When capital has got thirteen hours of labor daily out of a being, it can get nothing more. It would be a poor speculation in an industrial point of view to own the operative; for the trouble and expense of providing for times of sickness and old age would more than counterbalance the difference between the price of wages and the expenses of board and clothing. The far greater number of fortunes accumulated by the North in comparison with the South shows that hireling labor is more profitable for capital than slave labor.

Now let us examine the nature of the labor itself, and the conditions under which it is performed. Enter with us into the large rooms, when the looms are at work. The largest that we saw is in the Amoskeag Mills at Manchester. . . . The din and clatter of these five hundred looms, under full operation, struck us on first entering as something frightful and infernal, for it seemed such an atrocious violation of one of the faculties of the human soul, the sense of hearing. After a while we became somewhat used to it, and by speaking quite close to the ear of an operative and quite loud, we could hold a conversation and make the inquiries we wished.

The girls attended upon an average three looms; many attended four, but this requires a very active person, and the most unremitting care. However, a great many do it. Attention to two is as much as should be demanded of an operative. This gives us some idea of the application required during the thirteen hours of daily labor. The atmosphere of such a room cannot of course be pure; on the contrary, it is charged with cotton filaments and dust, which, we are told, are very injurious to the lungs.

On entering the room, although the day was warm, we remarked that the windows were down. We asked the reason, and a young woman answered very naively, and without seeming to be in the least aware that this

129

privation of fresh air was anything else than perfectly natural, that "when the wind blew, the threads did not work well." After we had been in the room for fifteen or twenty minutes, we found ourselves, as did the persons who accompanied us, in quite a perspiration, produced by a certain moisture which we observed in the air, as well as by the heat. . . .

The young women sleep upon an average six in a room, three beds to a room. There is no privacy, no retirement, here. It is almost impossible to read or write alone, as the parlor is full and so many sleep in the same chamber. A young woman remarked to us that if she had a letter to write, she did it on the head of a bandbox, sitting on a trunk, as there was no space for a table.

So live and toil the young women of our country in the boardinghouses and manufactories which the rich an influential of our land have built for them.

Letters to the *Voice of Industry* (1846)

March 13, 1846

The Female Department

NOTICE

The Female Labor Reform Association will meet every Tuesday evening, at 8 o'clock, at their Reading Room, 76 Central Street, to transact all business pertaining to the Association, and to devise means by which to promote the common interests of all the Laboring Classes. Also to discuss all subjects which shall come before the meeting. Every *Female* who realizes the great necessity of a *Reform* and improvement in the condition of the worthy, toiling classes, and who would wish to place woman in that elevated status intellectually and morally, which a bountiful Creator designed her to occupy in the scale of being, is most *cordially* invited to attend and give her influence on the side of *virtue* and *suffering humanity*.

Huldah J. Stone, Sec'y

April 24, 1846

To the Female Labor Reform Association In Manchester

SISTER OPERATIVES

As I am now in the "City of Spindles," out of employment, I have taken the liberty to occupy a few of your leisure moments in addressing the members of your Association, and pardon me for giving you a few brief hints of my own experiences as a factory Operative, before proceeding to make some remarks upon the glorious cause in which you are so arduously engaged. It would be useless to attempt to portray the hardships and privations which are daily endured, for all that have toiled within the factory walls, must be well acquainted with the present system of labor, which can be properly termed slavery.

I am a peasant's daughter, and my lot has been cast in the society of the humble laborer. I was drawn from the home of my childhood at an early age, and necessity obliged me to seek employment in the Factory . . . I have heard with the deepest interest, of your flourishing Association of which you are members, and it rejoices my heart to see so many of you contending for your rights, and making efforts to elevate the condition of your fellow brethren, and raising them from their oppressed and degraded condition, and seeing rights restored which god and Nature designed them to enjoy. Do you possess the principles of Christianity? Then do not remain silent; but seek to ameliorate the condition of every fellow being. Engage laboriously and earnestly in the work, until you see your desires accomplished. Let the proud aristocrat who has tyrannized over your rights with oppressive severity, see that there is ambition and enterprise among the "spindles," and show a determination to have your plans fully executed. Use prudence and discretion in all your ways; act independently and no longer be a slave to petty tyrants, who, if they have an opportunity, will encroach upon your privileges.

Some say that "Capital will take good care of labor," but don't believe it; don't trust them. Is it not plain, that they are trying to deceive the public, by telling them that your task is easy and plead that there is no need of reform? Too many are destitute of feeling and sympathy, and it is a great pity that they are not obliged to toil one year, and then they would be glad to see the "Ten Hour Petition" brought before the Legislature. This is plain, but true language. . . .

131

Harriet Hanson Robinson, *Lowell Textile Workers* (1898)

In 1831 Lowell was little more than a factory village. Several corporations were started, and the cotton mills belonging to them were building. Help was in great demand; and stories were told all over the country of the new factory town, and the high wages that were offered to all classes of workpeople—stories that reached the ears of mechanics' and farmers' sons, and gave new life to lonely and dependent women in distant towns and farmhouses. Into this Yankee El Dorado, these needy people began to pour by the various modes of travel known to those slow old days. The stagecoach and the canal boat came every day, always filled with new recruits for this army of useful people. The mechanic and machinist came, each with his homemade chest of tools, and oftentimes his wife and little ones. The widow came with her little flock and her scanty housekeeping goods to open a boarding-house or variety store, and so provided a home for her fatherless children. Many farmers' daughters came to earn money to complete their wedding outfit, or buy the bride's share of housekeeping articles. . . .

The laws relating to women were such, that a husband could claim his wife wherever he found her, and also the children she was trying to shield from his influence; and I have seen more than one poor woman skulk behind her loom or her frame when visitors were approaching the end of the aisle where she worked. Some of these were known under assumed names, to prevent their husbands from trusteeing their wages. It was a very common thing for a male person of a certain kind to do this, thus depriving his wife of *all* her wages, perhaps, month after month. The wages of minor children could be trusteed, unless the children (being fourteen years of age) were given their time. Women's wages were also trusteed for the debts of their husbands, and children's for the debts of their parents. . . .

It must be remembered that at this date woman had no property rights. A widow could be left without her share of her husband's (or the family) property, a legal "encumbrance" to his estate. A father could make his will without a reference to his daughter's share of the inheritance. He usually left her a home on the farm as long as she remained single. A woman was not supposed to be capable of spending her own or of using other people's money. In Massachusetts, before 1840, a woman could not legally be treasurer of her own sewing society, unless some man were responsible for her.

The law took no cognizance of woman as a money spender. She was a ward, an appendage, a relict. Thus it happened, that if a woman did not choose to marry, or, when left a widow, to re-marry, she had no choice but to enter one of the few employments open to her, or to become a burden on the charity of some relative.

In almost every New England home could be found one or more of these women, sometimes welcome, more often unwelcome, and leading joyless, and in many instances unsatisfactory, lives. The cotton factory was a great opening to these lonely and dependent women. From a condition approaching pauperism they were at once placed above want; they could earn money and spend it as they please; and could gratify their tastes and desires without restraint, and without rendering an account to anybody. . . .

Among the older women who sought this new employment were very many lonely and dependent women, such as used to be mentioned in old wills as "encumbrances" and "relicts," and to whom a chance of earning money was indeed a new revelation. How well I remembered some of these solitary ones! As a child of eleven years, I often made fun of them—for children do not see the pathetic side of human life—and imitated them for their limp carriage and inelastic gait. I can see them now, even after sixty years, just as they looked—depressed, modest, mincing, hardly daring to look one in the face, so shy and sylvan had been their lives. But after the first pay-day came, and they felt the jungle of silver in their pockets, and had begun to feel its mercurial influence, their bowed heads were lifted, their necks seemed braced with steel, they looked you in the face, and moved blithely among their looms or frames, and walked with elastic step to and from their work. And when Sunday came, homespun was no longer their only wear; and how sedately gay in their new attire they walked to church, and how proudly they dropped their silver fourpences into the contribution-box! It seemed as if a great hope impelled them—the harbinger of the new era that was about to dawn for them and for all woman-kind.

One of the first strikes of cotton-factory operatives that ever took place in this country was that in Lowell, in October, 1836. When it was announced that the wages were to be cut down, great indignation was felt, and it was decided to strike, *en masse*. This was done. The mills were shut down, and the girls went in procession from their several corporations to the "grove" on Chapel Hill, and listened to "incendiary" speeches from early labor reformers.

One of the girls stood on a pump, and gave vent to the feelings of her companions in a neat speech, declaring that it was their duty to resist all attempts at cutting down the wages. This was the first time a woman had spoken in public in Lowell, and the event caused surprise and consternation among her audience.

Cutting down the wages was not their only grievance, nor the only cause of this strike. Hitherto the corporations had paid twenty-five cents a week towards the board of each operative, and now it was their purpose to have the girls pay the sum; and this, in addition to the cut in wages, would make a difference of at least one dollar a week. It was estimated that as many as twelve or fifteen hundred girls turned out, and walked in procession through the streets. They had neither flags nor music, but sang songs, a favorite (but rather inappropriate) one being a parody on "I won't be a nun."

> "Oh! isn't it a pity, such a pretty girl as I—
> Should be sent to the factory to pine away and die?
> Oh! I cannot be a slave,
> I will not be a slave
> For I'm so fond of liberty
> That I cannot be a slave."

My own recollection of this first strike (or "turn out" as it was called) is very vivid. I worked in a lower room, where I had heard the proposed strike fully, if not vehemently, discussed; I had been an ardent listener to what was said against this attempt at "oppression" on the part of the corporation, and naturally I took sides with the strikers. When the day came on which the girls were to turn out, those in the upper rooms started first, and so many of them left that our mill was at once shut down. Then, when the girls in my room stood irresolute, uncertain what to do, asking each other, "Would you?" or "Shall we turn out?" and not one of them having the courage to lead off, I, who began to think they would not go out, after all their talk, became impatient, and started on ahead, saying, with childish bravado, "I don't care what you do, *I* am going to turn out, whether anyone else does or not;" and I marched out, and was followed by the others.

1. What were the various motivations for women to voluntarily work in the mills?

2. How did conditions of the workers in factories compare with slave labor?

3. What were the typical conditions of labor in the textile mills?

4. What elements of the textile mills and nineteenth-century society mitigated against a successful workers' protest for reform?

5. What elements from the passages indicated that these women did not claim equality with men, but asserted a unique quality of character for women?

133

C H A P T E R   1 0

THE TRIUMPH OF WHITE MEN'S DEMOCRACY

SUMMARY

The 1820s and 1830s witnessed the rise of popular democracy and a swelling of national political involvement. European visitors were amazed at the equalizing tendencies that were exposed in everything from hotels to the legal and clerical professions.

DEMOCRACY IN THEORY AND PRACTICE

The nation's founders had believed that "democracy" contained dangerous impulses, but by the 1820s and '30s the term had become more acceptable and applicable to American institutions. Alexis de Tocqueville noticed the decline of deference and the elevation of popular sovereignty in America. "Self-made" men could now rise in stature.

The Democratic Ferment

By 1820, most states had eliminated property requirements for manhood suffrage, and as public political involvement swelled, a permanent two-party system became a forum for political ideas. It became understood that a "loyal opposition" was essential to democratic government. Economic questions (prompted by the Panic of 1819) and the role of the federal government were major concerns that assisted a great swelling of popular political interest. Workingmen's parties and trade unions emerged as workers became convinced that the government should protect the rights of labor as well as those of the producers. Abolitionists sought an end to slavery and supported the civil rights of free African Americans and women.

Democracy and Society

Social equality became the dominant principle of the age. Special privilege and family connections could no longer be counted on the guarantee success. Industrialization, however, perpetuated inequality, not in the traditional sense of birth or privilege, but rather in terms of wealth and attainment.

Democratic Culture

Romanticism in American literature often appealed to the feelings and intuitions of ordinary people. A mass reading audience developed, and poets, writers, and artists directed their work to a democratic populace. American artists (although striving to elevate popular tastes) were encouraged to contribute to the general welfare by supporting virtue and middle-class sentiments.

JACKSON AND THE POLITICS OF DEMOCRACY

Andrew Jackson symbolized the triumph of democracy and egalitarianism from the 1820s to the 1840s.

The Election of 1824 and J.Q. Adams's Administration

Popular hero Andrew Jackson rose to prominence as a result of "popular sovereignty." Despite winning a plurality of popular votes, Jackson was denied the presidency by the House of Representatives, in favor of Adams. Rumors of a "corrupt bargain" between Adams and Henry Clay and controversy over tariff policy damaged Adam's administration.

Jackson Comes to Power

Supported by the newly organized Democratic party, Jackson returned to defeat Adams convincingly in 1828 in an election that featured a massive popular turnout. Possessed of indomitable will, Jackson became one of the most forceful presidents in history. He endorsed the "spoils system" as a way to provide himself with loyal advisors.

Indian Removal

Beginning in 1830, Jackson ordered the swift and forceful removal of all Indian tribes to reservations located west of the Mississippi River. Jackson ignored humanitarian protests. By 1838, the last of the southeastern tribes, the Cherokee, were forced to abandon ancestral grounds and embark on the "Trail of Tears."

The Nullification Crisis

Although an advocate of states' rights, Jackson regarded nullification as a major threat to federal authority. After South Carolina nullified the Tariff Acts of 1828 and 1832 in defiance of federal authority, Jackson threatened forceful intervention to bring the nullification crisis to an end. Appeased by the protests of lower tariffs, South Carolina suspended its nullification ordinance in 1833.

THE BANK WAR AND THE SECOND PARTY SYSTEM

Jackson's successful attack on the Bank of the United States aroused great controversy and called into question the president's power over the nation's finances.

Mr. Biddle's Bank

When Nicholas Biddle, president of the Bank of the United States, sought recharter in 1832, Jackson declared war on this "monster" corporation, which he was convinced violated the fundamental principles of a democratic society.

The Bank Veto and the Election of 1832

When Biddle tried to force an early recharter bill through Congress, Jackson responded by vetoing the bill and calling on the people for support. Jackson's overwhelming victory in the 1832 election was considered to be a mandate for the Bank's destruction.

Killing the Bank

Jackson proceeded to order that federal deposits in the Bank be removed and deposited in selected "pet banks." Strong opposition to Jackson's fiscal policy developed in Congress as fear spread that the destruction of the Bank would be disastrous for the nation's economy.

The Emerging of the Wings
Using the cry of "executive usurpation," and opposition party, the Whigs, emerged in Jackson's second term. Led by Clay and Daniel Webster, the Whigs, opposed the growth of presidential power and prerogative under "King Andrew." When over speculation and currency devaluation staggered the country's economy, Jackson ordered the "specie circular," as economic depression set in.

The Rise and Fall of Van Buren
Martin Van Buren with Jackson's endorsement, gained the presidency in 1836. Van Buren attempted to improve the faltering economy with his creation of an "independent subtreasury," but the persistent depression was beyond the control of governmental policies. The state of the economy cost Van Buren reelection in 1840 to the Whig candidate William Henry Harrison.

HEYDAY OF THE SECOND PARTY SYSTEM
Promoting the idea of the "positive liberal state," the Whigs challenged the Democrats on equal terms in the 1840s. The Whigs called for a government that was active and responsive in economic affairs. Although they supported a market economy, the Whigs wanted to restrain disorder and selfish individualism by calling on the government to enforce high moral standards and community values. The Democrats appealed to small farmers, workers, rising capitalists, immigrants, and Catholics with their support for individualism and personal liberty.

De Toqueville's Wisdom
Although De Toqueville was impressed by the American talent for local self-government, he was a keen observer of the limitations of the "white man's democracy," pointing out that the restricted roles assigned to women and the continued oppression of people of color marred the American democratic experiment.

LEARNING OBJECTIVES

After mastering this chapter, you should be able to

1.   Explain factors that contributed to the rise of democracy in the 1820s and 1830s.

2.   Describe how the diffusion of political power among the masses encouraged reform initiative and inspired new literary, artistic, and professional trends.

3.   Evaluate the main political and economic issues brought forth in the 1824 and 1828 elections and explain the outcomes of those presidential elections.

4.   Determine the political characteristics and personality traits that contributed to Jackson's image as a "man of the people."

5.   Summarize the problems encountered under Jackson's Indian-removal policy.

6.   Contrast the arguments put forth by the states' rightists and the unionists regarding the nullification crisis.

7.   Explain why South Carolina seized the tariff issue to mount its support for states' rights.

8.   Summarize the arguments used by the Jacksonians in their attack against the Bank of the United States

9.   Evaluate the causes for the Depression of 1837 and the steps taken by Van Buren to straighten out the financial disorder.

10.   Compare and contrast the ideologies and objectives of the Whigs and Democrats and identify the socioeconomic groups from which they drew their support.

11.   Reveal how the conflict over the Bank recharter was the dominant political issue of its time.

12.   Evaluate Jackson's strategy in "killing the Bank" and his use of state banks as depositories.

13.   Understand the reasons for political realignment in the 1830s and the emergence of the Whigs.

14.   Paraphrase both the blessings and perils of American democracy according to Toqueville.

GLOSSARY

To build your social science vocabulary, familiarize yourself with the following terms:

1.   **Natural aristocracy** those of well-born status naturally destined to direct economic and political institutions. ". . . a well-balanced republic led by a 'natural aristocracy' ".

2.   **popular sovereignty** authority based on popular support. "Besides evoking a heightened sense of 'popular sovereignty,' the democratic impulse . . .".

3.   **social leveling** a process to create equality by denying special privilege. "the democratic impulse stimulated a process of social leveling".

4.   **deference** giving decision making or authority to another person or group. "The decline of deference meant that 'self-made men' of lowly origins could now rise more readily . . .".

5. **entrepreneurs** those who organize business ventures by investing capital. ". . . particularly emerging entrepreneurs, saw salvation in government aid and protection for venture capital".

6. **tyrannical** characterized by excessive or arbitrary power. ". . . alleged 'rabble-rousers' who gulled the electorate into ratifying high-handed and tyrannical actions . . .".

7. **laissez-faire** the noninterference by government in economic affairs. ". . . by divorcing the government from the economy in the name of laissez-faire . . .".

8. **plurality** having more in number than any other, but not more than half of the total. "In the election Jackson won a plurality of the electoral votes".

9. **nullification** the process of declaring something to be void or inapplicable. "He . . . issued a proclamation denouncing nullification as a treasonous attack . . .".

10. **positive liberal state** that the state (government) would encourage and support economic development to bring about prosperity. "Whigs stood for a 'positive liberal state' ".

11. **elitism** leadership by a powerful or wealthy group. "...traditional forms of privilege and elitism were indeed under strong attack."

12. **ostracism** banishment or exclusion. "The vice president and his wife were viewed by Jackson as prime movers in the ostracism of Peggy Eaton"

13. **logrolling** political bargaining or trading of favors. "... the process of legislative bargaining known as logrolling."

14. **aristocratic art** style that reflected aristocratic tendencies of tastes. "... rather that the traditional subjects of 'aristocratic art.'"

15. **centralized state** government in which power flows from a centralized source and has predominance over state of local governments. "... and he praised Americans for not conceding their liberties to a centralized state."

IDENTIFICATION

Briefly identify the meaning and significance of the following terms.

1. Jacksonianism _____

_____

2.   Corrupt Bargain _____

_____

3.   "Spoils System" _____

_____

4.   independent subtreasury _____

_____

5.   Indian Removal _____

_____

6.   "Trail of Tears" _____

_____

7.   Nullification Crisis _____

_____

8.   The Bank War _____

_____

9.   The Whigs _____

_____

10.   "Specie Circular" _____

_____

MATCHING

A.   Match the following public figures with the appropriate description.

    1. John C. Calhoun   **a.** champion of states rights and leading proponent of nullification during the tariff crisis

2. Thomas Hart Benton

b. Jackson's secretary of state, who resigned over the Peggy Eaton affair

3. Amos Kendall

c. secretary of treasury under Jackson who withdrew federal funds from the Bank of the United States

4. Nicholas Biddle

d. Kentucky editor who marshaled opposition to Henry Clay and helped build the Jacksonian Democratic party

5. Roger Taney

e. Jacksonian senator from Missouri and leading opponent of Bank recharter

f. president of the Bank of the United States, who sought recharter four years early

B. Match the following public acts with the appropriate description.

1. *Worcester v. Georgia*

a. issued by Jackson, requiring that only gold and silver be accepted in payment for public lands

2. Maysville Road Bill

b. vetoed by Jackson on grounds of strict construction of the Constitution

3. Specie circular

c. passed by Congress to give the president the military powers to enforce the tariff laws

4. Tariff of 1828

d. issued by the Supreme Court, denying states the right to extend jurisdiction over Indian lands

5. Force Bill

e. overwhelmingly nullified by the South Carolina state legislature on the grounds of unconstitutionality

f. provided substantial across-the-board duty increases to protect manufacturers

COMPLETION

Answer the question or complete the statement by filling in the blanks with the correct word or words.

140

1. The rise of democracy meant that _____ could rise more easily to positions of importance and status.

2. In the first quarter century of the republic, political leaders had regarded _____ as obstructionist and threatening to Republican virtue.

3. During the 1830s and 1840s, a mass market became available for popular literature due to the increase in _____.

4. The dominant genre in the theater during the Jacksonian period was _____.

5. In preparing for the 1828 election, Jacksonians laid the groundwork for the first modern political party, the _____.

6. The unofficial set of advisors from whom Jackson constantly sought advice was known as the _____.

7. The first _____ was begun in Philadelphia to organize workers in 1827.

8. The Indian tribe that presented the greatest obstacle to voluntary relocation under Jackson's plan because of its settled agrarian way of life was the _____.

9. That government should support enterprises that contribute to prosperity was the Whig support for the _____.

10. Southern free traders and planters referred to the Tariff of 1828, which increased rates across-the-border, as the _____.

TRUE/FALSE

Mark the following statements either T (True) or F (False).

_____ 1. By the 1820s, most states still had property qualifications to determine manhood suffrage.

_____ 2. In the presidential elections from 1824 through 1840, the percentage of males voting remained relatively the same.

_____ 3. Industrialization created a permanent class of poorly paid wage earners primarily in the cities.

_____ 4. The Jacksonians were convinced that a "corrupt bargain" between Adams and Clay in 1824 had deprived their candidate of the presidential election.

_____ 5. The election of 1828 indicated clearly that there was more anti-Adams sentiment nationwide than pro-Jackson support.

_____ 6. The main issue before Congress in the late 1820s was the tariff issue.

_____ 7. A major advantage for any presidential aspirant during the Jacksonian period was to be portrayed as a self-made man from a humble background.

_____ 8. Being a confirmed states' rightist and a southerner, Jackson sided with South Carolina in its opposition to the Tariff of 1828.

_____ 9. Because political parties were acknowledged by practically everyone by 1832, Jackson approved of a competitive two-party system.

_____ 10. The Bank War illustrated Jackson's flexibility and his ability to compromise on key economic issues.

MULTIPLE CHOICE

Circle the one alternative that best completes the statement or answers the question.

1. Regarding industrialization, workingmen's parties and trade union leaders condemned
   a. the growing gap between rich and poor.
   b. the subjugation of workers under parasitic nonproducers.
   c. the lack of governmental support for workers.
   d. all of the above

2. The tariff law of 1828 can best be historically explained by saying that
   a. a complicated Jacksonian plot was revealed to discredit the Adams administration.
   b. since the tariff was perceived to be judicious and compromising, it was supported by all groups except the southern planters.
   c. the tariff revealed the growing world desire for protectionism.
   d. the tariff showed how special interest groups can achieve their goals through congressional "give and take."

3. What gave the Jacksonians the edge in the 1828 election was their portrayal of Jackson as
   a. an aristocratic gentleman in the mold of Washington and Jefferson.
   b. an intellectual despite his limited formal education.
   c. a military hero determined to make the United States a world power.
   d. an authentic man of the common people.

4. Jackson defended the "spoils system" by saying that the system
   a. insured that the best qualified men would be placed in important advisory positions.
   b. had been used successfully in Britain to determine appointment of ministers.
   c. was a legitimate application of democratic principle in that the duties of public office are simple enough for any man of intelligence to accomplish.
   d. policies would be established with greater continuity and consistency.

5. The difference between Jackson's Indian policy and those of previous presidents was that Jackson
   a. wanted to relocate the Indians to the west of the Mississippi.
   b. was the first president to support the Cherokee autonomy assertion.
   c. demanded a much speedier and thorough removal of all eastern tribes to reservations west of the Mississippi.
   d. was the first president to oppose the rights of separate states to assert their jurisdiction over the tribes within their borders.

6. The main economic reason why the South opposed the protective tariff was because it
   a. raised the price of manufactured products on which they depended and led to foreign counter protection against southern crops.
   b. would encourage economic modernization and the birth of the factory system in the South.
   c. would insure economic preeminence of the northern industrial states.
   d. contradicted the unqualified southern commitment to free trade.

7. The nullification crisis revealed
   a. the hatred in the South for Jackson.
   b. the acceptance in the South of the supremacy of the federal government over the states.
   c. that the remaining southern states would back South Carolina's stand with military support
   d. that southerners would not tolerate any federal policies that threatened their interests or challenged the existence of slavery.

8. The most forceful objection to the existence of the Bank of the United States was that
   a. it served eastern interests at the expense of the rest of the nation.
   b. its board of directors had contributed heavily to the John Quincy Adams campaign.
   c. it had loaned out so much money that devaluation and inflation resulted.
   d. it possessed great power and influence without being under popular, democratic control.

9. Regarding Jackson's banking and fiscal policies, Henry Clay and his supporters in Congress contended that the president had
   a. exceeded the powers of his office.
   b. supported western speculative interests at the expense of the rest of the nation.
   c. been wrong all along about the bank's excessive power.
   d. been wrong to pursue the issue as a personal vendetta against Biddle.

10. According to the Democrats of the 1840s, the role of the federal government should be to
    a. support state and private banking and "hard money" interests.
    b. erect a system of high protective tariffs to support industrial interests.
    c. make the United States a world power after the example of Britain.
    d. remove obstacles to individual economic, moral, and religious rights.

11. What new political trend was considered by Van Buren to be essential to Democratic government?
    a. universal manhood suffrage
    b. the spoils system
    c. the rise of a permanent two-party system
    d. the emphasis on economic issues

12. The romantic movement
    a. emphasized aristocratic more than plain folk's activities.
    b. stressed the equality of race and gender.
    c. valued emotionalism and intuition over rationality.
    d. always paralleled the growth of democracy.

13. The election of 1828 revealed
    a. widespread opposition to Adam's presidency.
    b. the birth and triumph of mass democracy.
    c. that certain issues were more important than personalities.
    d. that two political parties had become well organized.

14. The new Whig party believed that the role of the government in regard to the economy was to
    a. become a "positive liberal state" with the responsibility of protecting industry and contributing to economic progress.
    b. remain passive to economic progress.
    c. protect the hard money interests against the greedy desires of speculators.
    d. provide a welfare system for the poor and recognize the rights of trade unions.

15. The new hotels of the 1820s were "obviously democratic" because they were
    a. were all built according to the same architectural concepts.
    b. were squalid, shabby, and poorly built.
    c. welcomed anyone regardless of race, sex, or ability to pay.
    d. extended personal service previously available only to the privileged classed to practically anyone who could afford to pay.

THOUGHT QUESTIONS

To check your understanding of the key issues of this period, solve the following problems:

1. Why was "democracy" no longer thought of as a dangerous tendency by the 1820s? What democratic features of American life would have amazed European visitors?

2. Why was Jackson considered to be representative of this popular democratic movement? What were his political strengths and weaknesses?

3. How was industrialization transforming the American economy as well as altering social classes and functions?

4. Why did South Carolina resort to nullification over the tariff controversy of the early 1830s? What deeper sectional and political issues were exposed by the nullification crisis?

5. What economic principles did the Whig party stand for? In what ways were its objectives more modern than those of the Democrats? Do you think that the government should be the moral guardian of the people?

6. What do you think were the underlying reasons for Jackson's war on the Bank of the United States? Do you think he was justified in his actions?

CRITICAL THINKING EXERCISES

Using the material in Chapter 10 of the text and the Primary Source noted below, please answer the following questions.

Elizabeth Emery and Mary P. Abbott, "Letter to *The Liberator.*"

Elizabeth Emery and Mary P. Abbott, Letter to *The Liberator* (1836)

Andover, Massachusetts, August 22, 1836

Mr. Editor:

In these days of women's doings, it may not be amiss to report the proceedings of some ladies in Andover. The story is now and then told of a new thing done here, as the opening of a railroad, or the building of a factory, but we have news better than all—it is the formation of a "Female Antislavery Society."

The call of our female friends across the waters—the energetic appeal of those untiring sisters in the work of emancipation in Boston—above all, the sighs, the groans, the deathlike struggles of scourged sisters in the South—these have moved our hearts, our hands. We feel that woman has a place in this Godlike work, for women's woes, and women's wrongs, are borne to us on every breeze that flows from the South; woman has a place, for she forms a part in God's created intelligent instrumentality to reform the world. God never made her to be inactive nor in all cases to follow in the wake of man. When man proves recreant to his duty and faithless to his Maker, woman, with her feeling heart, should rouse him—should start his sympathies—should cry in his ear, and raise such a storm of generous sentiment, as shall never let him sleep again. We believe God gave woman a heart to feel—an eye to weep—a hand to work—a tongue to speak. Now let her use that tongue to speak on slavery. Is it not a curse—a heaven-daring abomination? Let her employ that hand, to labor for the slave. Does not her sister in bonds, labor night and day without reward? Let her heart grieve, and her eye fill with tears, in view of a female's body dishonored—a female's mind debased—a female's soul forever ruined! Woman nothing to do with slavery! Abhorred the thought!! We will pray to abhor it more and more. Is not woman abused—women trampled upon—woman spoiled of her virtue, her probity, her influence, her joy! And this, not in India—not in China—not in Turkey—not in Africa but in America—in the United States of America, in the birthplace of Washington, the father of freedom, the protector of woman, the friend of equality and human rights!

Woman out of her place, in feeling, playing, and acting for the slave! Impious idea! Her oppressed sister cries aloud for help. She tries to lift her manacled hand—to turn her bruised face—to raise her tearful eye, and by all these, to plead a remembrance in our prayers—an interest in our labors. . . . Woman then may not be dumb. Christian sisters of Boston! We gladly respond to your call. We will "leave no energy unemployed—no righteous means untried. We will grudge no expense—yield to no opposition—forget fatigue, till by the strength of prayer and sacrifice, the spirit of love shall have overcome sectional jealousy—political rivalry—prejudice against color—cowardly concession of principle—wicked compromise with sin—devotion to gain, and spiritual despotism, which now bear with a mountain's weight upon the slave." As Christian women, we will do a Christian woman's duty.

The Constitution of our Society is so similar to that of other Antislavery Societies, it may not be necessary to give a copy of it. Our preamble gives our creed:

"We believe American Slavery is a sin against God—at war with the dictates of humanity, and subversive of the principles of freedom, because it regards rational beings as goods and chattel; robs them of compensation for their toil—denies to them the protection of law—disregards the relation of husband and wife, brother and sister, parent and child; shuts out from the intellect the light of knowledge; overwhelms hope in despair and ruins the soul—thus sinking to the level of brutes, more than one million of American females, who are created in God's image, a little lower than the angels', and consigns them over to degradation, physical, social, intellectual and moral: consequently, every slaveholder is bound instantly to cease from all participation in such a system. We believe that we should have no fellowship with these works of darkness, but rather reprove them—and that the truth spoken in love, is mighty to the removal of slavery, as of all other sins."

On such a creed, we base the constitution, which binds us together, and which we omit. . . .

[M]ay fearful foreboding lead the slave holder to timely repentance.

Elizabeth Emery, President
Mary P. Abbott, Rec. Secretary

1. Using the text, describe the character and beliefs of a typical "Jacksonian." What were his major motivations and fears? What kinds of things would most likely stimulate his interest in the new political opportunities of the Jacksonian period?

2. In what ways does the text author believe that the democratic spirit of the Jacksonian period was indicated in the emergence of new forms of literature and art--the so-called "democratic culture?'

3. According to the text, one of Andrew Jackson's most important and controversial actions as president was his war against the Bank of the United States. From your reading of the text what evidence can you cite to suggest that Jackson's actions were justified or unjustified? In what ways did Jackson use the power of the "democratic spirit" to oppose and ultimately kill the bank?

4. Read "Letter to *The Liberator*." Although it is clearly an expression of moral outrage against slavery, in what ways is it also an expression of outrage against women's exclusion from the democratic spirit and reforms of the period?

CHAPTER 11

THE PURSUIT OF PERFECTION

SUMMARY

Social and economic upheaval in the early nineteenth century resulted in religious fervor, moral reform, and sometimes confusion.

The Rise of Evangelicalism
During the early nineteenth century turmoil was common for American Protestantism.

The Second Great Awakening: The Frontier Phase
Beginning on the frontier, a revival movement known as the Second Great Awakening provided an emotional outlet, a right of passage, and social cohesion.

The Second Great Awakening in the North
In both New England and upstate New York, other evangelical revivals spread doctrines emphasizing free choice and free will.

From Revivalism to Reform
The evangelical revivals of the North often spawned middle-class reform movements, such as the temperance movement, which emphasized self-improvement.

Domesticity and Changes in the American Family
Increasingly reformers celebrated the family and especially the mother as important to society.

Marriage and Sex Roles
In the nineteenth century, love became important in choosing a marital partner. Women also gained some measure of power, especially in their sphere, the home. This glorification of the role of the wife/mother was referred to as the "cult of true womanhood."

The Discovery of Childhood
Lower birthrates and smaller families led parents to place more emphasis on affectionate child rearing.

Institutional Reform
Responsibility for the reform of the individual eventually spread from the family to the larger community and society's important institutions.

The Extension of Education
Public education developed, especially in the North, under the leadership of reformers such as Horace Mann.

Discovering the Asylum
Reformers worked for rehabilitation of those who exhibited deviant behavior by placing them in asylums. Dorothea Dix worked to raise the level of care for the inmates.

Reform Turns Radical
Some of the reformers insisted on reforms so extreme that many considered them radical.

Divisions in the Benevolent Empire
Arguments between the adherents of moderate reform and those supporting quicker change split many organizations.

The Abolitionist Enterprise
Growing out of the evangelical movement, the abolitionist movement succeeded, especially in the North.

From Abolitionism to Women's Rights
Women served in the abolitionist movement and consequently began to work for their own liberation, and organized the first gathering for women's rights in the United States at Seneca Falls in 1840.

Radical Ideas and Experiments
Some Americans in the early to mid-nineteenth century sought a perfect social order and formed utopian socialist communities.

Fads and Fashions
Other Americans promoted fads such as phrenology, vegetarianism, and spiritualist seances.

Counterpoint on Reform
Hawthorne, in his writing in this period, underlined the observation that the dreams of reformers promised more than they could deliver.

LEARNING OBJECTIVES

After mastering this chapter, you should be able to:

1. List the factors that caused the Second Great Awakening.

2. Show how the religious revivals became reform movements.

3. Describe the "Cult of True Womanhood."

4. Analyze the impact the reform of family life had on lower-, middle-, and upper-class women.

5. Explain the purpose of public education according to Horace Mann.

6. Describe the factors and events which led to the rise of the women's rights movement.

7. Evaluate the results of the Seneca Falls Convention of 1848.

GLOSSARY

To build your social science vocabulary, familiarize yourself with the following terms:

1. **rite of passage** a ceremony, ritual, or formal act conferring adult status on an individual. "Conversion at a camp meeting could be a rite of passage . . ."

2. **expose** the revelation of a scandal, secret, or cover-up. "As a result of this expose, an asylum was established . . ."

3. **piety** reverence, devotion, and obedience to the will of a supreme being. "The ideal wife and mother was . . . a model of piety and virtue . . ."

4. **corporal punishment** physical or bodily punishment, such as spanking. "Corporal punishment declined, partially displaced by shaming or withholding of affection."

5. **indoctrination** the act of instructing or teaching a doctrine or certain principles. "Purely intellectual training at school was regarded as less important than moral indoctrination . . ."

6. **lyceum** an organization that provides concerts, lectures, or cultural events. "Every city and almost every town or village had a lyceum . . ."

7. **schism** a division or a split. ". . . but the schism did weaken Garrison's influence . . ."

8. **secular humanist one** who advocates a philosophical system that exalts human values without appeal to religion or the divinity of Christ. "Some were secular humanists carrying on the free-thinking tradition of the Enlightenment . . ."

9. **transcendentalism** a philosophical system that maintains that realities exist beyond the physical world. ". . . philosophical movement known as transcendentalism."

10. **phrenology** a doctrine that alleges that the shape of the skull determines character traits and

talents. ". . . the craze for phrenology--a popular pseudoscience . . ."

IDENTIFICATION

Briefly identify the meaning and significance of the following terms or names:

1. Charles G. Finney_____

_____

2. Second Great Awakening_____

_____

3. Peter Cartwright_____

_____

4. American Temperance Society_____

_____

5. Horace Mann_____

_____

6. Dorothea Dix_____

_____

7. William Lloyd Garrison_____

_____

8. Frederick Douglass_____

_____

9. Seneca Falls_____

_____

10. Brook Farm_____

_____

MATCHING

A. Match the following abolitionist leaders with the appropriate description:

_____1. William Lloyd Garrison

    a. midwestern abolitionist preacher who founded Oberlin College

_____2. Theodore Dwight-Weld

    b. daughter of a South Carolina slaveholder who worked for the abolition of slavery and the struggle for equal rights for women

_____3. Lewis Tappan

    c. leading abolitionist and founder of the American Anti-Slavery Society

_____4. Elijah Lovejoy

    d. absolute pacifist who repudiated all types of governmental coercion

_____5. Sarah Grimké

    e. antislavery editor who was shot and killed for his beliefs

    f. split with the American Anti-Slavery Society and organized the American and Foreign Anti-Slavery Society with no women on the executive board

B. Match the following religious leaders with the appropriate description:

_____1. Charles Finney

    a. first itinerant evangelist for the Congregationalists

_____2. Timothy Dwight

    b. first practitioner of evangelical Calvinism

_____3. Nathaniel Taylor

    c. president of Yale College in 1795, who opposed rationalism and Unitarianism

_____4. Lyman Beecher

    d. spellbinding preacher of revivals in upstate New York

_____5. Samuel John Mills

    e. most important theologian of neo-Calvinism

    f. leader of the American Bible Society

COMPLETION

Answer the question or complete the statement by filling in the blanks with the correct word or words.

1. The religious revival that began around 1801 on the southern frontier was called the
    _____.

2. The first preacher to adopt into his work the ideas of the new evangelical Calvinism was
    _____.

3. The organization that tried to convince people to abstain from drinking hard liquor was the
    _____.

4. The woman who campaigned to make school teaching a woman's occupation was
    _____.

5. The primary school reading book that was introduced in 1836 and also taught the "Protestant ethic" was called the _____.

6. William Lloyd Garrison published a leading abolitionist journal called the _____.

7. The political party that was based on antislavery sentiment was the _____.

8. British industrialist and socialist Robert Owen established a utopian community at
    _____, _____.

TRUE/FALSE

Mark the following statements either T (True) or F (False):

_____1.   American Protestantism was extremely stable in the early nineteenth century.

_____2.   Camp meetings served only religious purposes.

_____3.   Northeastern revivalism was less emotional than the camp meetings of the Southwest.

_____4.   Neo-Calvinism held to a rigid concept of absolute predestination.

_____5.   Charles G. Finney emphasized human reason and theological logic rather than emotional appeals and human feelings.

_____ 6. The temperance movement can be considered somewhat successful because alcohol consumption declined during the 1830s.

_____ 7. New work patterns had little or no effect on sex roles in the nineteenth century.

_____ 8. The availability of various methods of birth control and easy access to abortion resulted in smaller families in the nineteenth century.

_____ 9. Horace Mann viewed education as more moral indoctrination than intellectual training.

_____ 10. Leaders of the abolition movement also favored complete equality for women.

MULTIPLE CHOICE

Circle the one alternative that *best* completes the statement or answers the question.

1. Pious Protestants of the early nineteenth century were concerned about
   a. the spread of secular humanism.
   b. the lack of respect for the example of Christian orthodoxy set by the founding fathers.
   c. the increase in established state churches.
   d. declining membership in frontier churches, such as the Baptist and the Methodist.

2. Camp meetings on the frontier provided all of the following *except*
   a. an emotional outlet
   b. a sense of community
   c. a rational appeal to moral behavior
   d. a rite of passage for a young man or woman

3. The Second Great Awakening in the North especially appealed to
   a. Unitarians, searching for a revival theology consistent with their view of the Trinity.
   b. small- to medium-sized town dwellers with New England Puritan backgrounds.
   c. urban workers and mechanics, looking to revivals for relief from daily work problems and perhaps their dreary home life.
   d. rural planters, seeking a method to help them with their drinking problems.

4. Temperance reformers opposed public drunkenness because it
   a. spawned crime and vice.
   b. was a threat to the family.
   c. was a threat to private property and public order.
   d. all of the above.

5. The "cult of true womanhood" or the "ideology of domesticity" achieved
    a. true equality for men and women.
    b. some equality for women, especially in the ownership of property.
    c. some equality for women, especially in religion and morals for the family and as companion for their husbands.
    d. nothing that was not already accomplished in the colonial era.

6. The rise of the "cult of true womanhood" was caused by
    a. a division in the working lives of men and women.
    b. successful Supreme Court decisions.
    c. the high number of women in the teaching profession.
    d. agitation by organized groups.

7. The new literature that glorified the "cult of true womanhood" appealed especially to
    a. relatively affluent women.
    b. single women.
    c. working-class wives.
    d. rural and mountain wives.

8. The nineteenth century has been called the "century of the child" for which of the following reasons?
    a. The average family had more children.
    b. Birth control and abortion were not available.
    c. Children were an economic asset to the urban family.
    d. The family became more child-centered.

9. The purpose of public education as seen by Horace Mann was to teach
    a. cultural plurality.
    b. morality and discipline.
    c. freedom, liberty, and other ideals of the American Revolution.
    d. that the rights of private property are absolute.

10. The "discovery of the asylum"
    a. occurred because economic development led to the rise of urban areas and the decline of cohesive villages.
    b. resulted in placing lunatics and paupers with families in small towns.
    c. led to the abolition of solitary confinement.
    d. happened after a Calvinist revival meeting.

11. William Lloyd Garrison and the American Anti-Slavery Association advocated
    a. gradual emancipation with compensation to owners.
    b. gradual emancipation without compensation to owners.

c. immediate abolition of slavery and colonization of African Americans in Africa.

d. immediate abolition of slavery without emigration.

12. Which of the following caused a formal split in the American Anti-Slavery Association?
    a. Garrison's attack on the clergy
    b. Garrison's support for women's rights
    c. racism in the North
    d. African American leadership in the organization

13. The primary catalyst for the women's rights movement of the 1830s was the
    a. "cult of true womanhood."
    b. rise of free public education.
    c. abolitionist movement.
    d. Second Great Awakening.

14. The "Declaration of Sentiments" of the Seneca Falls meeting of 1848 stated that
    a. men had established a tyranny over women.
    b. men should willingly accept the cult of domesticity.
    c. women should have equal rights but only in their own spheres.
    d. women should have the right to vote, but not necessarily equality within the family.

15. The utopian socialist communities of the 1830s and 1840s were
    a. all secular with no religious basis.
    b. variable in organization and leadership.
    c. based on the idea of "free love."
    d. based on a purely American idea.

THOUGHT QUESTIONS

To check your understanding of the key issues of this period, solve the following problems:

1. What are some of the social, political, and economic similarities of the eras of American history that have experienced revivalism?

2. What was the relationship between the rise of capitalism and the temperance movement?

3. What do modern feminists have in common with the leaders of the women's movement of the 1830s and 1840s?

4. To what extent does public education in America still resemble that described by Horace Mann?

5. Speculate on the factors that caused the utopian communities to be short-lived.

CRITICAL THINKING QUESTIONS

After reading William Lloyd Garrison, from *The Liberator* (1831), Frederick Douglass, Independence Day Speech, and George Fitzhugh, "The Blessings of Slavery" (1857), answer the following questions:

William Lloyd Garrison, from The Liberator (1831)

During my recent tour for the purpose of exciting the minds of the people by a series of discourses on the subject of slavery, every place that I visited gave fresh evidence of the fact that a great revolution in public sentiment was to be effected in the free states-and particularly in New England-than at the South. I find contempt more bitter, opposition more active, detraction more relentless, prejudice more stubborn, and apathy more frozen, than among slaveowners themselves. Of course, there were individual exceptions to the contrary.

This state of things afflicted but did not dishearten me. I determined, at every hazard, to lift up the standard of emancipation in the eyes of the nation, within sight of Bunker Hill and in the birthplace of liberty. That standard is now unfurled; and long may it float, unhurt by the spoliations of time or the missiles of a desperate foe-yea, till every chain be broken, and every bondman set free! Let Southern oppressors tremble-let all the enemies of the persecuted blacks tremble. . . .

Assenting to the "self-evident truth" maintained in the American Declaration of Independence "that all men are created equal, and endowed by their Creator with certain inalienable rights-among which are life, liberty, and the pursuit of happiness," I shall strenuously contend for the immediate enfranchisement of our slave population. . . . In Park Street Church, on the Fourth of July, 1829, in an address on slavery, I unreflectingly assented to the popular but pernicious doctrine of gradual abolition. I seize this opportunity to make a full and unequivocal recantation, and thus publicly to ask pardon of my God, of my country, and of my brethren the poor slaves, for having uttered a sentiment so full of timidity, injustice, and absurdity. . . .

I am aware that many object to the severity of my language; but is there not cause for severity? I will be as harsh as truth, and as uncompromising as justice. On this subject I do not wish to think, or speak, or write, with moderation. No! No! Tell a man whose house is on fire to give a moderate alarm; tell him to moderately rescue his wife from the hands of the ravisher; tell the mother to gradually extricate her babe from the fire into which it has fallen-but urge me not to use moderation in a cause like the present. I am in earnest-will not equivocate-I will not excuse-I will not retreat in a single inch-and I will be heard. The apathy of the people is enough to make every statue leap from its pedestal, and to hasten the resurrection of the dead.

It is pretended that I am retarding the cause of emancipation by the coarseness of my invective and the precipitancy of my measures. The charge is not true. On this question my influence-humble as it is-is felt at this moment to a considerable extent, and shall be felt in coming years-not perniciously, but beneficially-not as a curse, but as a blessing. And posterity will bear testimony that I was right.

Frederick Douglass, Independence Day Speech (1852)

Fellow citizens above your national, tumultuous joy, I hear the mournful wail of millions! whose chains, heave and grievous yesterday, are, today, rendered more intolerable by the jubilee shouts that reach them. If I do forget, it I do not faithfully remember those bleeding children of sorrow this day, "may my right hand forger her cunning, and may ny tongue cleave to the roof of my mouth"! To forget them, to pass lightly over their wrongs, and to chime in with the popular theme would be treason most scandalous and shocking, and would make me a reproach before God and the world. My subject, them, fellow citizens, is American Slavery. I shall see this day and its popular characteristics from the slav;s point of view. Standing there identified with the American bondman, making his wrongs mine. I do not hesitate to declare with all my soul that the character and conduct of this nation never looked blacker to me than on this Fourth of July! Whether we turn to the declarations of the past or to the professions of the present, the conduct of the nation seems equally hideous and revolting. America is false to the past, false to the present, and solemnly binds herself to be false to the future. Standing with God and the crushed and bleeding slave on this occasion, I will,in the name of humanity which is outraged, in the name of liberty which is fettered, in the name of the Constitution and the Bible which are disregarded and trampled upon, All the emphasis I can command, everything that serves to perpetuate slavery the great sin and shame of America! "I will not equivocate, I will not excuse"; I will use the severest of language I can command; and yet not one word shall escape that any man, whose judgment is not blinded by prejudice, or who is not at heart a slaveholder, shall not confess to be right and just.

But I fancy I hear someone of my audience say, "It is just in this circumstance that your and your brother abolitionists fail to make a avorable impression on the public mind. Would you argue more and denounce less, would you persuade more and rebuke less, your cause would be much more likely to succeed." But, I submit, where all is plain, there is nothing to be argued. What point in the antislavery creed would you have me argue? On what branch of the subject do the people of this country need light? Must I undertake to prove that the slave is a man? That point is conceded already. Nobody doubts it. The slaveholders themselves acknowledge it the enactment of laws for their government. They acknowledge it when they punish disobedience on the part of the slave. There are seventy-two crimes in the state of Virginia which, if committed by a black man (no matter how ignorant he be), subject him to the punishment of death, while only two of the same crimes will subject a white man to the like punishment. What is this but the acknowledgment that the slave is a moral, intellectual, and responsible being? The
manhood of the slave is conceded. It is admitted in the fact that the Southern statute books are covered with enactments forbidding, under severe fines and penalties, the teaching of the slave to read or to write. When you can point to any such laws in reference to the beasts of the field, then I may consent to argue the manhood of the slave. When the dogs in your streets, when the fowls of the air, when the cattle on your hills, when the fish of the sea and the reptiles that crawl shall be unable to distinguish the slave from a brute, then will I argue with you that the slave is a man!

For the present, it is enough to affirm the equal manhood of the Negro race. It is not astonishing that, while we are plowing, planting, and reaping, using all kinds of mechanical tools erecting houses, constructing bridges, building ships, working in metals of brass, iron, copper and silver, and gold; that, while we are reading, writing, and ciphering, acting as clerks, merchants and secretaries, having among us lawyers, doctors,
ministers, poets, authors, editors, orators, and teachers; that, while we are engaged in all manner of enterprises common to other men, digging gold in California, capturing the whale in the Pacific, feeding sheep and cattle on the hillside, living, moving, acting, thinking, planning, living in families as husbands, wives, and children, and, above all, confessing and worshipping the Christian's God, and looking hopefully for life and
immortality beyond the grave, we are called upon to prove that we are men!

Would you have me argue that man is entitled to liberty? That he is the rightful owner of his own body? You have already declared it. Must I argue the wrongfulness of slavery? Is that a question for republicans? Is it to be settled by the rules of logic and argumentation, as a matter beset with great difficulty, involving a doubtful application of the principle of justice, hart to be understood? How should I look today, in the presence of Americans, dividing and subdividing a discourse, to show that men have a natural right to freedom? speaking of it relatively and positively, negatively and affirmatively? To do so would be to make myself ridiculous and to offer an insult to your understanding. There is not a man beneath the canopy of heaven that does not know that slaver is wrong for him.

What, am I to argue that is wrong to make men brutes, to rob them of their liberty, to work them without wages, to keep them ignorant of their relations to their fellow men, to beat them with sticks, to flay their flesh with the last, to load their limbs with irons, to hunt them with dogs, to sell them at auction, to sunder their families, to knock out their teeth, to burn their flesh, to starve them into obedience and submission to their masters?
Must I argue that a system them marked with blood, and stained with pollution, is wrong? No! I will not. I have better employment for my time and strength than such arguments would imply.

What, then remains to be argued? Is it that slavery is not divine; that God did not establish it; that our doctors of divinity are mistaken? There is blasphemy in the thought. That which is inhuman cannot be divine? Who can reason on such a proposition? They that can may; I cannot. The time for such argument is past.

At a time like this, scorching iron, not convincing argument, is needed. O! had I the ability, and could I reach the nation's ear, I would today pour out a fiery stream of biting ridicule, blasting reproach, withering sarcasm, and stern rebuke. For it is not light that is needed, but fire; it is not the gentle shower, but thunder. We need the storm, the whirlwind, and the earthquake. The feeling of the nation must be quickened, the conscience of the nation must be startled; the hypocrisy of the nation must be exposed; and its crimes against God and man must be proclaimed and denounced.

What, to the American slave is your Fourth of July? I answer: a day that reveals to him, more than all other days in the year, the gross injustice and cruelty to which he s the constant victim. To him, your celebration is a sham; your boasted liberty an unholy license; your national greatness, swelling vanity; your sound of rejoicing are empty and heartless; your denunciation of tyrants, brass-fronted impudence; your shouts of liberty and equality, hollow mockery; your prayers and hymns, your sermons and thanksgivings with all your religious parade and solemnity, are, to Him, mere bombast, fraud, deception, impiety, and hypocrisy a thin veil to cover up crimes which would disgrace a nation of savages. There is not a nation of savages. There is not a nation on earth guilty of practices more shocking and bloody than are the people of the United States at this very hour.

Go where you may, search where you will, roam through all the monarchies and despotisms of the Old World, travel through South America, search out every abuse, and when you have found the last, lay your facts by the side of the everyday practices of this nation, and you will say with that, for revolting barbarity and shameless hypocrisy, America reigns without a rival.

George Fitzhugh, "The Blessings of Slavery" (1857)

The negro slaves of the South are the happiest, and in some sense, the freest people in the world. The children and the aged and infirm work not at all, and yet have all the comforts and necessaries of life provided for them. They enjoy liberty, because they are oppressed neither by care or labor. The women do little hard work, and are protected from the
despotism of their husbands by their masters. The negro men and stout boys work, on the average, in good weather, no more than nine hours a day. The balance of their time is spent in perfect abandon. Besides, they have their Sabbaths and holidays. White men, with som muh of license and abandon, would die of ennui; but negroes luxuriate in corporeal and mental repose. With their faces upturned to the sun, they can sleep at any hour; and quiet sleep is the gretest of human enjoyments. "Blessed be the man who invented sleep." 'Tis happiness in itself-and results from contentment in the present, and confident assurance of the future. We do not know whether free laborers ever sleep. They are fools to do so; for, whilst they sleep, the wily and watchful capitalist is devising means to ensnare and exploit them. The free laborer must work or starve. He is more of a slave than the negro, because he works longer and harder for less allowance than the slave, and has no holiday, because the cares of life with him begin when its labors end. He has no liberty and not a single right. . . .

Until the lands of America are appropriated by a few, population becomes dense, competition among laborers active, employment uncertain, and wages low, the personal liberty of all the whites will continue to be a blessing. We have vast unsettled territories; population may cease to increase slowly, as in most countries, and many centuries may elapse before the question will be practically suggested, whether slavery to capital be preferable to slavery to human masters. But the negro has neither energy nor enterprise, and, even in our sparser populations, finds with his improvident habits, that his liberty is a curse to himself, and a greater curse to the society around him. These considerations, and others equally obvious, have induced the South to attempt to defend negro slavery as an exceptional institution, admitting, nay asserting, that slavery, in the general or in the abstract, is morally wrong, and against common right. With singular inconsistency, after making this admission, which admits away the authority of the Bible, of profane history, and of the almost universal practice of mankind-they turn around and attempt to bolster up the cause of negro slavery by these very exploded authorities. If we mean not to repudiate all divine, and almost all human authority in favor of slavery, we must vindicate that institution in the abstract.

To insist that a status of society, which has been almost universal, and which is expressly and continually justified by Holy Writ, is its natural, normal, and necessary status, under the ordinary circumstances, is on its face a plausible and probable proposition. To insist on less, is to yield our cause, and to give up our religion; for if white slavery be morally wrong, be a violation of natural rights, the Bible cannot be true. Human and divine authority do seem in the general to concur, in establishing the expediency of having masters and slaves of different races. In very many nations of antiquity, and in some of modern times, the law has permitted the native citizens to become slaves to each other. But few take advantage of such laws; and the infrequency of the practice establishes the general truth that master and slave should be of different national descent. In some respects the wider the difference the better, as the slave will feel less mortified by his position. In other respects, it may be that too wide a difference hardens the hearts and brutalizes the feeling of both master and slave. The civilized man hates the savage, and the savage returns the hatred with interest. Hence West India slavery of newly caught negroes is not a very humane, affectionate, or civilizing institution. Virginia negroes have become moral and intelligent. They love their master and his family, and the attachment is reciprocated. Still, we like the idle, but intelligent
house-servants, better than the hard-used, but stupid outhands; and we like the mulatto better than the negro; yet the negro is generally more affectionate, contented, and faithful.

The world at large looks on negro slavery as much the worst form of slavery; because it is only acquainted with West India slavery. But our Southern slavery has become a benign and protective institution, and our negroes

159

are confessedly better off than any free laboring population in the world. How can we contend that white slavery is wrong, whilst all the great body of free laborers are starving; and slaves, white or black, throughout the world, are enjoying comfort? . . .

The aversion to negroes, the antipathy of race, is much greater at the North than at the South; and it is very probable that this antipathy to the person of the negro, is confounded with or generates hatred of the institution with which he is usually connected. Hatred to slavery is very generally little more than hatred of negroes.

There is one strong argument in favor of negro slavery over all other slavery; that he, being unfitted for the mechanic arts, for trade, and all skillful pursuits, leaves those pursuits to be carried on by the whites; and does not bring all industry into disrepute, as in Greece and Rome, where the slaves were not only the artists and mechanics, but also the merchants.

Whilst, as a general and abstract question, negro slavery has no other claims over other forms of slavery, except that from inferiority, or rather peculiarity, of race, almost all negroes require masters, whilst only the children, the women, and the very weak, poor, and ignorant, &c., among the whites, need some protective and governing relation of this kind; yet as a subject of temporary, but worldwide importance, negro slavery has become the most necessary of all human institutions.

The African slave trade to America commenced three centuries and a half since. By the time of the American Revolution, the supply of slaves had exceeded the demand for slave labor, and the slaveholders, to get rid of a burden, and to prevent the increase of a nuisance, became violent opponents of the slave trade, and many of them abolitionists. New England, Bristol, and Liverpool, who reaped the profits of the trade, without suffering from the nuisance, stood out for a long time against its abolition. Finally, laws and treaties were made, and fleets fitted out to abolish it; and after a while, the slaves of most of South America, of the West Indies, and of Mexico were liberated. In the meantime, cotton, rice, sugar, coffee, tobacco, and other products of slave labor, came into universal use as necessaries of life. The population of Western Europe, sustained and stimulated by those products, was trebled, and that of the North increased tenfold. The products of slave labor became scarce and dear, and famines frequent. Now, it is obvious, that to emancipate all the negroes would be to starve Western Europe and our North. Not to extend and increase negro slavery, pari passu, with the extension and multiplication of free society, will produce much suffering. If all South America, Mexico, the West Indies, and our Union south of Mason and Dixon's line, of the Ohio and Missouri, were slaveholding, slave products would be abundant and cheap in free society; and their market for their merchandise, manufactures, commerce, &c., illimitable. Free white laborers might live in comfort and luxury on light work, but for the exacting and greedy landlords, bosses, and other capitalists.

We must confess, that overstock the world as you will with comforts and with luxuries, we do not see how to make capital relax its monopoly-how to do aught but tantalize the hireling. Capital, irresponsible capital, begets, and ever will beget, the immedicabile vulnus of so-called Free Society. It invades every recess of domestic life, infects its food, its clothing, its drink, its very atmosphere, and pursues the hireling, from the hovel to the poor-house, the prison and the grave. Do what he will, go where he will, capital pursues and persecutes him. "Haeret lateri lethalis arundo!"

Capital supports and protects the domestic slave; taxes, oppresses, and persecutes the free laborer.

1.   Compare the antislavery arguments and emotional styles of Garrison and Douglass.

2.   In Douglass's speech what obvious points does he refuse to "argue"? Why does he approach these subjects in this way?

3.   From your reading on slavery, react to Garrrison's question " . . . is there not cause for severity?"

4.   What points mentioned by Fitzhugh show slavery was a "blessing"?

5.   Does there appear to be any middle ground or points of agreement between Garrison and Douglass on the one hand, and Fitzhugh on the other?

CHAPTER 12

AN AGE OF EXPANSIONISM

SUMMARY

A popular mood known as "Young America" emerged in the 1840s. Its adherents brashly promoted territorial and economic expansion and development of the United States, but displayed little concern or awareness of the practical consequences of such actions.

Movement to the Far West
Borderlands of the 1830s
Beginning in the 1820s, American traders and settlers were lured west of the American borders, attracted by adventure, the prospect of financial gain, and for the Mormons, religious freedom. A potential American thrust toward Canada was blunted with settlement of Anglo-American differences in the Webster-Ashburton Treaty of 1842.

The Texas Revolution
An influx of Americans into Mexican-owned Texas during the 1820s produced cultural, economic, and political conflict, resulting in Mexican restrictions on Anglo immigration and slaveholding. A revolution by the Texans followed in 1835-1836.

The Republic of Texas
Remembering defeats inflicted by the Mexicans at the Alamo and Goliad, Texans rallied for a major victory at San Jacinto, capturing Santa Anna and forcing his recognition of Texas independence. General Sam Houston became the first president of the "Lone Star Republic," a separate nation until 1845.

Trails of Trade and Settlement
Opened in 1821, the Santa Fe Trail introduced Americans to the riches of New Mexico. In the 1840s, over five thousand Americans traveled the famous Oregon Trail to that territory in the Northwest. Quickly outnumbering British residents, Americans demanded an end to the joint occupation of Oregon with Britain that had first been arranged in 1818 and indefinitely extended in 1827.

The Mormon Trek
Seeking relief from public hostility to their unorthodox beliefs and practices, the Mormons moved from New York to Ohio to Missouri to Illinois where leader and founder Joseph Smith was attacked and killed by an angry mob. Smith's successor, Brigham Young, led a group of Mormons into Mexican-owned Utah in 1847, establishing an effective community based on discipline and cooperation.

Manifest Destiny and the Mexican War
Tyler and Texas

Hoping for a popular issue to revive his sagging political fortunes, President John Tyler promoted the annexation of Texas by treaty in 1844. The Senate rejected the document, however, when Secretary of State John Calhoun linked Texas too closely to the interests of the South and slavery.

The Triumph of Polk and Annexation

In 1844, Americans had the rare opportunity to draw a rather clear-cut distinction between the platforms of presidential candidates. In contrast to the anti-expansionist Whig candidate Henry Clay, Democrats in 1848 nominated dark horse James K. Polk, an aggressive spokesman for the annexation of Texas and sole American occupation of Oregon. Ironically, the antislavery Liberty party candidate drew just enough votes away from Clay to throw the election to Polk. The "mandate" for expansion resulted in a joint resolution by Congress annexing Texas.

The Doctrine of Manifest Destiny

Journalist John L. O'Sullivan coined the phrase "manifest destiny" to signify the growing feeling among Americans in the 1840s that God intended them to extend their ideals of republican government and economic opportunities to the unsettled as well as "under-settled" portions of the continent.

Polk and the Oregon Question

British rejection of an American proposal to divide Oregon provoked cries of "Fifty-four forty or fight" among Americans who demanded all of the territory. Cooler heads prevailed, however, and Polk negotiated a treaty with Britain in 1846 dividing Oregon along the 49th parallel, giving the valuable Puget Sound to the United States while allowing Britain to retain Vancouver Island.

War with Mexico

Mexico's refusal to accept Texan (and American) claims to a Rio Grande boundary as well as refusal to sell additional lands led the United States to declare war in May 1846. American forces scored a succession of military victories under Zachary Taylor in northern Mexico, Stephen Kearney in New Mexico, John C. Frémont in California, and Winfield Scott in the decisive campaign to capture the capital of Mexico City.

Settlement of the Mexican War

Ignoring radical demands for the annexation of all Mexico, American diplomat Nicholas P. Trist negotiated a successful end to the Mexican War with the Treaty of Guadalupe Hidalgo in February 1848. The treaty provided for the Mexican cession of New Mexico and California to the United States for $15 million, recognition of the Rio Grande border, and the assumption by the United States government of American claims against Mexico.

162

Internal Expansionism
The Triumph of the Railroad

In the 1840s and the 1850s, railroads replaced canals as the means for hauling America's freight traffic. Expansion of the railroads stimulated the domestic iron industry and encouraged modern methods for financing business enterprise.

The Industrial Revolution Takes Off

Technological advances, especially the development of sophisticated machine tools, helped bring about mass production techniques in American industry and agriculture. The factory mode of production, first used in the textile industry, expanded to industries producing iron, shoes, firearms, clocks, and sewing machines.

Mass Immigration Begins

The growth of industrial work opportunities in the United States, combined with economic hardships in many parts of Europe, sparked a period of mass immigration, especially from Ireland and Germany. The Irish, mostly Catholic, poor, and unskilled, crowded into urban slums and accepted low-paying factory jobs, evoking scorn from those Americans whose descendants had earlier established themselves in the country.

The New Working Class

Considering wage labor a temporary condition, most workers resisted appeals for organization along class lines or workers' strikes. The new working class "protested" long hours and low pay, however, in more subtle and indirect ways-by tardiness, absenteeism, and drunkenness. An age of expansionism had extracted a price. External (territorial) expansion generated sectional conflict and internal (economic) expansion fueled class and ethnic rivalries.

LEARNING OBJECTIVES

After mastering this chapter, you should be able to:

1. Describe the conditions of the western "borderlands" of the 1830s as well as the factors attracting American settlers.

2. Explain the causes, events, and results of the Texas revolution.

3. Discuss the importance of the Santa Fe and Oregon Trails in expanding American trade and settlement.

4. Trace the development of the Mormon Church and the westward trek of its members.

5. Identify the candidates and issues and explain the outcome and consequences of the election of 1844.

6. Evaluate the successes and failures of James K. Polk's administration.

7. Discuss the rationale for expansion as expressed in the doctrine of manifest destiny.

8. Summarize the causes, events, and outcomes of the Mexican War.

9. Discuss the factors which contributed to American economic growth from 1830 to 1860.

10. Describe the changing composition and attitudes of the American working class during this era.

GLOSSARY

To build your social science vocabulary, familiarize yourself with the following terms:

1. **indigenous** living naturally in a particular region or environment. "The number represented only a small fraction of the original indigenous population . . ."

2. **empressarios** managers; promoters. "Some fifteen other Anglo-American empressarios were similarly granted land in the 1820s."

3. **disfranchisement** deprivation of a legal right, especially the right to vote. "news . . . accompanied by rumors of the impending disfranchisement . . ."

4. **sovereignty** supreme power over a body politic. "Five thousand Americans . . . were demanding the extension of full American sovereignty over the Oregon country."

5. **Zion** the ideal nation, heaven. ". . . a western Zion where they could practice their faith unmolested . . ."

6. **vigilante** one who takes the law into his own hands. The Mormons were "the target of angry mobs and vigilante violence . . ."

7. **dissident** differing from an opinion or a group. "held in jail . . . on a charge stemming from his quarrels with dissident Mormons. . . "

8. **joint resolution** a resolution passed by a majority vote of both houses of Congress. "Tyler then attempted to bring Texas into the Union through an alternative means - a joint resolution . . ."

9. **conclave** a gathering or convention of a group. "postponement of the Democratic conclave until May 1844 weakened his chances."

10. **dark horse candidate** a candidate whose ability is not known or whose chances for success are not good. "After several ballots a dark horse candidate—James K. Polk of Tennessee—emerged triumphant."

11. **polarization** division into opposite groups. "fear that growing numbers would lead to diminished opportunity and European-type polarization of social classes."

12. **abrogation** the act of abolishing or nullifying. " abrogation of the joint agreement implied that the United States would attempt to extend its jurisdiction . . ."

13. **emissary** one sent on a mission as the agent of another. "by dispatching John Slidell as an emissary to Mexico City . . ."

14. **cession** a yielding to another. "A short and decisive war . . . would force the cession of California and New Mexico to the United States."

15. **exacerbated** aggravated; made more severe or worse. "large numbers of immigrants exacerbated the already serious problems of America's rapidly growing cities."

IDENTIFICATION

Briefly identify the meaning and significance of the following terms:

1. "Young America"_____

_____

2. Stephen F. Austin_____

_____

3. Oregon Trail_____

_____

4. Joseph Smith_____

_____

5. John Tyler_____

6. James K. Polk_____

_____

7. Manifest Destiny_____

_____

8. "Fifty-four Forty or Fight"_____

_____

9. Zachary Taylor_____

_____

10. Treaty of Guadalupe Hidalgo_____

_____

MATCHING

A. Match the following leaders with the appropriate description:

1.	John Slidell	**a.**	led American settlers in California in revolt against Mexican authorities
2.	Zachary Taylor	**b.**	headed a diplomatic mission to Mexico in hopes of averting war
3.	John C. Frémont	**c.**	commanded the seizure of Vera Cruz and Mexico City
4.	Stephen Kearny	**d.**	captured control of northern Mexico
5.	Winfield Scott	**e.**	negotiated the Treaty of Guadalupe Hidalgo

f. captured Santa Fe and proclaimed the annexation of New Mexico by the United States

B.   Match the following inventors with the appropriate accomplishment:

1.   Samuel F. B. Morse

2.   Elias Howe

3.   Charles Goodyear

4.   Cyrus McCormick

5.   John Deere

a. invented the sewing machine in 1846, laying the basis for the modern clothing industry

b. invented the steel plow in 1837, enabling farmers to cultivate the prairie sod

c. demonstrated the steam locomotive in 1830 as practical and profitable

d. discovered the process for the vulcanization of rubber in 1839

e. in 1834, patented the mechanical reaper, an important labor-saving device for harvesting grain

f. perfected and demonstrated the electric telegraph in 1844

COMPLETION

Answer the question or complete the statement by filling in the blanks with the correct word or words.

1.   In 1818, the United States and Great Britain agreed to a ten-year joint occupation of _____.

2.   The Texans' hope for local self-government suffered a blow in 1834 when _____ made himself dictator of Mexico and abolished the federal system of government.

3.   The hero of San Jacinto and the first president of the Texas republic was _____.

4.   Americans traveled the Santa Fe Trail to exchange manufactured goods for Mexican goods as _____, _____, and _____.

5.   The Mormons were led to Utah by _____.

6. The first vice president to enter the White House upon the death of a president was _____.

7. The phrase *"manifest destiny"* was coined and popularized by journalist _____.

8. The most important single battle of the Mexican War came in April 1847 when General Winfield Scott led American forces to victory over the Mexican army at _____.

9. The most important factor in the transformation of the American economy during the 1840s and 1850s was the rise of the _____.

10. One and one-half million Irish left their homes for America between 1845 and 1854 when a series of blights hit the _____ crop, their principal source of subsistence.

TRUE/FALSE

Mark the following statements either T (True) or F (False).

_____1. The Webster-Ashburton Treaty helped resolve the conflict between the United States and Great Britain over the proper boundary line between Maine and Canada.

_____2. The Texas revolution can be accurately described as a fight for freedom after a long period of oppression.

_____3. The notion of manifest destiny coincided with the traditional Puritan belief that Americans were God's chosen people.

_____4. John C. Calhoun was successful in securing Senate approval of the treaty for the annexation of Texas.

_____5. The slogan "fifty-four forty or fight" indicated a willingness on the part of some Americans to go to war against Britain for control of British Columbia.

_____6. Nicholas Trist, negotiator of the Treaty of Guadalupe Hidalgo, was praised by President Polk for his efforts and acclaimed as a national hero.

_____7. Historian Norman Graebner contends that the major American objective of the Mexican War was acquisition of California ports to promote expanded American commerce on the Pacific.

_____8. By 1840, railroads had replaced canal boats as the major mode of freight transportation in the United States.

_____ 9. Peak periods of European immigration to the United States before the Civil War coincided very closely with times of domestic prosperity and high demand for labor.

_____ 10. By the 1850s, most factory workers were unionized, eagerly responding to appeals for solidarity along class lines.

MULTIPLE CHOICE

Circle the one alternative that *best* completes the statement or answers the question.

1. The "Young America" ideal came to be identified primarily with young Democrats who sought to purge their party of its traditional
   a. support for territorial expansion.
   b. fear of the expansion of commerce and industry.
   c. opposition to the institution of slavery.
   d. scorn for European literary models and themes.

2. In the 1820s and 1830s, California
   a. contained huge agricultural estates and large herds of cattle.
   b. contained a large portion of Indians who enjoyed a peaceful, profitable coexistence with Hispanic inhabitants.
   c. did not impress American visitors as a suitable site for expansion.
   d. all of the above

3. By 1829, American settlers in Texas had displeased Mexican authorities by
   a. refusing to emancipate their slaves.
   b. evading import duties on goods from the United States.
   c. failing to convert to Catholicism.
   d. all of the above

4. Which of the following events of the Texas revolution is true?
   a. Stephen F. Austin was imprisoned by Texans for his refusal to support revolution against Mexico.
   b. Juan Seguin led the Mexican attack on the Alamo.
   c. San Jacinto proved to be the decisive battle of the war due to the capture of Santa Anna by the Texan army.
   d. Texans executed an army of 350 Mexicans at Goliad in a desire to avenge Texan deaths at the Alamo.

5. During its years as the "Lone Star Republic," Texas
   a. attracted ever increasing numbers of American settlers with free grants of land.

b. suffered economic devastation following the Panic of 1837.

c. expanded trade with Mexico along the Santa Fe Trail.

d. received offers of financial aid from Britain in return for a pledge to abolish slavery.

6. The members of the Church of Jesus Christ of Latter Day Saints (Mormons)
   a. accepted the teachings of Brigham Young, founder of the church following a divine revelation in 1830.
   b. encountered hostility from neighboring "gentiles" because of their unorthodox beliefs and practices.
   c. abandoned the settlement of Nauvoo, Illinois because of economic bankruptcy.
   d. welcomed United States administration over the territory of Utah.

7. John Tyler could be characterized as a(n)
   a. antislavery advocate.
   b. "accidental" president, profoundly out of sympathy with the rest of his party.
   c. typical Whig who favored a strong national government in support of economic expansion.
   d. opponent to the annexation of Texas.

8. The major issue of the election of 1844 concerned
   a. recharter of the Bank of the United States.
   b. territorial expansion.
   c. abolition of slavery.
   d. nullification of the tariff.

9. Which of the following factors contributed to the defeat of Whig candidate Henry Clay in the election of 1844?
   a. A substantial number of Whigs defected from the party to support the independent candidacy of President John Tyler.
   b. Clay made a "gentleman's agreement" with Van Buren to avoid discussion of territorial expansion during the campaign.
   c. Clay failed to develop an adequate platform concerning proposals for economic recovery.
   d. Clay waffled on the issue of Texas annexation, losing the support of northern antislavery Whigs to the Liberty party.

10. A basic argument offered in support of Manifest Destiny was the idea that
    a. God favored American expansionism.
    b. American expansion would mean an extension of democracy.
    c. population growth necessitated territorial acquisitions.
    d. all of the above.

11. The United States and Great Britain agreed to
    a. a permanent joint occupation of Oregon in 1827.

b. allow the United States sole possession of Oregon up to the 54 40' parallel.

c. submit the dispute over Oregon to international arbitration in 1845.

d. a compromise arrangement splitting Oregon at the 49th parallel.

12. The U.S. war with Mexico was
   a. provoked by the Mexican slaughter of Texans at the Alamo.
   b. an unexpected and unwelcome development for the Polk administration.
   c. longer than expected because Mexico refused to make peace despite a succession of military defeats.
   d. prolonged by the attempt of the United States to capture control of all of Mexico.

13. Factors accounting for economic advances in the United States from 1830 to 1860 included all of the following *except*
   a. technological innovations and mass production techniques.
   b. rapidly increasing European immigration to the United States.
   c. a declining interest in agriculture.
   d. new techniques for the gathering and control of private capital.

14. Most European immigrants to America from 1840 to 1860 came from
   a. Ireland and Germany.
   b. Switzerland and the Netherlands.
   c. Sweden and Norway.
   d. Poland and Italy.

15. The invention of the telegraph by Samuel F. B. Morse
   a. resulted from the inventor's study of art.
   b. ensured a successful political career for the inventor.
   c. produced few economic changes for the country during the inventor's lifetime.
   d. helped create a stronger sense of connection among Americans.

THOUGHT QUESTIONS

To check your understanding of the key issues of this period, solve the following problems:

1. What factors lured Americans to the Far West - California, New Mexico, Oregon, and Utah - from the 1820s through the 1840s?

2. Were the Texans justified in revolting against Mexico in 1836?

3. Americans have seemingly always believed that their nation was blessed with a divine mission. Explain. How did that notion relate to the concept of Manifest Destiny? Does such a sense of mission persist today?

4. Define *imperialism.* Was the Mexican War an imperialistic venture by the United States? Why, given the expansionist spirit of the age, did the United States not seek to acquire all of Mexico?

5. What were the most important factors contributing to American economic growth from 1830 to 1860?

6. How did increasing industrialization affect the conditions and attitudes of the new working class?

CRITICAL THINKING QUESTIONS

Read the following selections: "The Great Nation of Futurity" (1845) by John L. O'Sullivan and "Testimony Before the Massachusetts Legislature" (1845) by the Female Labor Reform Association. Answer the questions following the reading selections.

John L. O'Sullivan, "The Great Nation of Futurity" (1845)

The American people having derived their origin from many other nations, and the Declaration of National Independence being entirely based on the great principle of human equality, these facts demonstrate at once our disconnected position as regards any other nation; that we have, in reality, but little connection with the past history of any of them and still less with all antiquity, its glories, or its crimes. On the contrary, our national birth was the beginning of a new history, the formation and progress of an untried political system, which separates us from the past and connects us with the future only; and so far as regards the entire development of the natural rights of man, in moral, political, and national life, we may confidently assume that our country is destined to be the great nation of futurity.

It is so destined, because the principle upon which a nation is organized fixes its destiny, and that of equality is perfect, is universal. It presides in all the operations of the physical world, and it is also the conscious law of the soul-the self-evident dictate of morality, which accurately defines the duty of man to man, and consequently man's rights as man. Besides, the truthful annals of any nation furnish abundant evidence that its happiness, its greatness, Its duratlon, were always proportionate to the democratlc equallty In Its system of government.

How many nations have had their decline and fall because the equal rights of the minority were trampled on by the despotism of the majority; or the interests of the many sacrificed to the aristocracy of the few; or the rights and interests of all given up to the monarchy of one? These three kinds of government have figured so frequently and so largely in the ages that have passed away that their history, through all time to come, can only furnish a resemblance. Like causes produce like effects, and the true philosopher of history will easily discern the principle of equality, or of privilege, working out its inevitable result. The first is regenerative, because it is natural and right; and the latter is destructive to society, because it is unnatural and wrong.

What friend of human liberty, civilization, and refinement can cast his view over the past history of the monarchies and aristocracies of antiquity, and not deplore that they ever existed? What philanthropist can contemplate the oppressions, the cruelties, and injustice inflicted by them on the masses of mankind and not turn with moral horror from the retrospect?

America is destined for better deeds. It is our unparalleled glory that we have no reminiscences of battlefields, but in defense of humanity, of the oppressed of all nations, of the rights of conscience, the rights of personal enfranchisement. Our annals describe no scenes of horrid carnage, where men were led on by hundreds of thousands to slay one another, dupes and victims to emperors, kings, nobles, demons in the human form called heroes. We have had patriots to defend our homes, our liberties, but no aspirants to crowns or thrones; nor have the American people ever suffered themselves to be led on by wicked ambition to depopulate the land, to spread desolation far and wide, that a human being might be placed on a seat of supremacy.

We have no interest in the scenes of antiquity, only as lessons of avoidance of nearly all their examples. The expansive future is our arena and for our history. We are entering on its untrodden space with the truths of God in our minds, beneficent objects in our hearts, and with a clear conscience unsullied by the past. We are the nation of human progress, and who will, what can, set limits to our onward march? Providence is with us, and no earthly power can. We point to the everlasting truth on the first page of our national declaration, and we proclaim to the millions of other lands that "the gates of hell"-the powers of aristocracy and monarchy-"shall not prevail against it."

The far-reaching, the boundless future, will be the era of American greatness. In its magnificent domain of space and time, the nation of many nations is destined to manifest to mankind the excellence of divine principles; to establish on earth the noblest temple ever dedicated to the worship of the Most High, the Sacred, and the True. Its floor shall be a hemisphere, roof the firmament of the star-studded heavens, and its congregation of Union of many Republics, comprising hundreds of happy millions, calling owning no man master, but governed by God's natural and moral law of equality, the law of brotherhood-of "peace and good will amongst men."

Yes, we are the nation of progress, of individual freedom, of universal enfranchisement. Equality of rights is the cynosure of our union of states, the grand exemplar of the correlative equality of individuals; and, while truth sheds its effulgence, we cannot retrograde without dissolving the one and subverting the other. We must onward to the fulfillment of our mission-to the entire development of the principle of our organization-freedom of conscience, freedom of person, freedom of trade and business pursuits, universality of freedom and equality. This is our high destiny, and in nature's eternal, inevitable decree of cause and effect we must accomplish it. All this will be our future history, to establish on earth the moral dignity and salvation of man-the immutable truth and beneficence of God. For this blessed mission to the nations of the world,

which are shut out from the lifegiving light of truth, has America been chosen; and her high example shall smite unto death the tyranny of kings, hierarchs, and oligarchs and carry the glad tidings of peace and good will where myriads now endure in existence scarcely more enviable than that of beasts of the field. Who, then, can doubt that our country is destined to be the great nation of futurity?

Female Labor Reform Association, *Testimony Before the Massachusetts Legislature* (1845)

The first petitioner who testified was Eliza R. Hemmingway. She had worked 2 years and 9 months in the Lowell Factories; 2 years in the Middlesex, and 9 months in the Hamilton Corporations. Her employment is weaving—works by the piece. The Hamilton Mill manufactures cotton fabrics. The Middlesex, woolen fabrics. She is now at work in the Middlesex Mills, and attends one loom. Her wages average from $16 to $23 a month exclusive of board. She complained of the hours for labor being too many, and the time for meals too limited. In the summer season, the work is commenced at 5 o'clock, a.m., and continued till 7 o'clock, p.m., with half an hour for breakfast and three-quarters of an hour for dinner. During eight months of the year, but half an hour is allowed for dinner. The air in the room she considered not to be wholesome. There were 293 small lamps and 61 large lamps lighted in the room in which she worked, when evening work is required. These lamps are also lighted sometimes in the morning. About 130 females, 11 men, and 12 children (between the ages of 11 and 14) work in the room with her. She thought the children enjoyed about as good health as children generally do. The children work but 9 months about of 12. The other 3 months they must attend school. Thinks that there is no day when there are less than six of the females out of the mill from sickness. Has known as many as thirty. She, herself, is out quite often, on account of sickness. There was more sickness in the Summer than in Winter months; though in the Summer, lamps are not lighted. She thought there was a general desire among the females to work but ten hours, regardless of pay. Most of the girls are from the country, who work in the Lowell Mills. The average time there is about three years. She knew one girl who had worked there 14 years. Her health was poor when she left. Miss Hemmingway said her health was better where she now worked, than it was when she worked on the Hamilton Corporation.

She knew of one girl who last winter went into the mill at half past 4 o'clock, a.m., and worked til half past 7 o'clock p.m. She did so to make more money. She earned from $25 to $30 per month. There is always a large number of girls at the gate wishing to get in before the bell rings. On the Middlesex Corporation one-fourth part of the females go into the mills before they are obliged to. They do this to make more wages. A large number come to Lowell and work in the mills to assist their husbands to pay for their farms. The moral character of the operatives is good. There was only one American female in the room with her who could not write her name.

Miss Sarah G. Bagley said she had worked in the Lowell Mills eight years and a half—six years and a half on the Hamilton Corporation, and two years on the Middlesex. She is a weaver, and works by the piece. She worked in the mills three years before her health began to fail. She is a native of New Hampshire, and went home six weeks during the summer. Last year she was out of the mill a third of the time. She thinks the health of the operatives is not so good as the health of females who do housework or millinery business. The chief evil, so far as health is concerned, is the shortness of time allowed for meals. The next evil is the length of time employed—not giving them time to cultivate their minds. She spoke of the high moral and intellectual character of the girls. That many were engaged as teachers in the Sunday schools. That many attended the lectures of the Lowell Institute; and she thought, if more time was allowed, that more lectures would be given and more girls attend. She thought that the girls generally were favorable to the ten hour system. She had presented a petition, same as the one before the Committee, to 132 girls, most of whom said that they would prefer to work but ten hours. In a pecuniary point of view, it would be better, as their health would be improved. They would have more time for sewing. Their intellectual, moral, and religious habits would also be benefited by the change.

Miss Bagley said, in addition to her labor in the mills, she had kept evening school during the winter months, for four years, and thought that this extra labor must have injured her health.

1.   What "evidence" does O'Sullivan use to justify his claim that the United States is "the great nation of futurity"?

2.   What groups of people does O'Sullivan seemingly disregard when he proclaims the United States as "the nation of progress, of individual freedom, of universal enfranchisement"?

3.   Describe the working conditions for female workers in the factories of Lowell, Massachusetts during the 1840s.

4.   What particular factory conditions does Sarah Bagley cite as detrimental to the health and well-being of female workers?

5.   Why do you think the testimony of the Lowell factory women achieved such limited results at the time?

CHAPTER 13

MASTERS AND SLAVES

SUMMARY

In the South in the first half of the nineteenth century, an elite group of whites dominated the society and made profits on the labor of black slaves, who nonetheless were able to develop a rich culture of their own.

SLAVERY AND THE SOUTHERN ECONOMY

The staple crop cotton and the labor of slaves dominated the economy of the lower South prior to the Civil War. During this time, however, the upper South sold slaves and diversified their agriculture.

Economic Adjustments in the Upper South

As tobacco farming became less important, the states of Virginia, Maryland, and Kentucky raised other crops and began infant industries.

The Rise of the Cotton Kingdom

The invention of the cotton gin and the introduction of "short-staple" cotton to the lower South made cotton the single most important export and the most profitable business in the United States.

Slavery and Industrialization

Although many Southerners considered methods to diversify and industrialize their region, most investment dollars went into cotton.

The "Profitability" Issue

The cotton/slavery system profited the planter directly, but it probably limited the South's development.

THE SLAVE HOLDING ECONOMY

Plantation culture was clearly dominated by an elite class of Slave holding planters.

Planters and Slaves

Hardworking business people, they treated their slaves in a manner consistent with a desire to maximize profits.

The World of the Plain Folk

Below this elite, several classes of whites scratched out a living, some with, but most without the aid of slaves.

A Closed Mind and a Closed Society
After 1831, the elites, threatened by the slightest challenge to slavery, increasingly used nearly any means to end discussion or debate on the subject.

The Black Experience Under Slavery
Slaves, struggling against tremendous odds, managed to create a full, rich culture.

Forms of Slave Resistance
Because violence and escape were not often successful strategies, African-American slaves resisted passively or by sabotage and thus maintained their self-respect.

The Struggles of Free Blacks
Free blacks from both the North and the South faced many legal restrictions, and generally sympathized with the slaves.

African-American Religion
Slaves established their own distinctive religion which became a foundation of their unique culture.

The Slave Family
Strong family ties supported the individual slave when facing an essentially hostile white culture.

LEARNING OBJECTIVES

After mastering this chapter, you should be able to

1. Compare and contrast the role of slavery in the Chesapeake with the Deep South.

2. Analyze the effects of short-staple cotton and the cotton gin on the South.

3. Explain the arguments and issues surrounding the profitability and efficiency of slavery.

4. Discuss the relevant statistics about slave ownership in the South.

5. Describe the daily lives of a typical planter, a small slave holder, a yeoman farmer and a mountaineer.

6. List the arguments for and against slavery offered by Southerners.

7. Explain the various methods used by slaves to resist the oppression of their masters.

8. Discuss the life of free blacks in the North and the South during the days of slavery.

9. Compare black religion with its white Protestant counterparts.

10. Describe the main features of black slave family life.

GLOSSARY

To build your social science vocabulary, familiarize yourself with the following terms:

1. **oppressor**   who one burdens another with unjust, unreasonable, or cruel hardships ". . . divine wrath was about to be visited upon the white oppressor".

2. **abolitionism**   the principle favoring an immediate end to slavery. ". . . 1831 also saw the emergence of a more militant northern abolitionism".

3. **sectionalism**   the principle that politics should be based on arcs or districts with certain common geographic features. ". . . the growth of a more militant sectionalism . . . inspired threats to secede . . .".

4. **staple**   a crop grown regularly for marketing at a profit. ". . . landowners who sought to profit from expanding market opportunities by raising staple crops on a large scale".

5. **caste**   a distinct hereditary class. "...caste--inherited advantages or disadvantages associated with racial ancestry."

6. **paternalistic**   pertaining to treatment of one by another in a fatherly fashion. ". . . liked to think of themselves as kindly and paternalistic".

7. **patriarchal**   of or belonging to the father or father-like ruler of a group. "Often they referred to their slaves as if they were members of an extended patriarchal family."

8. **Spartan**   unadorned by luxuries. ". . . life was relatively Spartan".

9. **deportation**   exile, banishment, or removal of an undesirable from a country. ". . . program of gradual, voluntary emancipation accompanied deportation of the freedmen".

10. **regime**   a political system; a manner of management, government, or control. ". . . they needed some kind of . . . special regime equivalent to the asylums . . .".

11. **socialism**   a type of economic organization with central planning and some government ownership. "Worker insecurity . . . led inevitably to strikes, bitter class conflicts, and the rise of socialism . . .".

12. **armories**   a place where weapons are kept. ". . . conspiracy . . . to seize local armories . . ."

13. **Jacobins**   violent revolutionaries. "...the blacks were the Jacobins of the country."

14. **allegory**   a narration with personification, symbolism and an extended or continued metaphor.

IDENTIFICATION

Briefly identify the meaning and significance of the following terms.

1. Nat Turner _____

_____

2. Short-Staple Cotton _____

_____

3. Cotton Gin _____

_____

4. Hinton R. Helper _____

_____

5. American Colonization Society _____

_____

6. George Fitzhugh _____

_____

7. Cassius M. Clay _____

_____

8. Second Seminole War _____

_____

9. David Walker _____

_____

10. Harriet Tubman _____

_____

MATCHING

A. Match the following people with the appropriate description.

1. Hinton R. Helper   **a.** wrote a novel about a brutal slave owner named Simon Legree

2. George Fitzhugh   **b.** believed that his fellow white Southerners were victims of slavery and should fight against it

3. Cassius M. Clay   **c.** was a brave southern abolitionist from Kentucky

4. Frederick Douglass   **d.** defended slavery by attacking the wage labor system

5. Harriet Beecher Stowe   **e.** was probably the richest planter of the 1850s

                                         f. was an escaped slave who founded the newspaper *North Star*

B. Match the following people with the appropriate description.

1. Denmark Vesey   **a.** went into the South to help runaway slaves

2. David Walker   **b.** mobilized a large number of slaves in an unsuccessful rebellion in Richmond, Virginia

3. Harriet Tubman   **c.** was an escaped slave who became an orator for an antislavery organization

4. Reverend Richard   **d.** wrote a pamphlet denouncing slavery and calling for

a revolt

5. Gabriel Prosser   e. organized the African Methodist Episcopal church

           f. led an unsuccessful slave revolt in Charleston, South Carolina

COMPLETION

Answer the question or complete the statement by filling in the blanks with the correct word or words.

1. The leader of a violent slave rebellion in Virginia on August 22, 1831, was

   _____.

2. The original plantation crop of the upper South in colonial days was _____.

3. The most important domestic economic interest and the most valuable single export for the United States on the eve of the Civil War was _____.

4. Some Southerners were fans of the romantic cult of chivalry as described in the novels of

   _____.

5. The _____ favored gradual emancipation and deportation of blacks.

6. Lack of _____ was primarily responsible for the low standard of living of southern whites.

7. Proslavery advocates argued that the institution was sanctioned by the authority of the

   _____.

8. Many African-American fugitives fought along with the Indians in _____.

9. A network to assist escaped slaves in finding their way to freedom was called the

   _____

10. _____ was an ex-slave who made dangerous raids into the South to help runaway slaves.

TRUE/FALSE

Mark the following statements either T (True) or F (False).

_____ 1. From colonial days until the Civil War growing cotton was the most important enterprise in Tidewater Virginia and Maryland.

_____ 2. Although cotton was highly profitable, its profits were not widely distributed among Southerners.

_____ 3. The diversified economy of the South made slavery unprofitable.

_____ 4. Aside from the existence of slavery, the South was not a stratified society.

_____ 5. A substantial majority of southern whites owned slaves.

_____ 6. Most great planters were self-made men of wealth.

_____ 7. Most southern yeomen disliked both abolitionists and wealthy planters.

_____ 8. Black churches were simply copies of white Protestant churches.

_____ 9. The African-American family was an extremely important and strong institution for slaves.

_____ 10. Free blacks were treated as essentially equal to whites.

MULTIPLE CHOICE

Circle the one alternative that *best* completes the statement or answers the question.

1. By the 1850s the economy of the Deep South was
   a. based on a variety of agricultural crops mixed with light industry.
   b. growing because of the phenomenon of a long period of steady cotton prices.
   c. dependent upon the sale and export of short-staple cotton.
   d. declining because of the constant panics and bank failures of the 1840s.

2. The profits from cotton were mostly used to
   a. diversify southern agriculture.
   b. industrialize southern cities.
   c. phase out slavery slowly.

    d. support plantations and buy more slaves and land.

3.   In the Chesapeake or tidewater areas of Virginia and Maryland, farmers
    a. shifted from tobacco to wheat after the Revolution.
    b. continued growing tobacco but with fewer slaves.
    c. grew large amounts of both tobacco and cotton until the Civil War.
    d. actually grew more cotton than did farmers in the Deep South.

4.   Most southern whites
    a. owned between one and five slaves.
    b. were simple yeoman farmers.
    c. actually opposed the institution of slavery.
    d. were poor mountain folk surviving on the sale of corn whiskey.

5.   In their day-to-day activities most large plantation owners
    a. had much leisure time.
    b. were shrewd, hardworking businesspeople.
    c. spent their time drinking, gambling, and dueling.
    d. spent their cotton profits investing in diverse enterprises.

6.   The influential planters of the South
    a. added to their profits by selling the offspring of their slaves.
    b. often sold slaves and land to increase their net worth.
    c. found it in their own self-interest to give their slaves at least a minimum level of
       substinence so that they would be fit enough to work.
    d. were never close or friendly with a slave.

7.   The substantial class of southern white yeoman farmers was
    a. composed of degraded, shiftless, "poor white" squatters.
    b. concentrated in the rich, alluvial river bottoms of the South.
    c. composed of Jacksonian's who wanted to abolish slavery.
    d. composed of those who opposed both northern abolitionists and southern aristocrats.

8.   Most Southerners believed that
    a. slavery was essentially evil but necessary.
    b. slavery provided benefits to all involved, including the slaves.
    c. emancipation was inevitable.
    d. the slaves should live as close to the patterns of their African tribal life as possible.

9.   Free blacks in the North and the South
    a. generally opposed slavery.
    b. were essentially equal to whites.
    c. had political rights but struggled against economic deprivation.

    d. had no sympathy for slaves.

10. Free blacks in the North and white abolitionists
    a. agreed on goals and methods.
    b. conflicted over leadership in antislave organizations.
    c. often intermarried.
    d. agreed on a colonization and deportation program.

11. Violent slave revolts were
    a. uncommon throughout the South.
    b. common before 1831.
    c. common after 1831.
    d. uncommon in the upper South but frequent in the Deep South.

12. Which of the following does *not* explain why non-Slave holding whites supported slavery?
    a. They felt that slavery kept African Americans "in their place."
    b. They had respect and deference for the planters.
    c. They aspired to be planters and own slaves.
    d. They feared and disliked African Americans.

13. Regarding the debate over slavery, the southern white elite
    a. suppressed almost all opposition arguments with law, violence, and social pressure.
    b. confidently encouraged the debate.
    c. suppressed only obviously harmful, potentially dangerous arguments.
    d. did not resort to religious arguments to defend slavery.

14. The underground railroad aided
    a. escaped slaves and was a largely privately owned enterprise.
    b. escaped slaves and was a largely white-owned enterprise.
    c. whites in recovering runaway slaves.
    d. commuters in large urban communities.

15. The African-American family during slavery was
    a. loosely organized and resulted in much promiscuity.
    b. monogamous and stable.
    c. opposed to premarital sex.
    d. stable but polygamous.

THOUGHT QUESTIONS

To check your understanding of the key issues of this period, consider the following problems.

1. To what extent was it true that northern laborers were in as bad a condition as southern slaves?

2. Why were the yeoman farmers not opposed to slavery, but instead vigorously in support of it?

3. Was the South justified in suppressing free speech on the issue of slavery?

4. How democratic was the prewar South?

5. Compare the reaction of slaves to oppression with examples of passive resistance.

6. In what ways was the African-American family experience more loving and affectionate than that of its white counterpart?

CRITICAL THINKING EXERCISES

Using the material in Chapter 13 of the text and the Primary Sources provided below, please answer the questions which follow the Documents.

Frederick Douglass, "Whipping slaves"
Peter Randolph, "Culture and Religion in the Quarters"

Frederick Douglass, Whipping Slaves

It would astonish one, unaccustomed to a slaveholding life, to see with what wonderful ease a slaveholder can find things of which to make occasion to whip a slave. A mere look, word, or motion—a mistake, accident, or want of power—are all matters for which a slave may be whipped at any time. Does a slave look dissatisfied? It is said, he has the devil in him, and it must be whipped out. Does he speak loudly when spoken to by his master? Then he is getting high-minded, and should be taken down a button-hole lower. Does he forget to pull off his hat at the approach of a white person? Then he is wanting in reverence, and should be whipped for it. Does he ever venture to vindicate his conduct, when censured for it? Then he is guilty of impudence—one of the greatest crimes of which a slave can be guilty. Does he ever venture to suggest a different mode of doing things from that pointed out by his master? He is indeed presumptous, and getting above himself; and nothing less than a flogging will do for him. Does he, while plowing, break a plough—or, while hoeing, break a hoe? It is owing to his carelessness, and for it a slave must always be whipped.

Peter Randolph, Culture and Religion in the Quarters

Many say the Negroes receive religious education—that Sabbath worship is instituted for them as for others, and were it not for slavery, they would die in their sins—that really, the institution of slavery is a benevolent missionary enterprise. Yes, they are preached to, and I will give my readers some faint glimpses of these preachers, and their doctrines and practices. . . . The prominent preaching to the slave is, "'Servants, obey your masters.' Do not steal or lie, for this is very wrong. Such conduct is sinning against the Holy Ghost, and is base ingratitude to your kind masters, who feed, clothe, and protect you." All Gospel, my readers! It is great policy to build a church for the "dear slave," and allow him the wondrous privilige of such holy instruction! . . .
On the Sabbath, after doing their morning work, and breakfast over (such as it was), that portion of the slaves who belong to the church ask of the overseer permission to attend meeting. If he is in the mood to grant their request,

he writes them a pass, as follows: "Permit the bearer to pass and repass to __, this evening, unmolested." Should a pass not be granted, the slave lies down, and sleeps for the day—the only way to drown his sorrow and disappointment.

Others of the slaves, who do not belong to the church, spend their Sabbath in playing with marbles, and other games, for each other's food, etc. Some occupy the time in dancing to the music of the banjo, made out of a large gourd. This is continued till the after part of the day, when they separate, and gather wood for their log-cabin fires for the ensuing week.

Not being allowed to hold meetings on the plantation, the slaves assemble in the swamps, out of reach of the patrols. They have an understanding among themselves as to the time and place of getting together. This is often done by the first one arriving breaking from the trees, and bending them in the direction of the selected spot. Arrangements are then made for conducting the exercises. They first ask each other how they feel, the state of their minds, etc. The male members then select a certain space, in separate groups, for their division of the meeting. Preaching in order, by the brethren; then praying and singing all round, until they generally feel quite happy. The speaker usually commences by calling himself unworthy, and talks very slowly, until, feeling the spirit, he grows excited, and in a short time, there fall to the ground twenty or thirty men and women under its influence. Enlightened people call it excitement; but I wish the same was felt by everybody, so far as they are sincere.

The slave forgets all his sufferings, except to remind others of the trials during the past week, exclaiming: "Thank God, I shall not live here always!" Then they pass from one to another, shaking hands, and bidding each other farewell, promising, should they meet no more on earth, to strive and meet in heaven, where all is joy, happiness, and liberty. As they separate, they sing a parting hymn of praise.

Sometimes the slaves meet in an old log-cabin, when they find it necessary to keep a watch. If discovered, they escape, if possible; but those who are caught often get whipped. Some are willing to be punished thus for Jesus' sake. Most of the songs used in worship are composed by the slaves themselves, and describe their own sufferings.

1. Explain the reasons for the whipping of slaves as described by Douglass. What were the psychological effects of the beatings on the slave and on those observing?

2. According to your text, what role did religion play in "buffering" slaves against the cruelty of whipping?

3. According to your text, what role did the family play in protecting slaves against the effects of whipping?

4. According to Peter Randolph, how did slaves forge an "invisible institution" to help them endure slavery?

5. Are the views of your text and Randolph consistent in their description of the role played by religion in helping slaves face their hostile environment?

CHAPTER 14

THE SECTIONAL CRISIS

SUMMARY

The caning of Senator Charles Sumner of Massachusetts by Representative Preston Brooks of South Carolina demonstrated the growing sectional conflict of the 1850s and foreshadowed the violence on the battlefield between armies of the North and the South.

The Compromise of 1850
The Problem of Slavery in the Mexican Cession
The Constitution gave the federal government the right to abolish the international slave trade, but no power to regulate or destroy the institution of slavery where it already existed. Nonetheless, Congress had prevented the extension of slavery to certain territories in the Missouri Compromise of 1820. So long as both the free North and the slave South had some opportunities for expansion, compromise had been possible.

The Wilmot Proviso Launches the Free-Soil Movement
The Wilmot Proviso of 1846 proposed to ban African Americans, whether slave or free, from any territory acquired from the Mexican War. This blend of racist and antislavery sentiments appealed to many Northerners anxious to preserve new lands for free whites. Congress ultimately rejected both the proviso as well as the extreme alternative of allowing slavery in all of the Mexican cession.

Squatter Sovereignty and the Election of 1848
Rejecting the idea of an extension of the Missouri Compromise line as too beneficial to southern interests, many Northerners supported the idea of "squatter" or "popular sovereignty," leaving the question of slavery in a territory to the actual settlers. In the election of 1848, Whig Zachary Taylor, avoiding a stand but promising no executive interference with congressional legislation, defeated two challengers: Democrat Lewis Cass who urged "popular sovereignty," and Free-Soiler Martin Van Buren who favored the Wilmot Proviso.

Taylor Takes Charge
President Taylor proposed admitting California and New Mexico directly as states, bypassing territorial status and the arguments over slavery. The possibility, however, that only free states would emerge from the Mexican cession provoked southern resistance and talk of secession.

Forging a Compromise
Although Taylor resisted compromise until his death, his successor Millard Fillmore supported a series of resolutions known as the Compromise of 1850. Voting on the measures separately, members of Congress agreed to admit California as a free state, organize the territories of New

Mexico and Utah on the basis of popular sovereignty, retract the borders of Texas in return for assumption of the state's debt, and abolish the slave trade in the District of Columbia. The most controversial provision created a strong Fugitive Slave Law, denying suspected runaways any rights of self-defense, and requiring Northerners to enforce slavery.

Political Upheaval 1852-1856
The Party System in Crisis
The Compromise of 1850 robbed the political parties of distinctive appeals and contributed to voter apathy and disenchantment. Although a colorless candidate, Democrat Franklin Pierce won the election of 1852 over Winfield Scott, the candidate of a Whig party which was on the verge of collapse from internal divisions.

The Kansas-Nebraska Act Raises a Storm
In 1854, Democratic Senator Stephen Douglas, anxious to expand American settlement and commerce across the northern plains while promoting his own presidential ambitions, pushed an act through Congress organizing the territories of Kansas and Nebraska on the basis of popular sovereignty. This repeal of the long-standing Missouri Compromise, along with publication of the "Ostend Manifesto" urging the United States acquisition of Cuba, convinced an increasing number of Northerners that Pierce's Democratic administration was dominated by pro-southern sympathizers, if not conspirators.

An Appeal to Nativism: The Know-Nothing Episode
Appearing after the demise of the Whig party, the American, or Know-Nothing party appealed to the anti-immigrant sentiments of American citizens who feared and resented the heavy influx of European immigrants. Although enjoying temporary success, the Know-Nothing party soon lost influence and numbers because of inexperienced leaders, a lack of cohesion, and a failure to address the nation's major problems.

Kansas and the Rise of the Republicans
Formed in protest of the Kansas-Nebraska Act, the Republican party adopted a firm position opposing any further extension of slavery. Election fraud and violence in Kansas discredited the principle of popular sovereignty and strengthened Republican appeal in the North.

Sectional Division in the Election of 1856
In 1856, Democrat James Buchanan won the presidency over Republican John C. Frémont and Know-Nothing candidate Millard Fillmore. National unity was temporarily maintained, but the overwhelmingly sectional Republican party showed surprising strength for a fledgling organization in sweeping the upper North.

The House Divided, 1857-1860
Cultural Sectionalism

187

Before the actual political division of the nation occurred, American religious and literary leaders split into opposing camps. Southern intellectuals reacted defensively to outside criticism and rallied to the idea of southern nationalism.

The Dred Scott Case

In a controversial case, the Supreme Court ruled that Dred Scott was a slave and that African Americans (whether slave or free) had no rights as citizens. Further, the Court declared the Missouri Compromise unconstitutional, denying that Congress had any power to prohibit slavery in the territories. Rather than resolve disputes over the slavery question, the decision intensified sectional discord.

The Lecompton Constitution

Proslavery forces in Kansas resorted to electoral fraud to secure a convention to draft a slave state constitution. When finally submitted to a fair vote by the residents of Kansas in 1858, the Lecompton Constitution was overwhelmingly rejected.

Debating the Morality of Slavery

In the 1858 Illinois Senate race, Republican Abraham Lincoln asked Democrat Stephen Douglas how he could reconcile the idea of popular sovereignty with the Dred Scott decision. Douglas offered the "Freeport Doctrine," a suggestion that territories could dissuade slaveholders from moving in by providing no supportive legislation for slavery. Coupled with his stand against the Lecompton Constitution, Douglas's Freeport Doctrine guaranteed loss of southern support for his presidential bid.

The South's Crisis of Fear

Two events of 1859-1860 intensified southern fears of Republican intentions: northern expressions of sympathy at the execution of crazed abolitionist John Brown; and public endorsement by a prominent Republican politician of Hinton Rowan Helper's *Impending Crisis of the South*. The objective of John Brown's raid on the federal arsenal at Harpers Ferry, Virginia, had been to equip a slave army and Helper's book condemned slavery on economic grounds, urging lower-class whites of the South to unite against planter domination and abolish slavery.

The Election of 1860

Unable to agree on a platform or candidate in 1860, the Democrats split: a northern wing nominated Stephen Douglas and endorsed popular sovereignty, and a southern wing nominated John C. Breckinridge and demanded federal protection of slavery in the territories. Border state conservatives formed the Constitutional Union party and nominated John Bell of Tennessee. Republicans nominated Abraham Lincoln on a Free-Soil position and a broad economic platform. Although he won only 40 percent of the popular vote, Lincoln swept the North for a majority of the electoral votes and election as president. Political leaders of the lower South immediately launched the movement for secession.

Explaining the Crisis

Rather than arising out of the mistakes of irresponsible politicians or of irreconcilable economic views, southern secession was prompted by profound ideological differences between the North and South over the morality and utility of slavery.

LEARNING OBJECTIVES

After mastering this chapter, you should be able to:

1. List and analyze the following suggestions made to solve the problem of extending slavery to new territories after the Mexican War: (a) Wilmot Proviso, (b) extension of the Missouri Compromise line, (c) squatter sovereignty, and (d) President Taylor's solution.

2. Identify the candidates and explain the platforms and outcomes of the presidential elections from 1848 to 1860.

3. Describe the series of resolutions that resulted in the Compromise of 1850.

4. Explain the motivations for and the consequences of the Kansas-Nebraska Act of 1854.

5. Contrast the intent and results of the Ostend Manifesto.

6. Analyze the reasons for shifting political alignments in this era, specifically: (a) the rise and fall of the Free-Soil party, (b) the disintegration of the Whig party, (c) the appearance and brief success of the Know-Nothing party, and (d) the emergence and victory of the Republican party.

7. Trace the development of attempts to win Kansas by the proslavery and antislavery forces, noting specifically: (a) the "sack of Lawrence," (b) the role of John Brown, and (c) the Lecompton Constitution.

8. Discuss the effects of social and cultural sectionalism in preparing the path for southern secession.

9. Discuss the background, final decision, criticisms, and implications of the *Dred Scott* case of 1857.

10. Contrast the positions taken by Republican Abraham Lincoln and Democrat Stephen Douglas in the debates held for the Illinois Senate race of 1858.

11. Explain the intensification of southern fears regarding a possible Republican victory in the election of 1860, especially in light of John Brown's 1859 raid on Harpers Ferry, Virginia and the 1860 contest for Speaker of the House.

12. Contrast the various historical interpretations that have been advanced to explain the reasons for southern secession.

GLOSSARY

To build your social science vocabulary, familiarize yourself with the following terms:

1. **lionized** treated as an object of great interest or importance. "Brooks, denounced in the North as a bully, was lionized by his fellow Southerners."

2. **pacificator** peacemaker; appeaser. "Hoping that he could again play the role of the 'great pacificator,' Henry Clay of Kentucky offered a series of resolutions . . . "

3. **omnibus** a type of bill relating to or providing for many things at once. "a decision was made to abandon the omnibus strategy in favor of a series of measures that could be voted on separately."

4. **fugitive** runaway; escapee. "Southerners demanded strict northern adherence to the compromise, especially to the Fugitive Slave Law . . ."

5. **extradition** the surrender of an alleged criminal by one state or authority to another having jurisdiction to try the charge. "an antislavery mob . . . tried to free fugitive Anthony Burns from the courthouse where his extradition hearing was to take place."

6. **consensus** general agreement or solidarity in sentiment or belief. "The consensus of 1852 meant that the parties had to find other issues on which to base their distinctive appeals."

7. **manifesto** a public declaration of intentions, views, or motives. "A manifesto of 'independent Democrats' denounced the bill . . ."

8. **nativism** policy of favoring native inhabitants as opposed to immigrants. "Political nativism first emerged during the 1840s . . ."

9. **evangelical** Christian emphasizing salvation by faith through personal conversion, the authority of Scripture, and the importance of preaching as contrasted with ritual. "the party showed a clear commitment to the values of native-born evangelical Protestants."

10. **apologists** those who speak or write in defense of a particular faith, cause, or institution. "most southern church leaders . . . became influential apologists for the southern way of life."

11. **polemics** aggressive attacks on, or refutations of, the opinions or principles of another. "Southern men of letters . . . wrote proslavery polemics."

12. **cavaliers** gentlemen; aristocrats. "The notion that planter 'cavaliers' were superior to money-grubbing Yankees was the message . . . "

13. **arbiter** a person or agency with power to decide a dispute. "the Court under Chief Justice John Marshall effectively claimed the role of final arbiter of constitutional questions."

14. **gerrymandered** divided a territory into election districts so as to give one political party a majority. "the success of the plan required a rigged, gerrymandered election for convention delegates."

15. **impasse** a predicament or deadlock offering no obvious escape. "The impasse over the speakership was thus resolved . . ."

IDENTIFICATION

Briefly identify the meaning and significance of the following terms:

1. Preston Brooks_____

_____

2. Squatter Sovereignty_____

_____

3. Fugitive Slave Law _____

_____

4. Franklin Pierce_____

_____

5. Kansas-Nebraska Act_____

_____

6. Know-Nothings _____

_____

7. John Brown _____

_____

8. James Buchanan _____

_____

9. *Dred Scott* v. *Sanford* _____

_____

10. Abraham Lincoln _____

_____

MATCHING

A. Match the following unsuccessful presidential candidates with the appropriate description:

1. Martin Van Buren

2. Winfield Scott

3. John C. Frémont

4. John Bell

5. John Breckinridge

a. nominated by southern Democrats on a platform of federal protection for slavery in the territories

b. senator from Michigan who formulated the principle of "popular sovereignty"; nominated by the Democrats in 1848

c. military hero in the Mexican War who ran as the last candidate of the Whig party

d. nominee of the Constitutional Union party who ran on a platform of sectional compromise

e. former president who ran as the first candidate of the Free-Soil party

f. famed explorer of the West who ran as the first candidate of the Republican party

192

B. Match the following policy statements or publications with the appropriate description:

1. "Ostend Manifesto"

    a. enormously successful novel condemning slavery as a threat to the family and morality that was written by a woman

2. *Uncle Tom's Cabin*

    b. statement offered by Stephen Douglas providing territories with plan to prevent immigration of slaveholders

3. Compromise of 1850

    c. a memorandum drawn up by American ministers in Europe urging U.S. acquisition of Cuba

4. "Freeport Doctrine"

    d. proslavery novel glorifying southern civilization and sneering at that of the North

5. *The Impending Crisis of the South*

    e. a series of measures intended to reduce tensions between the North and the South by providing mutual concessions on a range of divisive issues

    f. document urging lower-class southern whites to resist planter dominance and abolish slavery in their own best interests

COMPLETION

Answer the question or complete the statement by filling in the blanks with the correct word or words.

1. In 1844, radical abolitionist _____ publicly burned a copy of the Constitution, condemning it as "a covenant with death, an agreement with hell."

2. The first significant effort to create a broadly based sectional party in opposition to the extension of slavery came with the founding of the_____ party.

3. Serving once again as the "great pacificator," Senator _____ of Kentucky offered a series of resolutions in 1850 meant to restore sectional harmony.

4. Presidential opposition to the Compromise of 1850 was broken when _____ succeeded to the White House upon the death of Zachary Taylor.

5. The first territorial elections in Kansas were controlled by proslavery settlers, aided by thousands of residents from _____ who crossed the border to vote illegally.

6. Proslavery adherents touched off a small-scale civil war in Kansas with a raid on the free-state capital, portrayed by northern propagandists as "the sack of _____."

7. The turmoil in Kansas associated with attempts to implement popular sovereignty contributed to the increased popularity of the _____ party in the North.

8. President Buchanan was denounced by Republicans as a _____, a prosouthern Democrat.

9. The raid by fervent abolitionist John Brown on the federal arsenal and armory in _____, _____, touched off a wave of fear, repression, and mobilization in the South.

10. Republicans rejected Senator _____ of New York as their presidential candidate in 1860 because of his radical positions against slavery and nativism.

TRUE/FALSE

Mark the following statements either T (True) or F (False).

_____1. Because of his discourteous behavior in the Senate, Charles Sumner was not reelected in his home state of Massachusetts.

_____2. Northerners rejected extension of the Missouri Compromise line because it would have opened most of the land in the Mexican Cession to slavery.

_____3. Because of a sustained business depression, economic issues preoccupied voters in the election of 1852.

_____4. Stephen Douglas hoped the Kansas-Nebraska Act would rekindle the spirit of Manifest Destiny and strengthen his prospects as a presidential candidate.

_____5. The "sack of Lawrence," a raid by pro-slavery adherents on the free-state captial of Kansas touched off a small scale civil war in that territory during the summer of 1856.

_____6. By transforming political questions into moral issues, northern and southern religious leaders enhanced the chances for compromise.

_____7.   Although Dred Scott lost his case before the Supreme Court, a subsequent master freed him and his wife, Harriet.

_____8.   Abraham Lincoln presented himself in his political campaign as an abolitionist, committed to the emancipation of slaves throughout the United States.

_____9.   Stephen Douglas enjoyed widespread southern approval until his "Freeport Doctrine" suddenly alienated supporters in that section.

_____10. The proportion of slave-owning white families in the South continued to increase through the decade of the 1850s.

MULTIPLE CHOICE

Circle the one alternative that *best* completes the statement or answers the question.

1.   During the 1840s, a majority of Northerners
     a. converted to the cause of gradual abolition of slavery.
     b. rejected the law of the land in favor of an immediate "higher law" prohibiting human bondage.
     c. disliked slavery, but were reluctant to accept large numbers of blacks as equal and free citizens.
     d. viewed slavery as a useful, desirable labor system.

2.   Northern Democrats were upset at the seeming policy of the Polk administration to
     a. increase tariffs.
     b. provide federal funds for the improvement of rivers and harbors.
     c. seek control of "all of Oregon."
     d. favor southern interests.

3.   Passage of the Wilmot Proviso of 1846 would have
     a. prohibited slavery in any territory acquired from the Mexican War.
     b. allowed the extension of slavery into any territory acquired from the Mexican War.
     c. extended the Missouri Compromise line to the Pacific.
     d. established "popular sovereignty" as the means for any future expansion of slavery.

4.   The principle of "popular sovereignty"
     a. would leave the determination of the status of slavery in a territory to the actual settlers.
     b. was interpreted differently in the North and the South.
     c. led to disruption and violence in the settlement of Kansas.
     d. all of the above.

5. Which of the following statements concerning the election of 1848 is true?
   a. Whig candidate Zachary Taylor proposed equal rights for slaveholders in federal territories.
   b. The Democrats nominated Senator Lewis Cass of Michigan, the major proponent of popular sovereignty.
   c. Martin Van Buren rejected the nomination of the Free-Soil party because of his support for the extension of slavery.
   d. all of the above.

6. The Compromise of 1850 was
   a. strongly supported by President Taylor.
   b. passed as a series of measures that could be voted on separately.
   c. passed by Congress as an omnibus bill.
   d. opposed by important congressional leaders such as Clay and Douglas.

7. Which of the following provisions was not included in the Compromise of 1850?
   a. admission of California to the Union as a free state
   b. organization of the New Mexico and Utah territories on the principle of "popular sovereignty"
   c. reopening of the international slave trade
   d. compensation to Texas for giving up certain land claims

8. Whig candidate Winfield Scott alienated the South in 1852 partly by his
   a. demand for immigration restrictions.
   b. alliance with northern antislavery leaders.
   c. support for laissez-faire economic policies.
   d. support of the Compromise of 1850.

9. A significant result of the Kansas-Nebraska Act was
   a. the formation of the Republican party.
   b. a new spirit of compromise.
   c. increased prestige for the Democratic party.
   d. reaffirmation of the Missouri Compromise.

10. The Know-Nothing party of the 1850s collapsed almost as rapidly as it had arisen because it
    a. failed to develop as an intersectional movement.
    b. sought to promote and protect the rights of immigrants.
    c. remained insensitive to the needs of the working class.
    d. neglected to provide answers to the country's major problems.

11. As president, James Buchanan
    a. accepted the advice of the "Ostend Manifesto" to pursue the acquisition of Cuba at all costs.

b. negotiated the Gadsden Purchase of southern Arizona from Mexico.

c. denounced the Lecompton Constitution as an obvious perversion of the principle of popular sovereignty.

d. urged the Supreme Court to settle once and for all the constitutional issues related to the extension of slavery in the territories.

12. The rapid rise of the Republican Party in the North can be partly attributed to the party's

    a. active support of issues at the local level geared to attract immigrant and Catholic votes.

    b. moral stance in demanding complete abolition of the institution of slavery.

    c. adept organizing and campaigning skills at the grass-roots level.

    d. consistently laissez-faire economic platform.

13. The *Dred Scott* decision of the Supreme Court

    a. granted citizenship to African Americans.

    b. declared the Missouri Compromise unconstitutional.

    c. allowed congressional control of slavery in the territories.

    d. won widespread approval in the North.

14. The Lecompton Constitution of Kansas was

    a. approved by the territory's residents in a fair referendum.

    b. vigorously defended by Senator Stephen Douglas.

    c. designed to protect slavery in the soon-to-be-admitted state.

    d. favored by a majority of the members of Congress.

15. During 1859-1860, southern extremists supported the

    a. release of John Brown after his raid on Harpers Ferry.

    b. election of John Sherman as Speaker of the House.

    c. election of Abraham Lincoln as president.

    d. reopening of the Atlantic slave trade.

THOUGHT QUESTIONS

To check your understanding of the key issues of this period, solve the following problems:

1. List and explain the alternative suggestions for the problem of extending slavery to new territories acquired by the United States in the Mexican War. Why did they fail to provide an adequate solution? What "ambiguity" doomed popular sovereignty as a solution?

2. How could Northerners detest slavery and yet not embrace abolitionism? Contrast the goals and appeal of the Free-Soil movement with those of the abolitionist movement.

3. The author suggests that the Compromise of 1850 "was really more like an armistice or a cease-fire." Explain.

4. How and why were the 1840s and 1850s a time of shifting political alignments in the United States? Account for the seeming dominance of the Democratic party during this era.

5. Assume the role of a northern politician in 1860. Give "evidence" of how a proslavery conspiracy has captured the Democratic party and why you are voting for Abraham Lincoln for president.

6. Assume the role of a southern slaveholder in 1860. Give "evidence" of how antislavery forces have attempted to ruin your way of life and why you oppose the election of Abraham Lincoln as president.

7. Why did Lincoln win the election of 1860? How did the South react?

CRITICAL THINKING QUESTIONS

Read the following selections: "The Testimony of a Former Slave" (1843) by Lewis G. Clarke and "Let Your Motto Be Resistance" (1848) by Henry Highland Garnet. Answer the questions following the reading selections.

Lewis G. Clarke, The Testimony of a Former Slave

Kentucky is the best of the slave States, . . . but the masters manage to fix things pretty much to their own liking. . . . The law gives him full swing, and he don't fail to use his privilege, I can tell you. . . . I can't tell these respectable people as much as I would like to, but think for a minute how you would like to have *your* sisters, and *your* wives, and *your* daughters, completely, totally, and altogether in the power of a master. You can picture to yourselves a little how you would feel, but oh, if I could *tell* you! A slave woman ain't allowed to respect herself, if she would I had a pretty sister; she was whiter than I am, for she took more after her father. When she was sixteen years old, her master sent for her. When he sent for her again, she cried, and did not want to go. She told her mother her troubles, and she tried to encourage her to be decent, and hold up her head above such things, if she could. Her master was so mad, to think she complained to her mother, that he sold her right off to Louisiana; and we heard afterward that she died there of hard usage.

Now, who would like to be a slave, even if there was nothing bad about it but such treatment of his sisters and daughters? But there's a worse thing yet about slavery, the worst thing in the whole lot, though it's all bad. . . . I mean the patter rollers [patrols]. I suppose you know they have *patter rollers* to go round o' nights, to see that the slaves are all in, and not planning any mischief? . . . They hire these patter rollers, and they have to take the meanest fellows above ground; and because they are so mortal sure the slaves don't *want* their freedom, they have to put all power into their hands, to do with the niggers jest as they like. If a slave don't open his door to them, at any time of night, they break it down. They steal his money, if they can find it, and act just as they please with his wives and daughters. If a husband dares to say a word, or even look as if he wasn't quite satisfied, they tie him up and give him thirty-nine lashes. If there's any likely young girls in a slave's hut, they're mighty apt to have business there, especially if they think any colored young man takes a fancy to any of 'em. Maybe he'll get a pass from his master, and go to see the young girl for a few hours. [If] the patter rollers break in and find him, they'll abuse the girl as bad as they can on purpose to provoke him. If he looks cross, they'll give him a flogging, tear up his pass, turn him out of doors, and then take him up and whip him for being out without a pass. If the slave says they tore it up, they swear he lies, and nine times out of ten the master won't come out agin 'em, for they say it won't *do* to let the niggers suppose they may complain of the patter rollers; they must be taught that it's their business to obey 'em in everything; and the patter roller knows that very well. Oh how often I've seen the poor girls sob and cry, when there's been such goings on! Maybe you think, because they're slaves, they ain't got no feeling and no shame! A woman's being a slave don't stop her genteel ideas; that is, according to their way, and as far as they *can*. They know they must submit to their masters; besides, their masters, maybe, dress 'em up, and make 'em little presents, and give 'em more priviliges, while the whim lasts; but that ain't like having a parcel of low, dirty, swearing, drunk patter rollers let loose among 'em, like so many hogs. This breaks down their spirits dreadfully, and makes 'em wish they were dead.

Now, who among you would like to have *your* wives, and daughters, and sisters, in *such* a situation? This is what every slave in all of these States is exposed to. Yet folks go from these parts down to Kentucky, and come back, and say the slaves have enough to eat and drink, and they are very happy, and they wouldn't mind it much to be slaves themselves. I'd like to have 'em to try it; it would teach them a little more than they know now.

Henry Highland Garnet, Let Your Motto Be Resistance

Brethren and Fellow Citizens:

Your brethren of the north, east, and west have been accustomed to meet together in National Conventions, to sympathize with each other, and to weep over your unhappy condition. In these meetings, we have addressed all classes of the free, but we have never, until this time, sent a word of consolation and advice to you. We have been contented in sitting still and mourning over your sorrows, earnestly hoping that before this day your sacred liberties would have been restored. But we have hoped in vain. Years have rolled on, and tens of thousands have been borne on streams of blood, and tears, to the shores of eternity. While you have been oppressed, we have also been partakers with you; nor can we be free while you are enslaved. We therefore, write to you as being bound with you. . . .

SLAVERY! How much misery is comprehended in that single word. What mind is there that does not shrink from its direful effects? Unless the image of God is obliterated from the soul, all men cherish the love of Liberty. The nice, discerning political economist does not regard the sacred right more than the untutored African who roams in the wilds of Congo. Nor has the one more right to the full enjoyment of his freedom than the other. In every man's mind the good seeds of liberty are planted, and he who brings his fellow down so low as to make him contented with a condition of slavery, commits the highest crime against God and man. Brethren, your oppressors aim to do this. They endeavor to make you as much like brutes as possible. When they have blinded the eyes of your mind—when they have embittered the sweet waters of life—when they have shut out the light which shines from the word of God—then, and not till then, has American Slavery done its perfect work.

TO SUCH DEGRADATION, IT IS SINFUL IN THE EXTREME FOR YOU TO MAKE VOLUNTARY SUBMISSION. The divine commandments, you are in duty bound to reverence and obey. If you do not obey them, you will surely meet with the displeasure of the Almighty. He requires you to love him supremely, and your neighbor as yourself—to keep the Sabbath day holy—to search the Scriptures—and to bring up your children with respect for his laws, and to worship no other God but him. But slavery sets all these at naught, and hurls defiance in the face of Jehovah. The forlorn condition in which you are placed does not destroy your moral obligation to God. You are not certain of heaven because you suffer yourselves to remain in a state of slavery, where you cannot obey the commandments of the Sovereign of the universe. If the ignorance of slavery is a passport to heaven, then it is a blessing, and no curse, and you should rather desire its perpetuity than its abolition. God will not receive slavery, nor ignorance, nor any other state of mind, for love and obedience to him. Your condition does not absolve you from your moral obligation. The diabolical injustice by which your liberties are cloven down, NEITHER GOD, NOR ANGELS, NOR JUST MEN COMMAND YOU TO SUFFER FOR A SINGLE MOMENT. THEREFORE, IT IS YOUR SOLEMN AND IMPERATIVE DUTY TO USE EVERY MEANS, BOTH MORAL, INTELLECTUAL, AND PHYSICAL, THAT PROMISE SUCCESS. If a band of heathen men should attempt to enslave a race of Christians, and to place their children under the influence of some false religion, surely heaven would frown upon the men who would not resist such aggression, even to death. If, on the other hand, a band of Christians should attempt to enslave a race of heathen men, and to entail slavery upon them, and to keep them in heathenism in the midst of Christianity, the God of heaven would smile upon every effort which the injured might make to disenthrall themselves.

Brethren, it is as wrong for your lordly oppressors to keep you in slavery as it was for the man thief to steal our ancestors from the coast of Africa. You should, therefore, now use the same manner of resistance as would have been just in our ancestors, when the bloody footprints of the first remorseless soul thief was placed upon the shores of our fatherland. The humblest peasant is as free in the sight of God as the proudest monarch that ever swayed a sceptre. Liberty is a spirit sent out from God and, like its great Author, is no respecter of persons.

199

Brethren, the time has come when you must act for yourselves. It is an old and true saying that, "if hereditary bondsmen would be free, they must themselves strike the blow." You can plead your own cause, and do the work of emancipation better than any other. The nations of the old world are moving in the great cause of universal freedom, and some of them at least will, ere long, do you justice. The combined powers of Europe have placed their broad seal of disapprobation upon the African slave trade. But in the slaveholding parts of the United States, the trade is as brisk as ever. They buy and sell you as if you were brute beasts. The North has done much—her opinion of slavery in the abstract is known. But in regard to the South, we adopt the opinion of the *New York Evangelist*—"We have advanced so far, that the cause apparently waits for a more effectual door to be thrown open than has been yet." We are about to point out to you that more effectual door. Look around you, and behold the bosoms of your loving wives beating with untold agonies! Hear the cries of your poor children! Remember the stripes your fathers bore. Think of the torture and disgrace of your noble mothers. Think of your wretched sisters, loving virtue and purity, as they are driven into concubinage and are exposed to the unbridled lusts of incarnate devils. Think of the undying glory that hangs around the ancient name of Africa—and forget not that you are native-born American citizens, and as such, you are justly entitled to the rights that are granted to the freest. Think how many tears you have poured out upon the soil which you have cultivated with unrequited toil and enriched with your blood; and then go to your lordly enslavers and tell them plainly that you ARE DETERMINED TO BE FREE. Appeal to their sense of justice, and tell them that they have no more right to oppress you than you have to enslave them. Entreat them to remove the grievous burdens which they have imposed upon you, and to remunerate you for your labor. Promise them renewed diligence in the cultivation of the soil, if they will render you an equivalent for your services. Point them to the increase in happiness and prosperity in the British West-Indies since the act of Emancipation. Tell them in language which they cannot misunderstand of the exceeding sinfulness of slavery, and of a future judgment, and of the righteous retributions of an indignant God. Inform them that all you desire is FREEDOM, and that nothing else will suffice. Do this, and forever after cease to toil for the heartless tyrants, who give you no other reward but stripes and abuse. If they then commence the work of death, they, and not you, will be responsible for the consequences. You had far better all die—*die immediately*—than live slaves, and entail your wretchedness upon your posterity. If you would be free in this generation, here is your only hope. However much you and all of us may desire it, there is not much hope of redemption without the shedding of blood. If you must bleed, let it all come at once—rather *die freemen, than live to be slaves*. It is impossible, like the children of Israel, to make a grand exodus from the land of bondage. . . . In the name of the merciful God, and by all that life is worth, let it no longer be a debatable question whether it is better to choose LIBERTY OR DEATH. . . .

Brethren arise, arise! Strike for your lives and liberties. Now is the day and the hour. Let every slave throughout the land do this, and the days of slavery are numbered. You cannot be more oppressed than you have been—you cannot suffer greater cruelties than you have already. RATHER DIE FREEMEN, THAN LIVE TO BE SLAVES. Remember that you are THREE MILLIONS!

It is in your power to torment the God-cursed slaveholders, that they will be glad to let you go free. If the scale was turned, and black men were the masters and white men the slaves, every destructive agent and element would be employed to lay the oppressor low. Danger and death would hang over their heads day and night. Yes, the tyrants would meet with plagues more terrible than those of Pharaoh. But you are a patient people. You act as though you were made for the special use of these devils. You act as though your daughters were born to pamper the lusts of your masters and overseers. And worse than all, you tamely submit, while your lords tear your wives from your embraces and defile them before your eyes. In the name of God, we ask, are you men? Where is the blood of your fathers? Has it all run out of your veins? Awake, awake; millions of voices are calling you! Your dead fathers speak to you from their graves. Heaven, as with a voice of thunder, calls on you to arise from the dust.

Let your motto be RESISTANCE, RESISTANCE, RESISTANCE! No oppressed people have ever secured their liberty without resistance. What kind of resistance you had better make, you must decide by the circumstances that surround you, and according to the suggestion of expediency. Brethren, adieu! Trust in the living God. Labor for the peace of the human race, and remember that you are three millions.

1. How would Clarke have responded to the defenders of slavery who claimed that slaves were content and well-cared for by their masters?

2. Who were the "patter rollers?" What purposes did they serve?

3. According to Garnet, why did slaveholders endeavor to make slaves "as much like brutes as possible?"

4. What steps did Garnet propose that slaves take in resistance to their condition? How does he justify these steps of resistance?

5. Why do you think Garnet's appeal evoked such controversy, even among abolitionists? What is different about Garnet's opposition to slavery from that of Harriet Beecher Stowe, author of *Uncle Tom's Cabin* (1852)?

CHAPTER 15

SECESSION AND THE CIVIL WAR

SUMMARY

Lincoln effectively guided the Union through the Civil War by inspiring Northerners with his conviction that the struggle would be won. The war tested the American ideal of democracy. It was a defense of political liberalism at a time when much of Europe had rejected it.

THE STORM GATHERS

The war came after a compromise effort failed and the North resolved to fight to preserve the Union.

The Deep South Secedes

With the election of Lincoln, the states of the Deep South seceded from the Union to better secure slavery.

The Failure of Compromise

When northern moderates attempted a reconciliation of the sections, Lincoln led the Republicans in rejecting the proposed compromise because it would have permitted the spread of slavery to the Southwest.

And the War Came

Lincoln then carefully avoided firing the first shot by shifting the burden of decision to the South Carolinians, who fired on Fort Sumter.

ADJUSTING TO TOTAL WAR

The northern war aim, to force the South physically back into the Union, required a "total war" of societies and economies as well as armies. This formidable task required all of the North's demographic and economic advantages.

Prospects, Plans, and Expectations

The South chose to fight "an offensive defense," while the North had two main goals: the Confederate capital in the East and the Mississippi Valley in the West.

Mobilizing the Home Fronts

Both the North and the South faced enormous difficulties in raising, equipping, and financing armies on such a large scale.

Political Leadership: Northern Success and Southern Failure
Lincoln exercised extraordinary powers to achieve his aims. Jefferson Davis took a more narrow--and less successful--view of his role as Confederate president.

Early Campaigns and Battles
The northern effort stalled in the East, where Lee turned back successive attempts to capture Richmond, but in the West the Union took much of the Mississippi Valley and established its naval supremacy.

The Diplomatic Struggle
At the same time, the South failed in its attempt to use its cotton supply to attract the substantial European support necessary if the South was to continue to hold out against the more powerful North.

Fight to the Finish
In the final two and one-half years of the war, the North adopted increasingly extreme war measures to overcome determined southern resistance.

The Coming of Emancipation
Lincoln moved slowly to emancipate the slaves, and did so more from military, political, and diplomatic expediency than moral purpose.

African American Roles in the War
Almost 200,000 African Americans served in the Union armies and contributed significantly to a northern victory.

The Tide Turns
Southern armies, economy, diplomacy and society could no longer resist the superior demographic and economic forces of the North.

Last Stages of the Conflict
The resulting Northern victories achieved the Union's several military objectives, including the capture of Richmond, and turned back a Northern peace movement, assuring Lincoln's reelection and the successful conclusion of the war.

Effects of War
Four years of struggle had changed the status of women, African Americans, and working people. Most clearly, the war had broadened federal powers, channeling them into a new corporate, industrial economy. The war effort also encouraged a shift away from traditional individualism toward social discipline and collective action.

LEARNING OBJECTIVES

After mastering this chapter, you should be able to

1. Explain why Lincoln was so effective as the Union's wartime leader.

2. Trace the development of southern secession from Lincoln's election through the decision of the upper South to join the Confederacy.

3. Evaluate the Republican decision to reject the Crittenden compromise plan.

4. Describe the development of the North's resolve to fight if necessary to defeat secession.

5. Analyze the opposing strategies of the Civil War.

6. Define the concept of "total war," then explain its effect on the efforts of the North and the South to mobilize their home fronts for the war effort.

7. Compare and contrast the leadership of the Union and Confederate presidents.

8. Describe the relative success of the Union and Confederate armies in the early campaigns in the eastern theater of war.

9. Describe the relative success of the Union and Confederate armies in the western theater of war.

10. Explain why "King Cotton Diplomacy" failed.

11. Trace and explain Lincoln's gradual movement toward the emancipation of the slaves.

12. Describe the role played by African-American troops in the Union armed forces during the Civil War.

14. List and describe the principal social and economic changes that accompanied the Civil War.

GLOSSARY

To build your social science vocabulary, familiarize yourself with the following terms:

1. **unilateral**   involving only one of two or more sides. ". . . South Carolina's unilateral action set a precedent . . .".

2. **reactionary** favoring movement toward political and social conservatism. ". . . the goal of the new converts . . . was not to establish a slave holders' reactionary utopia".

3. **martial law** military law over a civilian population, usually for a temporary emergency. ". . . ruthless methods . . . included the use of a martial law . . .".

4. **demographic** related to the scientific study of the statistics of human population. "The South had some advantages...counterbalancing the North's demographic...superiority."

5. **blockade** the closing of passage to and from an area. "Lincoln also attached great importance to the coastal blockade . . .".

6. **commissary** a department that supplies provisions and equipment. "...the Confederate commissary resorted to the impressment of...produce...."

7. **writ of habeas corpus** a judicial order requiring a government to present an individual to a court for explanation of his detention. ". . . suspended the writ of habeas corpus . . .".

8. **belligerency** a state of being at war. "The Confederate commissioners . . . succeeded in gaining recognition of southern `belligerency' . . .".

9. **privateers** privately owned ships commissioned by a government to fight an enemy. "...it permitted the South to...outfit privateers in neutral ports."

10. **mediation** the process of acting as an intermediary between two parties. ". . . the British would cosponsor his plan to offer European mediation of the American conflict . . .".

11. **resolution** the adoption by vote of an assembly's expression of will or opinion. "Congress voted...."

12. **emancipation** the act or process of freeing, as from slavery. ". . . he was reluctant to commit his administration to a policy of immediate emancipation".

13. **contraband** illegal trade or goods. ". . . in accordance with the theory that they were contraband of war . . .' ".

14. **conscription** drafting for military service. "The Enrollment Act . . . provided for outright conscription . . .".

15. **cease-fire** an agreement to halt military hostilities. "Their platform appealed to war weariness by calling for a cease-fire...."

IDENTIFICATION

Briefly identify the meaning and significance of the following terms.

1. Confederate States of America _____

_____

2. Crittenden Plan _____

_____

3. Fort Sumter_____

_____

4. "Total War"_____

_____

5. Jefferson Davis_____

_____

6. George McClellan_____

_____

7. Robert E. Lee_____

_____

8. Ulysses S. Grant_____

_____

9. "King Cotton Diplomacy"_____

_____

10. Emancipation Proclamation_____

_____

MATCHING

A.   Match the following ships with the appropriate description.

_____ 1. *Virginia*

                                               a. Union ship that resupplied Fort Sumter

_____ 2. *Merrimack*

      b. Confederate ironclad destroyed near Hampton Roads, Virginia

_____ 3. *Monitor*

      c. armored Union gun ship that sank Confederate ironclad vessel

_____ 4. *Alabama*

      d. U.S. ship taken, renamed, and armored by the Confederacy

_____ 5. *Trent*

      e. British steamer boarded by U.S. warship

      f. Confederate privateer built in a British shipyard

B.   Match the following battles with the appropriate description.

_____ 1. Antietam

      a. Grant's 1863 victory took control of the Mississippi for the Union

_____ 2. Vicksburg

      b. Grant's 1864-1865 siege took this rail center near Richmond

_____ 3. Gettysburg

      c. Sherman's 1864 victory occupied the "hub of the Deep South"

_____ 4. Petersburg

      d. Lee's 1862 invasion of Maryland stopped here

_____ 5. Atlanta

      e. Lee's 1863 victory over Hooker cost him the life of one of his best generals

      f. Lee's 1863 loss during invasion of the North helped "turn the tide" of the war

COMPLETION

Answer the question or complete the statement by filling in the blanks with the correct word or words.

1. Southerners who supported secession by individual states were opposed by _____, who argued that their states should act together rather than singly.

2. Fort Sumter was located in the harbor of _____, _____.

3. The four border states that remained in the Union were _____, _____, and _____.

4. General Winfield Scott recommended squeezing the South into submission with an _____.

5. Politicians who called for restoration of the Union by negotiation rather than war were called _____.

6. Union naval forces that captured New Orleans were led by Flag Officer _____.

7. Lincoln replaced _____ because he thought the general was suffering from a case of "the slows."

8. The Union captured, held and then released two Confederate envoys to Britain; they were _____ and _____.

9. An American ambassador to Britain helped prevent the recognition of the Confederacy; he was _____.

10. In 1864, the Democrats nominated _____ _____.

TRUE/FALSE

Mark the following statements either T (True) or F (False).

____ 1. The southern states' righters produced a Confederate constitution strikingly different from that of the United States.

____ 2. Conflicting views on slavery determined the final division of states into Union and Confederate.

____ 3. Under the pressure of Union blockade, the Confederacy sponsored a program that produced enough munitions to supply southern troops throughout the war.

____ 4. Both the North and the South resorted to heavy taxation to maintain their fiscal integrity in spite of the financial demands of the war.

____ 5. When South Carolina seceded, southern "cooperationists" proposed that all southern states cooperate by immediately seceding from the Union.

____ 6. Immediately after the secession of South Carolina, northern business united behind the Union war effort.

____ 7. States of the upper South had to decide on secession when Lincoln asked them for troops to help "coerce" the southern states.

____ 8. A Union conscription law provoked the worst domestic disturbance in our history when a New York antidraft riot led to at least 120 deaths.

____ 9. The Civil War improved the economic situation of working Americans by providing high wages.

____ 10. While President Buchanan theoretically opposed the right of secession, he did little to oppose it in fact.

MULTIPLE CHOICE

Circle the one alterative that *best* completes the statement or answers the question.

1. The secession movement was dominated by
   a. hill country white supremacists who feared black social competition.
   b. southern radical nationalists who hoped to establish a plantation "utopia."
   c. southern moderates intent on securing slavery from northern political interference and federal control.
   d. moderates from the Upper South who gave up on the Union with the election of Lincoln in 1860.

2. The Republicans rejected the Crittenden plan for compromise because they
   a. wanted to defeat the South militarily.
   b. hoped to demoralize southern moderates.
   c. feared driving southern extremists to war.
   d. insisted on resolving the crisis over the future of slavery.

3. The firing on Fort Sumter
   a. brought European aid for the South.
   b. demonstrated Union naval power.
   c. unified northern opinion for defense of the Union.
   d. demonstrated the Union's will to fight.

4. Which was *not* an advantage enjoyed by the North at the beginning of the war?
   a. a better transportation system
   b. greater industrial production
   c. a larger population
   d. better military leadership

5. Which of the following best describes Lincoln's military strategy?
   a. the "anaconda" policy of starving the South into submission by cutting off its supplies of commodities and food
   b. winning the war with a quick strike at the Confederate capital
   c. an attempt to capture control of the Mississippi Valley
   d. a two-front policy keeping the pressure on Richmond while also advancing in the Mississippi Valley

6. During the Civil War, the South suffered shortages in all of the following *except*
   a. cash and other liquid assets.
   b. transportation facilities.
   c. foodstuffs.
   d. munitions.

7. The superior training and supply of Northern troops was offset by
   a. the large number of seasoned troops in Confederate ranks.
   b. the superior fighting ability of Southern troops.
   c. the large number of fresh troops in the Confederate ranks.
   d. all of the above

8. Which best describes Jefferson Davis's major weaknesses as a war leader?
   a. inability to deal with home-front problems
   b. excessive tact in dealing with field commanders
   c. abusive exercise of Confederate government power

d. obsession with popular political support

9. Why did the North have so little success in its eastern military campaigns during the early part of the war?
   a. Lincoln's constant meddling in the details of battle
   b. the Union's constant shortage of munitions and other essential supplies
   c. Winfield Scott's overly aggressive campaign to capture Richmond
   d. George McClellan's overly cautious approach in the campaign to capture Richmond

10. "King Cotton Diplomacy" failed because
    a. Britain started growing its own cotton.
    b. British mill workers willingly suffered to help destroy slavery.
    c. the textile industry no longer used much cotton.
    d. the British economy gained more than it lost from neutrality.

11. Why was Lincoln so reluctant to support immediate freedom for the slaves?
    a. He preferred gradual and compensated emancipation.
    b. He feared alienating border-state Unionists.
    c. He knew many northerners were racially prejudiced.
    d. all of the above

12. Which of the following best describes Ulysses S. Grant's approach in his campaign against Robert E. Lee?
    a. forcing Lee to take the offensive so Grant could capitalize on his superior defensive talents
    b. keeping the pressure on Lee with constant assault or siege
    c. taking Richmond in a single overpowering strike against Lee
    d. holding Lee in northern Virginia while William T. Sherman marched from Georgia to Richmond

13. Which of the following Civil War battles and campaigns are in the correct chronological order?
    a. Peninsula campaign, Vicksburg and Gettysburg, the siege of Petersburg
    b. Vicksburg and Gettysburg, Peninsula campaign, siege of Petersburg
    c. the siege of Petersburg, Vicksburg and Gettysburg, Peninsula campaign
    d. None of the above.

14. Civil War Republicans enacted all of the following policies *except*
    a. a low tariff for free trade.
    b. free land with a homestead act.
    c. land grants for railroad construction.
    d. a national banking system with standardized currency.

15. Which of the following was *not* an effect of the Civil War?
    a. broadening "the woman's sphere"
    b. broadening the scope of federal power
    c. improving the industrial workers' standard of living
    d. enacting government support for business and agriculture

THOUGHT QUESTIONS

To check your understanding of the key issues of this period, solve the following problems:

1. Considering that the Southerners faced such a formidable military task in a war with the North, why did they secede?

2. Could the Southerners have better defended their interests through a political struggle within the Union, rather than a military struggle outside the Union?

3. Could the South have won the Civil War, or was its defeat inevitable?

4. Discuss the social and economic effects of the "total war" between North and South.

5. Do American social and ethnic minorities make significant gains during our wars? During the Civil War?

CRITICAL THINKING EXERCISE

Using material in Chapter 15 of the text and the Primary Sources provided below, please answer the questions which follow the Documents.

Clara Barton, "Medical Life at the Battlefield"
Lucy Breckinridge, "Diary"

Clara Barton, Medical Life at the Battlefield (1862)

I was strong and thought I might go to the rescue of the men who fell. . . . What could I do but go with them, or work for them and my country? The patriot blood of my father was warm in my veins. The country which he had fought for, I might at least work for. .

But I struggled long and hard with my sense of propriety-with the appalling fact that I was only a woman whispering in one ear, and thundering in the other the groans of suffering men dying like dogs-unfed and unsheltered, for the life of every institution which had protected and educated me!

I said that I struggled with my sense of propriety and I say it with humiliation and shame. I am ashamed that I thought of such a thing.

When our armies fought on Cedar Mountain, I broke the shackles and went to the field. . . .

Five days and nights with three hours sleep-a narrow escape from capture-and some days of getting the wounded into hospitals at Washington, brought Saturday, August 30. And if you chance to feel, that the positions I occupied were rough and unseemly for a woman-I can only reply that they were rough and unseemly for men. But under all, lay the life of the nation. I had inherited the rich blessing of health and strength of constitution-such as are seldom given to woman-and I felt that some return was due from me and that I ought to be there. . . .

. . . . Our coaches were not elegant or commodious; they had no seats, no platforms, no steps, a slide door on the side the only entrance, and this higher than my head. For my man attaining my elevated position, I must beg of you to draw on your imaginations and spare me the labor of reproducing the boxes, boards, and rails, which in those days, seemed to help me up and down the world. We did not criticize the unsightly helpers and were thankful that the stiff springs did not quite jostle us out. This need not be limited to this particular trip or train, but will for all that I have known in Army life. This is the kind of conveyance which your tons of generous gifts have reached the field with the freights. These trains through day and night, sunshine and heat and cold, have thundered over heights, across plains, the ravines, and over hastily built army bridges 90 feet across the stream beneath.

At 10 o'clock Sunday (August 31) our train drew up at Fairfax Station. The ground, for acres, was a thinly wooded slope-and among the trees on the leaves and grass, were laid the wounded who pouring in by scores of wagon loads, as picked up on the field the flag of truce. All day they came and the whole hillside was red. Bales of hay were broken open and scattered over the ground littering of cattle, and the sore, famishing men were laid upon it.

And when the night shut in, in the mist and darkness about us, we knew that standing apart from the world of anxious hearts, throbbing over the whole country, we were a little band of almost empty handed workers literally by ourselves in the wild woods of Virginia, with 3,000 suffering men crowded upon the few acres within our reach.

After gathering up every available implement or convenience for our work, our domestic inventory stood 2 water buckets, 5 tin cups, 1 camp kettle, 1 stew pan, 2 lanterns, 4 bread knives, 3 plates, and a 2-quart tin dish, and 3,000 guest to serve.

You will perceive by this, that I had not yet learned to equip myself, for I was no Pallas, ready armed, but grew into my work by hard thinking and sad experience. It may serve to relieve your apprehension for the future of my labors if I assure you that I was never caught so again.

But the most fearful scene was reserved for the night. I have said that the ground was littered with dry hay and that we had only two lanterns, but there were plenty of candles. The wounded were laid so close that it was impossible to move about in the dark. The slightest misstep brought a torrent of groans from some poor mangled fellow in your path.

Consequently here were seen persons of all grades from the careful man of God who walked with a prayer upon his lips to the careless driver hunting for his lost whip,-each wandering about among this hay with an open flaming candle in his hands.

The slightest accident, the mere dropping of a light could have enveloped in flames this whole mass of helpless men.

How we watched and pleaded and cautioned as we worked and wept that night! How we put socks and slippers upon their cold feet, wrapped your blankets and quilts about them, and when we no longer these to give, how we covered them in the hay and left them to their rest! . . .

The slight, naked chest of a fair-haired lad caught my eye, dropping down beside him, I bent low to draw the remnant of his blouse about him, when with a quick cry he threw his left arm across my neck and, burying his face in the folds of my dress, wept like a child at his mother's knee. I took his head in my hands and held it until great burst of grief passed away. "And do you know me?" he asked at length, "I am Charley Hamilton, we used to carry your satchel home from school!" My faithful pupil, poor Charley. That mangled right hand would never carry a satchel again.

About three o'clock in the morning I observed a surgeon with a little flickering candle in hand approaching me with cautious step up in the wood. "Lady," he said as he drew near, "will you go with me? Out on the hills is a poor distressed lad, mortally wounded, and dying. His piteous cries for his sister have touched all our hearts none of us can relieve him but rather seem to distress him by presence."

By this time I was following him back over the bloody track, with great beseeching eyes of anguish on every side looking up into our faces, saying so plainly, "Don't step on us."

Lucy Breckinridge, Diary (1862)

Sunday, August 12th, 1862

It rained so steadily today that we could not go to church. I sat all the morning in the library with George talking about "reds" and marriages. He said very earnestly, "Well, Luce, take my advice and do not get married until the war is over. There are many reasons why you should not; for instance, you might be a widow in a short time."" Then, after thinking a few minutes, it seemed to strike him that it would not be such a bad thing to be a pretty young widow. He has an idea that I am engaged, and seems to take a great deal more interest in me; treats me with marked respect and unwonted tenderness. He is a funny boy and a very sweet one. I never loved him so much before, because all my special love was given to John [Lucy's brother]. He and I were so nearly the same age, and never were separated in any way until the last two or three years. I loved him better than anyone on earth. Though we were playmates from our babyhood, I do not ever remember having been angry with John. I was more intimate with him and stayed with him more than I did with Eliza [Lucy's sister]. We never formed a plan for the future in which we were not connected. Everything seems changed to me since he died. He was the noblest of us all, and all his life had been the favorite with his brothers and sisters. "God takes our dearest even so; the reason why we cannot know; helpless he leaves us crushed with woe."

Eliza and Emma went over to the graveyard and put up a white cross with John's name on it and the date of the Battle of Seven Pines with the inscription, "He hath entered into peace," and put garlands of ivy on it. It is only a temporary mark for the grave. All of his brothers and sisters wish to raise a monument to his memory, the first of our band who has been taken from us. What a sad summer this has been.

1. Explain the failure the North and South to reach a compromise that would have prevented war.

2. Describe, explain and evaluate the employment of "total war".

3. Describe both of the battlefield work of Clara Barton and reaction to the carnage.

4. Describe and explain the wartime difficulties faced by Lucy Breckinridge.

5. Are your answers to questions 3 and 4 above related to that of question 2? If so, how

CHAPTER 16

THE AGONY OF RECONSTRUCTION

SUMMARY

After the Civil War, the South faced a difficult period of rebuilding its government and economy and of dealing with the newly freed African Americans.

THE PRESIDENT VERSUS CONGRESS

In the absence of constitutional guidelines, the president and Congress waged a bitter fight over how best to reconstruct the Union.

Wartime Reconstruction

By 1863, Lincoln and Congress had begun to debate two divisive issues: the reconstruction of the southern states and the status of the freedmen. Lincoln proposed a minimal program to restore the southern states to the Union and showed some willingness to compromise with Congress in the months before his death. But the Reconstruction issues remained unresolved.

Andrew Johnson at the Helm

Johnson's ascent to the presidency led to a bitter clash with Congress. There was a uniform hope of breaking the power of the planter class, but Congress supported federal guarantees for black citizenship, and Johnson insisted that the South be permitted to reestablish white supremacy.

Congress Takes the Initiative

Determined to crush the old southern ruling class, the Republican-led Congress extended the life of the Freedmen's Bureau and passed a civil rights bill to grant equal benefits and protection to the freedmen. Fearing that Johnson would not enforce the civil rights act, Congress passed the Fourteenth Amendment guaranteeing equal rights under the law to all Americans and defining national citizenship. After the southern states rejected the Fourteenth Amendment, and the president vetoed two Reconstruction bills, Congress initiated its own radical program.

CONGRESSIONAL RECONSTRUCTION PLAN ENACTED

The First Reconstruction Act of 1867 temporarily placed the South under military rule and allowed for the readmittance of southern states once African American suffrage was legitimized.

The Impeachment Crisis

When the president obstructed the plan's implementation, Congress retaliated with an attempt to remove him from office. Johnson narrowly avoided removal, preserving the office from congressional domination, but insuring also that Congress would have the upper hand in the reconstruction process.

RECONSTRUCTION IN THE SOUTH

The South devastated and demoralized after the war, and dominated by southern whites who wanted to deny all rights to freedmen.

Social and Economic Adjustments
When Congress failed to enact a program of land redistribution, southern landowners initiated a new labor system that forced freedmen into virtual peonage. Most of the ex-slaves had no alternative but to return to white-owned fields under a contract labor system. While sharecropping extended black servitude and economic dependence on the farm, segregation of the races was imposed in the towns.

Political Reconstruction in the South
Politically, Reconstruction established southern governments of Republican business people, poor whites, and the freedmen. Although often corrupt, these radical regimes initiated significant progressive reforms. They failed however to achieve interracial equality; community pressure established a social system based on segregation.

THE AGE OF GRANT
Serving during one of the most difficult periods in American history, Grant lacked the strong principles, consistency, and sense of purpose to be an effective administrator.

Rise of the Money Question
What to do with the greenbacks (paper money issued during the war) became a major problem by 1868. Hard money advocates clashed with "green backers" who wanted government sponsored inflation. The panic of 1873 intensified the argument, and the Sherman Specie Resumption Act in 1874 failed to please either the inflationists or the hard-money advocates.

Retreat from Reconstruction
In the South, Grant's administration failed to sustain black suffrage against violent groups bent on restoring white supremacy. Organizations like the Ku Klux Klan used terrorism, insurrection, and murder to intimidate southern Republican governments and prospective black voters. With the Fifteenth Amendment severely threatened, Congress passed the "Force" Acts which allowed the president to use military force to quell insurrections.

Spoilsmen versus Reformers
The idealism of radical republicanism waned as new leaders -"spoilsmen"- came to power determined to further their own private interests. The Credit Mobilier scandal, the "Whiskey Ring," and the impeachment of Secretary of War Belknap for accepting bribes left liberal reform Republicans aghast and the Grant administration in shambles.

REUNION AND THE NEW SOUTH

The reconciliation of the sections came at the expense of southern blacks and poor whites.

The Compromise of 1877

In the 1876 presidential election, Samuel Tildenm the Democratic candidate, won the popular majority as well as the uncontested electoral vote. But disputed returns in the three Republican-controlled southern states threw the election into turmoil. The Compromise of 1877 ended military rule and insured that conservative "home rule" would be restored in the South. With southern Democratic acquiescence, Republican candidate Rutherford Hayes assumed the presidency.

The New South

In the South, upper-class "Redeemers" took power in the name of white supremacy and industrial development and then initiated a "New South." The economy was dominated by northern capital and southern employers, landlords, and creditors. Economic and physical coercion, including hundreds of lynchings, effectively disenfranchised people of color. Some blacks, justifiably bitter at the depth of white racism, supported black nationalism and emigration to Africa, but most chose to struggle within American society.

LEARNING OBJECTIVES

After mastering this chapter, you should be able to

1. Contrast the presidential and congressional wartime reconstruction programs.

2. Explain how Andrew Johnson's background shaped his attitudes and policies on Reconstruction.

3. Describe the processes by which Andrew Johnson lost support in Congress, and the Radical Republicans gained control of Reconstruction.

4. Summarize the goals of Radical Reconstruction and evaluate the success with which these goals were achieved.

5. Define the sections of the Fourteenth Amendment and understand why its enforcement was crucial to Reconstruction efforts.

6. Describe the Radicals' attempt to remove President Johnson from office.

7. Define the southern systems of contract labor and sharecropping with emphasis on their effects upon African Americans.

8. Evaluate Grant's handling of the major problems of his administration: the money question, enforcement of Reconstruction, and governmental corruption.

9. Analyze the important results of the impeachment crisis on the federal government and the Reconstruction process.

10. Identify the social and economic adjustments in the South during the Reconstruction years.

11. Evaluate the achievements and list reasons for the ultimate failure of the southern Republican governments.

12. Summarize the worst of the scandals which rocked the Grant administration.

13. Explain the nature of the political crisis involving the election of 1876.

14. Discuss the terms and results of the "Compromise of 1877."

15. Describe the social and political effects of the "Redeemer" regimes in the New South.

GLOSSARY

To build your social science vocabulary, familiarize yourself with the following terms:

1. **crop lien** use of a farmer's crop as collateral for a loan. ". . . the notorious 'crop lien' system . . .".

2. **disfranchisement** the act of depriving a citizen of the right to vote. "Full-scale disfranchisement . . .".

3. **impeachment** the act of bringing charges against a government officer for official misconduct. ". . . to call for his impeachment".

4. **Jim Crow** segregated. ". . . black, or 'Jim Crow,' cars . . .".

5. **laissez faire** government noninterference in the economy. ". . . advocated strict laissez-faire economic policies . . .".

6. **patronage** political control of the distribution of jobs and other favors. ". . . the corruption breeding patronage system . . .".

7. **referendum** the practice of referring a matter to the electorate for adoption or rejection. ". . . served as a referendum to the Fourteenth Amendment"

8. **specie** coined money, usually of gold or silver. ". . . redeemed in specie payments."

9. **amnesty** a pardon granted for past crimes. "...a Proclamation of Amnesty and Reconstruction...."

10. **habeas corpus** a legal writ used to protect individuals against unlawful detention. "... suspend the writ of habeas corpus..."

11. **rider** a clause added to a bill as it passes a legislative body. "...a rider to an army appropriations bill-sought to limit Johnson's authority to issue orders to military commanders."

12. **revisionism** proposing a revised historical interpretation. "The most powerful example of this early revisionism was W. E. B. Dubois' *Black Reconstruction in America.*"

13. **provisional** temporary, until a permanent replacement is made. "...appointed provisional governors...."

14. **sharecropping** the status of working a piece of land in return for a portion of the crop. "...an alternative capital-labor relationship-sharecropping..."

15. **autonomy** the right and power of self-government. "The president's case for state autonomy...."

IDENTIFICATION

Briefly identify the meaning and significance of the following terms.

1. Jim Crow _____

    _____

2. Wade-Davis Bill _____

    _____

3. Freedmen's Bureau _____

    _____

4. Fourteenth Amendment _____

_____

5. Thaddeus Stevens _____

_____

6. First Reconstruction Act _____

_____

7. "Carpetbaggers" _____

_____

8. John Sherman _____

_____

9. Horace Greeley _____

_____

10. New South _____

_____

MATCHING

A. Match the following public figures with the appropriate description.

____ 1. Orville Babcock

____ 2. William Belknap

____ 3. Schyler Colfax

____ 4. Jay Gould

a. secretary of war who resigned to prevent a Senate trial for taking bribes in the sale of Indian trading posts

b. senator from Missouri who helped lead the crusade for civil service reform

c. president's private secretary who was indicted for his role in the "Whiskey Ring"

d. Speaker of the House and later vice-president who

220

was implicated in the Credit Mobilier scandal

____ 5. Carl Schurz

e. financier who, with the help of a relative of the president, tried to corner the gold market

f. New York City "boss" who headed a corrupt Democratic political "machine"

B. Match the following bills and acts with the appropriate description.

____ 1. Wade-Davis Bill

a. congressional legislation designed to limit the authority of President Andrew Johnson

____ 2. Black Codes

b. a series of laws designed to protect black suffrage by authorizing use of the army against the KKK

____ 3. Tenure of Office Act

c. initial congressional plan for Reconstruction vetoed by Lincoln

____ 4. Force Acts

d. congressional attempt to provide the freedman "full and equal benefit of all laws

____ 5. Civil Rights Bill of 1866

e. southern state laws passed during Reconstruction to impose restrictions on former slaves

f. congressional legislation creating a federal agency to aid the former slaves

COMPLETION

Answer the question or complete the statement by filling in the blanks with the correct word or words.

1. The 1915 epic film of D. W. Griffith that presented Reconstruction as a "tragic era" of misrule and corruption was entitled _____.

2. Slavery was abolished with the ratification of the _____.

3. Lincoln refused to sign the Wade-Davis Bill of 1864 by exercising a _____.

4. The physical destruction of the South would not have been so devastating had there been sufficient _____ available for rebuilding.

5. The _____ Amendment restricted the power of the Fourteenth states to violate the life, liberty, or property of any citizen.

6. By the 1870s, most African Americans were relegated to the position of _____, an arrangement whereby they agreed to work a small piece of land in return for a fixed share of the crop.

7. In 1874, President Grant discouraged inflation by vetoing a modest new issue of

    _____.

8. The _____ was a southern society bent on restoring white supremacy by intimidating politically active African Americans.

9. The southern Republican party consisted of the following three groups _____.

10. By the 1870s, leadership of the Republican party had passed to opportunistic politicians called _____, who were more interested in personal gain than in public service.

TRUE/FALSE

Mark the following statements either T (True) or F (False).

____ 1. Lincoln favored a lenient plan for Reconstruction in order to shorten the war by attracting southern support.

____ 2. The dominant view of the Republican-led Congress toward the Reconstruction process was that strong executive leadership would be required.

____ 3. Andrew Johnson abandoned Lincoln's plans for Reconstruction by doing away with the requirement of an oath of allegiance for southern whites.

____ 4. Women's rights leaders Elizabeth Cady Stanton and Susan B. Anthony campaigned against ratification of the Fifteenth Amendment.

____ 5. As a result of his impeachment trial, Andrew Johnson became the first president to be removed from office.

____ 6. Physical reconstruction of the South was difficult because its per capita wealth in 1865 was only about half of what it had been in 1860.

____ 7. The "Green backers" in the credit-hungry West favored sound money policies.

_____ 8. The Fifteenth Amendment to the Constitution prohibited any state from denying any citizen the right to vote because of race, color, or previous condition of servitude.

_____ 9. During Grant's first term, the greatest threat to southern Republican governments came from white supremist societies like the KKK.

_____ 10. The factor which most contributed to Democrat Samuel Tilden's defeat in the presidential election in 1876 was the continued strength of the Republican regimes in the South and his consequent lack of popular support there.

MULTIPLE CHOICE

Circle the one alternative that best completes the statement or answers the question.

1. Which of the following statements reflects Lincoln's view of Reconstruction?
    a. Amnesty would for those Southerners who had never willingly aided the Confederacy.
    b. Reconstruction would guarantee full political and civil equality for southern blacks.
    c. Congress would determine the terms for readmission of the seceded states.
    d. Pardon would be granted to all Southerners taking an oath of allegiance to the Union and acknowledging the legality of emancipation.

2. President Andrew Johnson's plan for Reconstruction called for the southern states to
    a. declare their ordinances of secession illegal.
    b. repay their Confederate war debts.
    c. ratify the Fourteenth Amendment.
    d. prohibit former Confederates from holding government offices.

3. The Fourteenth Amendment to the Constitution
    a. prohibited slavery in the United States.
    b. provided for franchise regardless of race, color, or past servitude.
    c. defined national citizenship and prohibited the states from abridging the constitutional rights of people without due process of law.
    d. restored the former slave states to the union after congressional requirements were met.

4. President Johnson antagonized Republicans in Congress by
    a. calling for an extension of the Freedmen's Bureau.
    b. supporting a civil rights bill meant to guarantee equality for African Americans.
    c. urging confiscation and redistribution of land.
    d. campaigning against Radical Republicans in the elections of 1866.

5. After rejecting Johnson's Reconstruction plan, Congress enacted a program based on

a. the social and moral regeneration of the South.

b. the confiscation and redistribution of land.

c. immediate enfranchisement of both the freedmen and ex-Confederates.

d. guarantees for the rights of all citizens with the Fourteenth Amendment.

6. The House of Representatives impeached President Johnson on the grounds that he
    a. dismissed officers in the southern military districts.
    b. challenged the Tenure of Office Act by removing Secretary of War Edwin Stanton.
    c. vetoed the Reconstruction Bill.
    d. attempted to abolish the Freedmen's Bureau.

7. "Regeneration before Reconstruction" referred to
    a. restructuring southern state governments before readmission to the union.
    b. funding the rehabilitation of those areas in the South damaged during the war.
    c. transforming southern society, including land reform to the freedmen, before readmission.
    d. repudiating the debts owed by the former Confederate states to the Union.

8. Hard-money proponents favored
    a. more money in circulation to spur economic growth.
    b. retirement of greenbacks as quickly as possible and payment in silver and gold only.
    c. redemption of much of the war debt in greenbacks.
    d. easy credit terms to encourage economic expansion in the West.

9. Farmers and debtors generally favored a monetary policy that
    a. expanded the currency and inflated prices.
    b. contracted the currency and deflated prices.
    c. legally backed all currency with gold only.
    d. kept commodity prices stable and dependable.

10. The main reason[s] for the Ku Klux Klan's success in the South after 1868 would be
    a. popular support from whites of all social classes for white supremacy.
    b. its centralized political organization.
    c. its support from the southern state Republican governments.
    d. the persistent threat of a violent black uprising against the white planter class.

11. The three social groups which formed the coalition of the southern Republican party were
    a. businesspeople, poor white farmers, and former slaves.
    b. wealthy planters, professionals, and urban laborers.
    c. urban middle class, independent small farmers, and carpetbaggers.
    d. white agricultural laborers, wealthy businessmen, and black sharecroppers.

12. In defending Republican governments in the South, President Grant
    a. was quick to react with the military to any threat of violence.
    b. intervened only to protect the civil rights of African Americans.
    c. was consistent and hesitant because of northern political realities.
    d. left these governments on their own to defend themselves.

13. How would you characterize Grant's personal role in the corruption that marked his administration?
    a. He should be considered completely blameless.
    b. He vigorously prosecuted all wrongdoing.
    c. He protected some corrupt officials from justice.
    d. He made a great deal of money from illegal activities.

14. To ensure the election of Rutherford Hayes, Republican leaders agreed to
    a. offer lucrative positions to members of the electoral commission.
    b. end federal support for southern radical regimes.
    c. support fraudulent elections with federal troops.
    d. continue federal support for southern radical regimes.

15. The "Redeemers" in the South favored
    a. egalitarian democracy and continued Republican leadership.
    b. government appropriations for schools and public services and economic diversification.
    c. strengthening the Black Codes and support for white supremacist organizations like the Klan.
    d. political restoration of white supremacy and the gospel of industrial progress.

THOUGHT QUESTIONS

To check your understanding of the key issues of this period, solve the following problems:

1. If Lincoln had lived, would the events and outcome of Reconstruction have been substantially different?

2. Was radical Reconstruction policy based more on humanitarian concern for the freedmen or on selfish political and economic interests?

3. Andrew Johnson was the only U.S. president impeached in our history. (Richard M. Nixon tendered a timely resignation.) What does it mean to impeach a president? Should Andrew Johnson have been convicted?

4. What factors contributed to the development of segregation in the late nineteenth century?

5. Government plays a role in determining the supply of money and, therefore, the general price levels. During Grant's administration what factors led the president to allow special interests to determine his policy on the money question?

6. Why did professional historians from the 1890s to the 1940s regard Reconstruction as a "tragic era"? In the eyes of the revisionists, what was the real tragedy of Reconstruction?

CRITICAL THINKING EXERCISE

Using material in Chapter 16 of the text and to Primary Sources provided below, please answer the questions which follow the Documents.

"The Freedman's Agenda for Reconstruction"
Bayley Wyatt, "A Right to the Land"
Henry Blake, "Working on Shares"

The Freedmen's Agenda for Reconstruction

1st. *Resolved*, That the rights and interests of the colored citizens of Virginia are more directly, immediately and deeply affected in the restoration of the State to the Federal Union than any other class of citizens; and hence, that we have peculiar claims to be heard in regard to the question of its reconstruction, and that we cannot keep silence without dereliction of duty to ourselves, to our country, and to our God.

2d. *Resolved*, That personal servitude having been abolished in Virginia, it behooves us, and is demanded of us, by every consideration of right and duty, to speak and act as freemen, and as such to claim and insist upon equality before the law, and equal rights of suffrage at the "ballot box."

3d. *Resolved*, That it is a wretched policy and most unwise statesmanship that would withhold from the laboring population of the country any of the rights of citizenship essential to their well-being and to their advancement and improvement as citizens.

4th. *Resolved*, That invidious political or legal distinctions, on account of color merely, if acquiesced in, or voluntarily submitted to, is inconsistent with our own self-respect, or to the respect of others, placing us at great disadvantages, and seriously retards our advancement or progress in improvement, and that the removal of such disabilities and distinctions are alike demanded by sound political economy, by patriotism, humanity and religion.

5th. *Resolved*, That we will prove ourselves worthy of the elective franchise, by insisting upon it as a right, by not tamely submitting to its deprivation, by never abusing it by voting the state out of the Union, and never using it for purposes of rebellion, treason, or oppression.

6th. *Resolved*, That the safety of all loyal men, black or white, in the midst of the recently slaveholding States, requires that all loyal men, black or white, should have equal political and civil rights, and that this is a necessity as a protection against the votes of secessionists and disloyal men.

7th. *Resolved*, That traitors shall not dictate or prescribe to us the terms or conditions of our citizenship, so help us God.

8th. *Resolved*, That as far as in us lies, we will not patronize or hold business relations with those who deny to us our equal rights.

Bayley Wyatt, A Right to the Land

We made bricks without straw under old Pharaoh. . . . We now, as a people desires to be elevated, and we desires to do all we can to be educated, and we hope our friends will aid us all they can. . . .

I may state to all our friends, and to all our enemies, that we has a right to the land where we are located. For why? I tell you. Our wives, our children, our husbands, has been sold over and over again to purchase the lands we now locate upon; for that reason we have a divine right to the land. . . .

And then didn't we clear the land and raise the crops of corn, of cotton, of tobacco, of rice, of sugar, of everything? And then didn't them large cities in the North grow up on the cotton and the sugars and the rice that we made? Yes! I appeal to the South and the North if I hasn't spoken the words of truth.

I say they have grown rich, and my people is poor.

Henry Blake, Working on Shares

After freedom, we worked on shares a while. Then we rented. When we worked on shares, we couldn't make nothing—just overalls, and something to eat. Half went to the white man, and you would destroy your half, if you weren't careful. A man that didn't know how to count would always lose. He might lose anyhow. The white folks didn't give no itemized statements. No, you just had to owe so much. No matter how good account you kept, you had to go by their account, and—now, brother, I'm telling you the truth about this—it's been that way for a long time. You had to take the white man's words and notes on everything. Anything you wanted you could get, if you were a good hand. If you didn't make no money, that's all right; they would advance you more. But you better not try to leave and get caught. They'd keep you in debt. They were sharp. Christmas come, you could take up twenty dollars in somethin'-to-eat and as much as you wanted in whiskey. You could buy a gallon of whiskey—anything that kept you a slave. Because he was always right and you were always wrong, if there was a difference. If there was an argument, he would get mad and there would be a shooting take place.

1. After reading the text, explain the labor system which put the freedmen back to work in the planters' fields. How free were the farmer slaves in the "New South."?

2. Were the resolutions of the "Freedmen's Agenda for Reconstruction" primarily political or economic?

3. Why, in Bayley Wyatt's view, did freedmen have a "divine right" to own land?

4. Describe the operation and effects of sharecropping as Henry Blake explains the system.

5. Given your answer on sharecropping in question 5, which plan would have promoted most effectively the welfare of freedom: that in question 2, or that in question 3?

ANSWER KEY

CHAPTER 1

Matching A
1. d
2. b
3. f
4. c
5. a

Matching B
1. c
2. e
3. f
4. b
5. a

Completion
1. maize (corn), beans, and squash
2. Algonquian
3. Vinland
4. caravels
5. printing press
6. Treaty of Tordesillas
7. *encomienda*

True/False
1. F
2. F
3. T
4. T
5. F
6. F
7. T
8. F
9. F
10. T

Multiple Choice
1. a
2. a
3. d
4. b
5. d
6. b
7. d
8. b
9. b
10. a
11. d
12. a
13. b
14. a

CHAPTER 2

Matching A
1. c
2. e
3. f
4. a
5. d

Matching B
1. e
2. b
3. a
4. f
5. c

Completion

1. Oliver Cromwell, Charles I
2. James I
3. Charles II
4. Jamestown
5. House of Burgesses
6. headright
7. indentured
8. quitrent
9. William Bradford
10. John Winthrop

True/False

1. F
2. T
3. T
4. F
5. T
6. F
7. F
8. F
9. T
10. T
11. F

Multiple Choice

1. d
2. a
3. b
4. c
5. a
6. d
7. d
8. a
9. c
10. c
11. b
12. a
13. d
14. c
15. b

CHAPTER 3

Matching A

1. c
2. d
3. e
4. f
5. a

Matching B

1. e
2. b
3. a
4. c
5. d

Completion

1. tobacco
2. families
3. *The Day of Doom*
4. Harvard College
5. Gullah
6. Adam Smith
7. trade
8. vice-admiralty
9. Metacomet
10. Salem

True/False

1. F
2. F
3. F
4. T
5. T
6. F
7. F
8. T

9. F
10. T

Multiple Choice
1. a
2. a
3. d
4. c
5. d
6. d
7. d
8. b
9. a
10. a
11. b
12. d
13. b
14. c
15. d

CHAPTER 4

Matching A
1. f
2. a
3. d
4. e
5. b

Matching B
1. b
2. c
3. d
4. a
5. f

Completion
1. Natural reproduction
2. Conestoga wagons
3. self evident, natural laws
4. practical experimentation
5. weekly journal
6. King George's War

7. assemblies
8. Quebec

True/False
1. T
2. T
3. F
4. F
5. F
6. T
7. T
8. F
9. F

Multiple Choice
1. b
2. a
3. b
4. c
5. a
6. d
7. c
8. d
9. d
10. a
11. c
12. d
13. a
14. c
15. a

CHAPTER 5

Matching A
1. b
2. f
3. a
4. c
5. d

Matching B
1. e
2. a

3. f
4. b
5. c

Completion
1. boycotts
2. "Christian Sparta"
3. Virginia Resolves
4. *Gaspee*
5. East India Company
6. Quebec Act
7. Lexington, Concord
8. minutemen
9. Prohibitory Act
10. Benjamin Franklin, John
    Adams, John Jay

True/False
1. F
2. T
3. F
4. F
5. T
6. F
7. F
8. T
9. F
10. F

Multiple Choice
1. c
2. c
3. b
4. d
5. d
6. d
7. d
8. b
9. a
10. c
11. a
12. a
13. b
14. a
15. d

CHAPTER 6

Matching A
1. d
2. c
3. a
4. e
5. b

Matching B
1. b
2. a
3. d
4. f
5. c

Completion
1. Sans Souci Club
2. Society of Cincinnati
3. divorce
4. written
5. legislative
6. Paxton Boys
7. township
8. Montsquieu
9. George Mason
10. Daniel Boone

True/False
1. F
2. F
3. F
4. F
5. T
6. T
7. T
8. F
9. T
10. T

Multiple Choice
1. c
2. d
3. b
4. d
5. c
6. a
7. c
8. a
9. c
10. a
11. b
12. a
13. c
14. d
15. c

CHAPTER 7

Matching A
1. c
2. a
3. e
4. b
5. d

Matching B
1. d
2. b
3. e
4. a
5. c

Completion
1. War, State, Treasury
2. John Jay
3. implied
4. Edmond Genet
5. Alexander Hamilton
6. Fallen Timbers
7. Gazette of the United States
8. whiskey
9. XYZ Affair
10. Twelfth

True/False
1. F
2. T
3. F
4. T
5. F
6. T
7. F
8. T
9. F
10. F

Multiple Choice
1. a
2. b
3. c
4. a
5. d
6. d
7. a
8. d
9. a
10. b
11. c
12. d
13. c
14. c
15. a

CHAPTER 8

Matching A
1. e
2. a
3. f
4. c
5. d

Matching B

1. c
2. a
3. b
4. f
5. e

Completion

1. Ohio
2. Horseshoe Bend
3. West Point
4. Haiti
5. Tertium Quids
6. General James Wilkinson
7. Orders in Council
8. *Chesapeake*
9. James Madison
10. McHenry

True/False

1. F
2. T
3. T
4. T
5. T
6. F
7. F
8. F

Multiple Choice

1. b
2. c
3. b
4. d
5. b
6. d
7. a
8. d
9. a
10. c
11. d
12. c
13. b
14. c
15. b

CHAPTER 9

Matching A

1. c
2. a
3. e
4. f
5. b

Matching B

1. b
2. e
3. f
4. c
5. a

Completion

1. Adams-Onís Treaty
2. Appalachian Mountains, Mississippi River
3. Black Hawk
4. river network
5. flatboats
6. New York City
7. Missouri
8. *Woodward*

True/False

1. F
2. F
3. F
4. F
5. F
6. T
7. F
8. F
9. T
10. T

Multiple Choice
1. c
2. d
3. b
4. c
5. a
6. a
7. b
8. a
9. b
10. c
11. a
12. a
13. b
14. a
15. c

CHAPTER 10

Matching A
1. a
2. e
3. d
4. f
5. c

Matching B
1. d
2. b
3. a
4. e
5. c

Completion
1. self-made man
2. parties
3. literacy
4. melodrama
5. Democratic
6. Kitchen Cabinet
7. labor movement

8. Cherokee
9. "positive liberal state"
10. Tariff of Abominations

4. **True/False**
   1. F
   2. F
   T
   T
5. F
6. T
7. T
8. F
9. F
10. F

Multiple Choice
1. d
2. d
3. d
4. c
5. c
6. a
7. d
8. d
9. a
10. d
11. b
12. b
13. b
14. a
15. d

CHAPTER 11

Matching A
1. c
2. a
3. f
4. e
5. b

Matching B
1. d
2. c
3. e
4. b
5. f

Completion
1. Second Great Awakening
2. Lyman Beecher
3. American Temperance Society
4. American Tract Society
5. *McGuffey Reader*
6. *Liberator*
7. Liberty Party
8. New Harmony, Indiana

True/False
1. F
2. F
3. T
4. F
5. T
6. T
7. F
8. T
9. T
10. F

Multiple Choice
1. a
2. c
3. b
4. d
5. c
6. a
7. a
8. d
9. b
10. a

11. d
12. c
13. b
14. a
15. b

CHAPTER 12

Matching A
1. b
2. d
3. a
4. f
5. c

Matching B
1. f
2. a
3. d
4. e
5. b

Completion
1. Oregon
2. Santa Anna
3. Sam Houston
4. furs, mules, precious metals
5. Brigham Young
6. John Tyler
7. John L. O'Sullivan
8. Cerro Gordo
9. railroad
10. potato

True/False
1. T
2. F
3. T
4. F
5. T
6. F

7. T
8. F
9. T
10. F

Multiple Choice
1. b
2. a
3. d
4. c
5. a
6. b
7. b
8. b
9. d
10. d
11. d
12. c
13. c
14. a
15. d

CHAPTER 13

Matching A
1. b
2. d
3. c
4. f
5. a

Matching B
1. f
2. d
3. a
4. e
5. b

Completion
1. Nat Turner
2. tobacco
3. cotton
4. Sir Walter Scott

5. American Colonization Society
6. transportation
7. Bible
8. Second Seminole War
9. underground railroad
10. Josiah Henson

True/False
1. F
2. T
3. F
4. F
5. F
6. T
7. T
8. F
9. T
10. F

Multiple Choice
1. c
2. d
3. a
4. b
5. b
6. c
7. d
8. b
9. a
10. b
11. a
12. b
13. a
14. a
15. b

CHAPTER 14

Matching A
1. e
2. c
3. f
4. d
5. a

Matching B
1. c
2. a
3. e
4. b
5. f

Completion
1. William Lloyd Garrison
2. Free-Soil
3. Henry Clay
4. Millard Fillmore
5. Missouri
6. Lawrence
7. Republican
8. doughface
9. Harpers Ferry, Virginia
10. William Seward

True/False
1. F
2. T
3. F
4. T
5. T
6. F
7. T
8. F
9. F
10. F

Multiple Choice
1. c
2. d
3. a

4. d
5. b
6. b
7. c
8. b
9. a
10. d
11. d
12. c
13. b
14. c
15. d

CHAPTER 15

Matching A
1. b
2. d
3. c
4. f
5. e

Matching B
1. d
2. a
3. f
4. b
5. f

Completion
1. cooperationist
2. Charleston, South Carolina
3. Maryland, Deleware, Kentucky, Missouri
4. anaconda policy
5. Peace Democrats
6. David Farragut
7. George McClellan
8. James Mason, John Slidell
9. Charles Francis Adams
10. George McClellan

True/False
1. F

2. F
3. T
4. F
5. F
6. F
7. T
8. T
9. F
10. T

Multiple Choice
1. c
2. d
3. c
4. d
5. d
6. d
7. a
8. a
9. d
10. d
11. d
12. b
13. a
14. a
15. c

CHAPTER 16

Matching A
1. c
2. a
3. d
4. e
5. b

Matching B
1. c
2. e
3. c
4. b
5. d

Completion
1. Birth of a Nation
2. Thirteenth Amendment
3. pocket veto
4. investment capital
5. Fourteenth
6. sharecropper
7. greenbacks
8. Ku Klux Klan
9. businessmen, poor white farmers, blacks
10. spoilsmen

True/False
1. T
2. F
3. F
4. T
5. F
6. T
7. F
8. T
9. T
10. F

Multiple Choice
1. d
2. a
3. a
4. d
5. d
6. b
7. c
8. b
9. a
10. a
11. a
12. c
13. c
14. b
15. d